Critical Practice in Working with Children

Critical Practice in Working with Children

Tony Sayer

palgrave
macmillan

First published 2008 by
PALGRAVE MACMILLAN
Houndmills, Basingstoke, Hampshire RG21 6XS and
175 Fifth Avenue, New York, NY 10010
Companies and representatives throughout the world

PALGRAVE MACMILLAN is the global academic imprint of the Palgrave Macmillan
division of St. Martin's Press, LLC and of Palgrave Macmillan Ltd. Macmillan® is a
registered trademark in the United States, United Kingdom and other countries.
Palgrave is a registered trademark in the European Union and other countries.

ISBN-13: 978–0–230–54319–5
ISBN-10: 0–230–54319–7

This book is printed on paper suitable for recycling and made from fully
managed and sustained forest sources. Logging, pulping and manufacturing
processes are expected to conform to the environmental regulations of the
country of origin.

A catalogue record for this book is available from the British Library.

A catalog record for this book is available from the Library of Congress.

10 9 8 7 6 5 4 3 2 1
17 16 15 14 13 12 11 10 09 08

Printed and bound in China

Contents

List of Boxes and Figures

Practice Contexts

Case Studies

Practice Boxes

Figures

Abbreviations

ADHD	attention deficit hyperactivity disorder
ASBO	anti-social behaviour order
ASSET	Assessment tool in Youth Justice
BAAF	British Association for Adoption and Fostering
BBC	British Broadcasting Corporation
Cafcass	Children and Family Courts Advisory and Support Service
CAMHS	Child and adolescent mental health service
CHE	community home with education
CPS	Crown Prosecution Service
CRA	Children's Rights Alliance (pressure group)
CRB	Criminal Records Bureau (checks police records, etc.)
CROA	children's rights officers and advocates
CSCI	Commission for Social Care Inspections (inspects adult social care services)
DfCSF	Department for Children, Schools and Families (government department responsible for children's work)
DfES	Department for Education and Skills (formerly controlled children's work)
DoH	Department of Health
DoJ	Department of Justice
ECM	'Every Child Matters' (policy agenda)
ECP	'End Child Poverty' (pressure group)
EDT	emergency duty team (out-of-hours social work)
EOC	Equal Opportunities Commission
EU	European Union
GCSE	General Certificate in Secondary Education
GSCC	General Social Care Council
GTC	General Teaching Council
HMSO	Her Majesty's Stationery Office (government publishers)
IPPR	Institute for Public Policy Research (think-tank)
IVF	in-vitro fertilisation (infertility treatment)
ISSO	intensive supervision and surveillance order
JRF	Joseph Rowntree Fund (research organisation)
LA	local authority
LAC	local authority circular (from government to local authorities)
LACS	looked-after children's system
LEA	local education authority
NAYJ	National Association of Youth Justice
NCB	National Children's Bureau

NCH	National Children's Homes (voluntary organisation)
NEET	not in education, employment or training
NFA	no further action (the decision to close a case)
NSPCC	National Society for Prevention of Cruelty to Children
NYA	National Youth Agency (quango advising on youth issues)
Ofsted	Office for Standards in Education (inspects children's services)
ONS	Office of National Statistics
PACE	Police and Criminal Evidence Act (sets procedures for police custody, etc.)
PCT	primary care trust
PQ	Post Qualifying social work award
quango	quasi-autonomous non-governmental organisation
'res care'	residential care (children's homes, etc.)
RIP	Research in Practice (government agency promoting evidence-based practice)
SATs	standard assessment tests (taken by schoolchildren aged 7–14)
SCIE	Social Care Institute of Excellence (disseminates good practice)
SEN	special educational needs
SEU	Social Exclusion Unit (government body)
UNCRC	United Nations Convention on the Rights of the Child
YJB	Youth Justice Board
yob	slang term for a problem teenager
YOI	young offenders institution (youth prison)
YOT	youth offending team

Acknowledgements

Thanks are due to the late Jo Campling, publishing consultant, who motivated me to produce this text; the first cohort of students on the BA Social Work degree course at Bournemouth University who consumed the early drafts and commented generously, particularly to Debbie Young, one of that group, who assisted with IT; Joan Revill, one of the Course Team who commented upon the draft; and to Professor Jonathan Parker, Associate Dean (Social and Community Work) at Bournemouth University for agreeing to mentor me on this work.

Introduction

The introduction sets out the tools for critical analysis used in the book and the value base underlying the work, discusses the use of evidence and outlines the book's structure.

Work with children at the start of the 21st century presents new and exciting challenges following the major reforms over the last two decades. Practice has been markedly influenced by the developing policy agenda which has seen major structural change, most notably the separation of adult and children's social services, the integration of the major services for children in Children's Trusts and the drive towards more inter-professional practice. Cutting across that has been the growth in managerialism, with its emphasis upon cost effectiveness and accountability. These changes bring risks and potential benefits to childcare practitioners which need evaluating as part of critical practice.

This book aims to provide a resource for students preparing for careers in children's social services and current practitioners wishing to develop their skills through critical analysis, and to provide an introduction to children's work for allied professionals, particularly appropriate at a time when those working with children are being expected to work more closely together and to diversify their skills. It aims to enable students to evaluate critically their workplace and working practices and to present ideas for implementing change in the complex and contested contexts of contemporary practice.

In considering professional practice or the wider organisational context in which it operates, there is a need for practitioners to be able to get beyond the 'how to do it' level towards critical analysis. The book aims to introduce some tools that can be used in critical analysis and to suggest how these can be applied in some complex areas of practice where moral and organisational dilemmas must inform practice decisions. Theoretical perspectives used in the book include social constructionism as a tool for understanding how and why dominant discourses develop and evolve, systemic approaches as a means of getting beyond daily concerns towards a more strategic approach to childcare management, and Marxist and feminist perspectives as examples of the 'conflict theories' of society which can be used to think critically about class and gender issues, which arguably are at the heart of childcare work. Policy will be analysed in terms of seeking winners and losers and identifying power imbalances that impact upon workers and service users.

Starting from a social work perspective, the book discusses a range of interventions with individual children, their families and other carers. It offers an examination of modern childcare work in terms of its strengths and weaknesses, particularly the importance of the underlying value base. It introduces the range of statutory interventions and discusses the roles of the private and voluntary sectors in the mixed economy of care. A consideration of current issues in childcare social work includes some of the most contested areas, including an evaluation of the culture of managerialism and the retreat from professionalism, and reflections on failures to protect (scandals in child protection and residential care), which suggest not only poor front-line practice but also systemic and multidisciplinary failings. The organisational context which recognises the importance of rationing resources as part of assessments of need and risk, and the present emphasis upon crisis intervention rather than strategy and planning is critically examined.

Although the material is relevant to all professional interventions with children, families and a wider range of carers, there is an emphasis upon issues raised by work with older children and adolescents. Apart from this being the professional background of the author, the rationale is that those defined as 'troubled' or 'troublesome' represent the sharp end of practice, both in terms of face-to-face work with service users and the complex professional dilemmas often presented. They are therefore a relevant group when considering critical practice.

Critical Analysis

Brayne and Preston-Shoot (2004) encapsulate the reason for promoting critical analysis by suggesting that social workers need to get beyond being competent technicians who are 'fixers', towards a broader concept of a well-rounded professional capable of using knowledge and judgement to make decisions in a strategic way.

Adams, Dominelli and Payne (2002: xxi) suggest that:

> Criticality enables us to question the knowledge we have and our own involvement with clients – including our taken for granted understandings. It enables us to assess situations so as to make structural connections that penetrate the surface of what we encounter and locate what is apparent within wider contexts.

Cottrell (2003, cited in Brown and Rutter 2006: 44) summarises the general principles for thinking critically:

- stand back from information;
- break things down into component parts;
- examine material in detail from many angles;

- check the accuracy of information;
- look for possible flaws in reasoning, evidence or the way conclusions are drawn;
- consider the same issue from different viewpoints;
- see and explain why different people arrive at different viewpoints;
- being able to argue why one set of opinions, results or conclusions is preferable to others;
- be on guard for devices such as misleading statistics or survey data that encourage us to accept questionable statements or lure us into agreement.

It is about:

- checking assumptions;
- questioning information – accuracy, completeness, data source, possible bias (e.g., who paid for the study?), values and attitudes of the author, perceptions, and the validity of judgements made;
- providing more than description of what others say;
- giving your own views on competing perspectives;
- supporting views with evidence;
- making careful judgements.

There is a strong link between critical analysis and the literature on 'reflective practice'. Being reflective is getting beyond the mechanics of doing to think about why you're doing, especially what evidence supports the practice, and evaluating the effectiveness of intervention in terms of both process and outcomes. It is possible to reflect within an uncritical model, perhaps asking how well you implemented set policies and procedures. However, critical analysis requires reflection with wider terms of reference, to view an intervention in its wider context and to question the systems that underpinned the work to identify how things could have been done better.

It is sometimes suggested that critical analysis seems a negative experience. I would argue the opposite, that by knowing what could be done to improve practice, a worker can have a real impact on service development. This can be through changing things over which you have immediate control, or through your team or management structure, seeking to change policies and practices that seem to inhibit quality work. There will always be factors over which we, as practitioners have little control, at least in the short term, for example resource levels and legislation, but through the wider political process contestation can eventually promote change. We need to have a clear analysis of the issues before we can operate at that level.

Tools for Critical Analysis

The key task for the critical thinker is to get beyond the descriptive (*what?* questions) towards seeking underlying influences, whether it is an individual practice dilemma or wider issues concerning the context in which a service user operates or the organisational structures in which the service is provided (*why?* questions). A number of theoretical frameworks can assist in that process. This book uses the terminology 'individual' and 'structural' in identifying the causes of problems and attributing blame. The individualist perspective looks for weaknesses within the individual that lead to problems, whether they are within or beyond the control of the individual. Factors such as laziness are within their control, whereas a disability would be largely beyond their control. The structuralist perspective looks for causes within the wider society: unemployment, poverty and wider forms of oppression. For example, the disability movement argues that it is barriers within society rather than individual impairments that exclude people with disabilities.

It is important to move beyond a functionalist view of society and consensus theories and consider instead the perspectives of conflict theories. The consensus approach supports the status quo and assumes that welfare is a politically neutral activity designed to 'help people'. Even within the broad consensus approach there will be debates about the level and nature of service provision, but wider factors around the 'rules of the game' are largely uncontested.

Among the conflict theories of society, Marxism and feminism offer two frameworks for considering class and gender inequalities. To apply them one does not need to be expert in the details of the underlying ideologies, merely to be able to apply the general concepts – that many situations are influenced by gender, class or wider status inequalities. Indeed, a very detailed knowledge can be confusing, as Marxism has to be seen in a historical context: some things Marx said could be considered oppressive in modern society. For example, the concept of the lumpenproletariat is quite similar to modern discourses emanating from the political right, that unemployed people are lazy, work-shy and unworthy.

Another valuable perspective is offered by social constructionism. This approach seeks to get beyond the common sense approach in an attempt to uncover why particular perspectives become the dominant discourse while competing perspectives become marginalised. It cuts across the other perspectives by seeking to uncover the unequal power relationships that structure our personal consciousness and wider social relations.

Many social work interventions with children and families are reactive, with decisions made in crisis. Although sometimes necessary to protect children, they can offer second-best solutions, especially if the right resources are lacking. The 'systems theories' provide a more strategic approach to decision-making by viewing activities as part of a complex system, which in turn is related to other external and internal systems. By understanding the structures and functioning of these systems and subsystems, real improvements can be made in the way a particular unit or organisation delivers on its objectives.

The theoretical perspectives in the book aim to uncover oppressive practice. The systems approach contributes by analysing how systems contribute to oppression. For example, black children are disproportionately represented in youth custody and adolescent mental health sytems (Wilson and Rees 2006; Youth Justice Board 2004). While this is unlikely to reflect overt racism among the professionals operating these systems, there are institutional factors at work which promote these undesirable outcomes. However, there is a danger in attributing a problem to one oppressed status when a more complex analysis might be necessary. For example, Evans (2006) suggests that we often attribute the relative educational failure of black boys to racial and cultural factors whereas class influences might be more significant. A key requirement for professionals is to avoid categorisation and instead base the search for oppression on the uniqueness of each individual.

Gender-based Analysis

Social work with children is not gender-neutral. There are gender differences across all stakeholders in children's services. For example, few men are employed in the sector; just 2–3 per cent of the 279,000 childcare workers (including child minders, playgroup workers and daycare staff) are men (Equal Opportunities Commission 2005). Men in care work tend to work where the service users are disproportionately males (in youth offending teams, for example), and tend to be over-represented in management roles (McLean 2003). Conversely, from a feminist perspective there is concern that women are exploited in low-status care work where they comprise the large majority of the labour force and suffer from low pay and poor progression opportunities.

There are gender stereotypes that women are 'caring', while men who choose to work with children have dubious motives and are possible child sex abusers (paedophiles). At a more subtle level we question whether men have the caring skills to undertake roles such as foster carer or adopter. This means that there are areas of practice where there are few male role models for male service users (see chapter 2).

A major concern of feminist writers has been the disproportionate emphasis upon mothers, rather than parents,' as service users (Dominelli 2002b). Where there are child welfare concerns or issues about badly behaved children, mothers tend to be blamed and become the focus of intervention. Chapter 3 discusses for example, how in child sexual abuse, the majority of perpetrators are men but it is mothers who often get accused of failing to protect their children.

Daniel et al. (2005) question the lack of gender analysis in the 'Every Child Matters' agenda. They highlight the gendered nature of modern parenting and modern childhood, and the need to consider the gendered nature of child maltreatment (see chapter 3).

Class-based Analysis

While some political scientists and sociologists argue that class is an outmoded concept, that we are all middle class now (Goldthorpe and Lockwood 1969), that argument is of little relevance to children's social work. Few service users would choose to consume children's services which are a highly targeted service; they use services only because they are in need or, in some cases, are required to. Most service users are from the lower social strata, although there are exceptions, for example childless couples seeking to adopt, and some consumers of services for children with disabilities.

Poorer people predominate as users of services such as child protection, and disproportionately become 'looked-after' children, but caution is required in assuming that problematic parenting is largely a working-class phenomenon; for example, the possibility that child protection services are better at 'policing the poor', and that middle-class families are more 'privatised' and adept at managing welfare systems and better at covering up abuse. The concentration of the police and welfare agencies upon 'policing the poor' is a recurrent theme in this book, and is discussed in connection with child protection in chapter 3 and in connection with education welfare and youth justice in chapter 8.

There is another methodological problem underlying the assumption that poor families are abusers. We tend to study *known* abused children and perpetrators, and assume that these are representative of all abuse. However, the 'iceberg phenomenon' (i.e.that around four-fifths of the iceberg is below the surface), cautions against assuming that what is invisible is the same as what is observed, that hidden abusers are the same as known abusers.

A further problem is found with predictive theories, for example the suggestion that it can be predicted which young children are destined to become delinquent teenagers, so that steps can be taken to prevent it. The dangers of this are highlighted by the system's approach to youth justice (see chapter 8): early intervention might propel children towards undesirable outcomes, for example custody, creating a self-fulfilling prophesy. Because the human condition is so complex, there will be some children predicted to become delinquent who won't fulfil expectations, and others who score low on predictive factors who do become delinquent (false positives and false negatives).

Despite these concerns, the 'Every Child Matters' policy agenda continues to focus upon poor families and neighborhoods where most 'preventative services' are targeted and where most individual casework is undertaken. While it is appropriate that the common assessment framework considers social disadvantage as a contributory factor in children's problems, it should not be assumed that affluent people are incapable of abuse or that large numbers of poor people are abusers.

A Search for Winners and Losers

Particularly in considering proposals for policy change, we need to consider who are the likely winners and losers. As an example, in chapter 8 recent educational reforms are used to illustrate how the current agenda of parental choice and managerialism favours certain groups of children at the expense of others, again based largely on factors of class, race and gender.

A Search for Oppressive Practices

As well as oppression based upon class and gender, a critical practitioner will seek to consider other forms of oppression, perhaps based upon race, religion,

disability or sexuality, to get beyond direct discrimination and identify institutionalised practices that disadvantage particular groups. Examples of ommisions
are failing to recognising homophobic bullying in residential care or schools,
and that ageism (usually seen as discrimination against older people) also
applies to young people who are the greatest victims of age discrimination (see
chapter 2).

Dominelli (2002a) develops a model, which discusses how people define
themselves in terms of the oppression they suffer. There are the accepters who
acknowledge their subordinate position, often blaming themselves for being
victims. There are those who adopt an accommodationalist perspective, critical
of the oppression suffered but accepting the norms and values of the society
that oppresses them, seeking and the best compromise solutions in their relationships with those in power. Lastly there are the rejecters whose critique of
the current system is so fundamental that they wish to radically change existing
structures and power relations through individual or collective action, although
this is difficult to achieve within the current authoritarian and managerialist
state. Childcare workers and service users can function at each level and move
between them, taking different attitudes to different forms of oppression. For
example, a gay social worker might not be active in the gay movement but
might be actively fighting against child poverty through membership of relevant pressure groups.

Many service users and front-line staff can suffer cumulative discrimination
based upon membership of several oppressed groups. The further one is from
the socially constructed concept of the norm – arguably a white, middle-aged,
heterosexual man without disabilities – the more 'other' one is and the more
oppression one is likely to suffer.

Radical Social Work

Radical social work dates largely from the 1970s. As a critique of social work in
a capitalist and patriarchal society it brought together a number of critical
models, particularly Marxism and feminism. Radical social work is 'understanding the position of the oppressed in the context of the social and
economic structure they live in' (Bailey and Brake 1975: 9).

Radical social workers argue that social work, rather than 'helping people' is
actually an establishment activity aimed at promoting conformity and social
order by individualising problems that have structural causes, blaming the
victims and offering 'help' so that they can return to conformity which serves
the needs of those in oppressive positions. In doing this, social work 'papers
over the cracks' of a system that might be better left to degenerate and collapse
(Corrigan and Leonard 1977).

The radical approach promoted interventions based upon structural changes
within society at a macro level by pointing out how systems oppress individuals and communities. Operationally, community work was the site for much
radical practice. At an individual case level the task was consciousness-raising,
assisting service users to understand the oppression they suffered. Rather than

being passive recipients of poor public services, service users were encouraged to engage in contestation and struggle using collective political action (such as demonstrating), and devices such as appeals and complaints at an individual level.

The demise of the radical approach dates largely from the Thatcher years. On the one hand the state was unwilling to continue to pay people whose aim was to criticise and undermine it, and on the other hand cuts in public service spending saw a retreat from more collective approaches to statutory duties and case work. Community work could not be justified as cost-effective under the new outcome-led performance measures (see chapter 7).

Social Constructionism

Concepts such as 'children in need' and even 'child abuse' and 'child protection' are not fixed absolutes but *social constructions*. We think we know what these terms mean whereas they have no uncontested definition, what we think we know as 'common sense' is specific to our culture at this time. For example, the dominant social construction around children in Victorian times, that they should be seen and not heard, could be seen today as being emotionally abusive.

To test the extent to which a phenomenon is socially constructed, as opposed to being 'natural' (or even biological), we should consider whether it is universal across cultures and historical periods. For example, in asking whether the 'family' is 'natural' or a social construction, we need to consider that most societies across time and cultures have had some form of 'family' as a basic unit of social organisation, although on closer analysis there are many constructions of a 'family', for example the extended family, and hence we could argue that what we currently perceive as being a family is indeed heavily socially constructed.

What we regard as abusive reflects the social constructions around childhood as a life stage. While maturation is clearly a biological process, how children are treated in our society and therefore how they experience their childhood are heavily socially constructed. The assumption that children are sexual innocents is one example (see chapter 2).

The term 'in need' provides an example of cultural variation. Compared with children in many developing countries, the UK has very few children in dire need and yet a whole range of circumstances are defined as being problematic in our society.

Systems Theory

In childcare work there are at least three concepts of systems theory:

- As part of family therapy, the family is seen as a system. All relationships and interactions between members are analysed in order to gain a deeper understanding of the roles each participant plays in creating and sustaining a particular problem. For example, if the presenting problem is a suicidal teenage daughter, rather than focusing upon her personal problems, the systems approach examines her place in the wider family unit (and wider external systems) and assesses the ways in which others are contributing to her situation.

■ A link with the ecological approach to assessment upon which the Assessment Triangle (Department of Health 2000) is based. This goes beyond a person's individual or family problems and takes a more holistic view of the structural and environmental systems that impact upon them (Jack 1997; see chapter 3).

■ As a management tool to assess the functioning of a process of care to ensure its effectiveness in delivering set goals. There is a similarity with 'strategic management' in that both aim to use organisational analysis to get beyond an immediate problem and short-term reactive responses towards longer-term solutions and a more productive system. This section and examples throughout the book are concerned with this concept of systemic analysis.

Systems theory probably started in engineering. It was seen as important when dealing with a problem to go beyond the immediate situation and see the wider context. Each subsystem is an integral component of a whole system, and systems also have external contexts, other systems with which they interact.

The basic systems model considers inputs from the external environment and outputs to the external environment and, most importantly, what happens in the conversion process in between (the 'value added' within a particular system).

In childcare social work, inputs are determined largely by referrals of potential service users and include staff and financial and other resources (such as buildings). The conversion process is what happens within the agency, how available resources are deployed to meet the needs of the referrals. The outputs are the products of the conversion process, what happens to the service users and other factors, for example staff turnover.

Systems can be dysfunctional in themselves. In one post as team manager, I spent half a day a week on filing and other basic administrative duties because of an under-allocation of administrative staff that was beyond my control. The consequence was chaotic paperwork and my being unable to respond adequately to enquiries. In local authorities a culture can exist where support staff are cut with the result that higher-paid professionals are forced to cover the shortfall.

Systems interact with their external environment. For example, a youth offending team worker building a package for a young person about to be released from custody is dependent upon the goodwill and resources of housing suppliers and employers.

Figure 0.1   The basic systems model

Assessing the success of a system by its output can present problems. It is assumed that poor output is the result of a poor conversion process. An alternative possibility is that, given the nature of the input, the conversion process worked well to produce poor results. For example, in failing to reach targets for improving the education of 'looked after' children the government has assumed that teachers and social workers and their systems have in some way functioned ineffectively, whereas perhaps the young people entering the system have already been so damaged that they don't possess the education readiness necessary to achieve set targets (see chapter 5).

The Use of Evidence

Evidence-based Practice

Social work used to be a largely intuitive activity with individual professionals able to stamp their own personalities and values on their work, but now under the new ethos of managerialism the aim is service standardisation. Practice now has to be based on evidence not instinct, on what research has suggested works. Basing practice upon evidence seems sensible, like many other managerialist concepts (for example, accountability and cost-effectiveness), but the effectiveness of the approach can be questioned, especially if it is applied inflexibly.

First, evidence is drawn largely from quantitative research, particularly statistical analysis. The problem is that what worked for a significant proportion of people might not work for a particular service user in their unique situation. The role of the professional is to apply knowledge to each unique situation.

Secondly, we have to ask what evidence is being presented. For example, as shown in chapter 8, the practice of youth offending teams is informed by evidence, but the effectiveness of current youth justice policies is questioned. An explanation of this apparent contradiction is that the 'evidence' is drawn from a micro-analysis of the effectiveness of individual interventions, rather than a macro (systemic) analysis of the effectiveness of the overall youth justice system, which is propelling more young people towards highly ineffective custodial sentences.

Resources on the World Wide Web

The information revolution, largely associated with the growth of the Internet, has seen a massive increase in the amount and availability of relevant information accessible on line. A cautionary note: when using Internet sources don't believe what you read any more than you would a tabloid newspaper. Be particularly sceptical of material that is offered by general search engines where there is no system to authenticate sources.

However, the Internet provides many credible sources of information, examples of which can be found on:

■ The websites of voluntary organisations, for example, the NSPCC, the Children's Society, Barnardo's, NCH, each specialising in particular areas of need. Generally these have website addresses in the format www. barnardos.org.uk.

■ Government websites. Children's services materials are now found on the DfCSF website www.dfcsf.gov.uk, which contains links to other specialist sites, for example the Social Exclusion Unit and the Office of National Statistics. The unfolding government agenda, including policy and practice guidance can be found on www.ecm.gov.uk.

■ Agencies specialising in social work research. These include SCIE (Social Care Institute for Excellence), including the database 'Social Care Online', a gateway to research material (www.scie.org.uk); Research in Practice, which produces a monthly summary of new research with online registration (www.rip.org.uk); Joseph Rowntree Foundation (www.jrf.org.uk).

Values of this Book

Everything in social work is contested, is one of the valuable lessons from social constructionism. It therefore seems appropriate to be explicit about the values underlying this book:

1   The book is optimistic about people, both the variety of professionals who work tirelessly to improve the lives of disadvantaged people, and service users who can be oppressed by care systems and who, given the right opportunities and assistance, would be able to make major strides towards improving their own lives and the functioning of their communities. That is not to deny the need to protect children from adults who either are intent on abusing them, or abuse them through neglect of their responsibilities.

2   Under-resourcing has been a major theme of work with children, and it has limited creativity in delivering services to children and families. This has been reflected mainly in the retreat from empowering structuralist and community interventions towards minimalist statutory duties with an inevitable emphasis upon case work and 'victim blaming'.

3   Every child has not mattered; there have been winners and losers in state provision for children. This can be seen in the emphasis upon work with individual poor families, rather than less stigmatizing structural interventions to tackle poverty and disadvantage. For example, it is argued that children in the child protection system (see chapter 3), those 'looked after'(see chapters 5 and 6), young offenders (see chapter 8) or those labelled as mentally ill (see chapter 9) are largely the same group of 'deprived children'. Which system admits them is largely a lottery.

There have been groups targeted for interventions, for example those falling within the orbit of child protection (see chapter 3) at the expense of preventative services (see chapter 7), and groups of children who remain largely outside the system, for example runaways and asylum-seeking children (see chapter 4). wider issues that make children miserable have often not received the attention they deserve, for example bullying (see chapter 3) and the plight of young people in custody (see chapter 4).

4   Professionals have felt undermined by the organisations and statutory frameworks in which they operate. Examples range from the managerialist agenda and the 'tick-box approach' (discussed in relation to assessment and care management in chapter 3), and 'looked after' children (chapters 5 and 6). Having taught emerging professionals in both social work and youth justice, I have found that students who start by being highly motivated to help people quickly become disillusioned by targets, forms and the lack of opportunities for effective face-to-face work with service users.

5   Children's rights: although the political rhetoric is about creating opportunities for all children, the reality is that children are constructed as sub-citizens who have a weak voice in controlling their own lives and have to defer to the wishes of parents and professionals, often following unnecessarily controlling practices. Broader systems have also been oppressive. Some are directly controlling within an authoritarian state (see chapter 8) and others more subtly so, for example the increasing trend towards defining 'troubled' or 'troublesome' young people as having mental health problems (see chapter 9).

6   Levels of intervention: in a 'civilised' society state intervention is legitimate to promote the welfare of all children and to protect those suffering harm. However, not all interventions are in the best interests of the children involved, for example the truancy and anti-social behaviour interventions discussed in chapter 8. The most damaging interventions are those that fail to achieve their own objectives and yet interfere with the rights and liberties of children and families. The term 'cascades of intervention' is used to show how one intervention leads to another, where often the damage caused by the end result can be worse than the harm originally identified.

Critical thinking can be seen to be coming from the left in politics, for example from a Marxist perspective. However, at a time when government policies have largely adopted perspectives from the political right – marketisation, choice and responsibilisation, for example – it seems inevitable that a critique will come largely from the opposite direction.

Organisation of the Book

The book consists of self-contained chapters that cover the major areas of childcare practice. They aim to describe and critically analyse current and proposed interventions, applying where appropriate the models of critical analysis already introduced. In order to minimise repetition, links are offered to other chapters.

The book contains case material and summaries of issues relevant to promoting good practice designed to be thought-provoking rather than as definitive statements as to 'how to do it'. Ideas developed early in the chapters are applied to relevant practice areas aimed at bringing to life the identified issues.

In discussing all the major areas of childcare practice, the book cannot cover each area and issue in depth. In order to promote further study, in addition to the full list of references at the end of the book, each chapter ends with a Resources section suggesting key sources of additional information, and starting points for further research, often downloadable. At least one gateway to further information is suggested for each major area. This is particularly important due to the rapidly developing policy and research literature.

Chapter 1 creates a context in which social care for children is delivered: the constraints upon decision-making and the organisational structures. Chapter 2 uses material largely from work with young people to illustrate how social constructions inform how we define issues and organise interventions. Chapters 3 and 4 are about protecting children both inside and beyond the child protection net, chapter 3 focusing upon those living at home, while chapter 4 considers organisations and systems that have failed children living away from home.

Chapters 5 and 6 critically assess the systems for 'looked after' children, including the debates about placement options. Chapter 7 considers the failure to provide services to many children in need, with services focused mainly upon statutory case work with children suffering 'significant harm' and those in public care. Chapters 8 and 9 critically assess the current highly interventionist policies that label increasing numbers of youngsters as 'troubled' or 'troublesome'. Chapter 8 considers authoritarian interventions in dealing with antisocial behaviour and delinquency and discusses parallels within the education system. Chapter 9 discusses child and adolescent mental health. The book ends by suggesting frameworks for considering the future of child welfare services in a globalised and postmodern world.

KEY POINTS

- Critical practice involves getting beyond the 'how to do it' to examine why things are as they are, and who the winners and losers are.
- Social work is disproportionately about poor people who are blamed for their problems.
- Women are disproportionately involved in children's social care, and can be blamed for their children's problems.
- Radical social work aimed to de-individualise problems by seeing them as products of the wider society.
- Social constructionism alerts us to the contested nature of problems and shows that how we view things is related to a particular culture at a particular time. There are no absolute definitions.
- Systems approaches aim to get beyond crisis management to a more strategic and planned approach to service delivery.
- We need to be cautious in using evidence.

RESOURCES

Critical thinking

A gateway to more specialist sources, for example on the psychology of critical thinking, is provided by Brown and Rutter (2006), *Critical Thinking and Analysis*.

Theory in social work
Payne, M. (2005), *Modern Social Work Theory*. This book discusses the theoretical perspectives used in this book and several other perspectives.

Social constructionism
Parton, N. and O'Byrne, P. (2000), *Constructive Social Work: Towards a New Practice*.

Systems Theory
Bilson, A. and Ross, S. (1999), *Social Work Management and Practice: Systems Principles*.

Feminist social work
Dominelli, L. (2002), *Feminist Social Work Theory and Practice*.

Radical social work
Although currently unfashionable, the ideas from radical social work present an interesting contrast to modern thinking and are therefore worthy of further study. Most of the literature dates from the 1970s. See, for example:

Alinsky, S. (1971), *Rules for Radicals*.
Baily, R. and Break, M. (1975), *Radical Social Work*.
Corrigan, P. and Leonard, P. (1977), *Social Work Practice under Capitalism: A Marxist Approach*.
Ryan, W. (1976), *Blaming the Victim*.

Some more recent texts are
Fook, J. (1992), *Radical Casework: A Theory of Practice*.
Langlan, M. and Lee, P. (1989), *Radical Social Work Today*.
Lavalette, M. and Ferguson, I. (2007), *International Social Work and the Radical Tradition*.

CHAPTER 1

The Context of Social Work with Children

This chapter introduces the operational context of modern work with children and families, policy agendas, the structure of the children's social care sector and the contextual factors that impact upon both policy-making and operational decision-taking in children's work. An important aim is to familiarise readers with the language of childcare.

Policy Context: Every Child Matters

Following the Laming Report into the death of Victoria Climbie (Laming 2003), the government launched a new agenda for children's services based upon a green paper 'Every Child Matters' (Department for Education and Skills 2003). Sister papers followed: 'Youth Justice: The Next Steps' (Home Office Youth Offenders Unit 2003) set the agenda for work with young offenders; 'Youth Matters' (Department for Education and Skills 2005) considered wider youth issues; and 'Care Matters' (2006b) proposed future policies for 'looked after' children. Legislation, especially regarding the structures for the delivery of services for children was enacted in the Children Act 2004. This saw the setting up of children's trusts which brought together the function of local education authorities and children's social services and integrated the relevant services provided by health and other agencies.

The Every Child Matters agenda is shown in Practice Context 1.1. Perhaps the biggest challenges will be delivering in the newer policy areas: 'enjoyment', given the pressure to achieve and linked emotional problems (see chapter 9), and 'health', given the unhealthy lifestyles chosen by many of the modern generation of children (see chapter 10) (Hunter and Payne, n.d.). Although the 'safeguarding children' agenda signals a shift in emphasis from child protection to a wider range of services for many children, concerns have been raised that child protection services could be undermined by reduced funding (Munro and Calder 2005). At the same time, an effective shift towards preventative services will be impossible without increased funding (see chapter 7).

The 'Every Child Matters' agenda

'Every Child Matters: Change for Children' is about the well-being of children and young people from birth to age 19. The government's aim is for every child, whatever their background or circumstances, to have the support they need to:

be healthy
stay safe
enjoy and achieve
make a positive contribution
achieve economic well-being

Organisations involved in providing services to children – from hospitals and schools to police and voluntary groups – will be working in new ways, sharing information and working together, to protect children and young people from harm and help them achieve what they want in life. Children and young people will have far more say on issues that affect them as individuals and collectively.

Every local authority will be working with its partners, through children's trusts, to find out what works best for children and young people in its area and to act on it. They will need to involve children and young people in this process, and when inspectors assess how local areas are doing, they will listen especially to the views of children and young people themselves.

Source: adapted from Department for Education and Skills 2003.

Organisational Context

In order to make sense of their working environment and place individual decisions within a wider context, it is important for practitioners to understand the organisational and social factors that locate children's services. This section discusses the various agencies in which contemporary childcare is carried out and the wider context in which the agencies and their practitioners operate.

Statutory Childcare Work

'Statutory childcare work' suggests activity in working with children, their families and other carers sanctioned by the state, usually through legislation. The word 'work' implies a paid task, a service provided by an individual or organisation with some degree of public accountability. Of course most childcare activity is outside that framework, care being provided by parents and other relatives. An important policy consideration is the extent to which these voluntary carers should be rewarded for rearing the next generation. Arguably the boundary is moving in the direction of state intervention with policies such as funded childcare places and tax credits. There are also numerous carers on the margins of the parent–professional spectrum: volunteers and those paid little for their services, for example child minders and some foster carers.

The main framework for the organisation, though not necessarily the direct provision of children's services is children's trusts, which are responsible for the childcare functions outlined in Practice Context 1.2.

PRACTICE CONTEXT 1.2

The functions of children's trusts

1. Child protection: the threshold according to the Children Act 1989 is 'significant harm'. There are close partnerships between social workers, the police, and health, education and other services.
2. Services to 'looked after' children, including managing placements for them.
3. After-care services under the Leaving Care Act 2000, often in partnership with the voluntary sector.
4. Services for children in need. In practice few resources are devoted to this due to budgetary constraints. Work with young children is targeted via children's centres and work with older children is evolving based on 'extended schools'. There may be some targeted preventative work, for example family support to avoid the need to provide 'accommodation'. Some funds might be allocated to specific groups, for example to provide respite care for children with disabilities.
5. Adoption services, although there are still numerous voluntary adoption agencies, which now place mainly special needs children.
6. Education social work.
7. Youth work, including Connexions.

In partnership with other agencies they provide:

8. Youth offending teams (YOT).
9. Child and adolescent mental health services (CAMHS).

In addition they provide education services, by far their largest function, and have a general strategic duty to meet the educational and welfare needs of children in their area. There are differing local organisational arrangements for such services as the youth service and child health which are integrated within children's trusts to a greater or lesser degree. There are often complex organisational arrangements for the provision of services to children with disabilities where health, social work and education are involved, and for interactions with adult services where the parents have separate problems from the child, for example in cases of parents with mental health problems or substance abuse. There are greater complexities about how such partnerships will work now that adult and children's social services are separate (see chapter 3).

Childcare workers are increasingly employed in specialist teams, often multi-disciplinary or multi-agency, covering one or more of the above functions. Children's social services also tend to have an assessment team which undertakes core assessments under the common assessment framework before handing over longer-term work to specialist teams.

The 'Mixed Economy of Care'

Although children's services have not formally adopted the care management model based upon the purchaser/provider split (as used in adult social care), there has always been a diversity of providers, from the large children's charities (Children's Society, Barnardo's, NSPCC and NCH), smaller voluntary agencies, private providers (most commonly residential homes) and individual carers (foster carers and child minders, for example). There is, however a move towards the 'contract culture', with services being commissioned from the private and voluntary sectors, and a trend for services to be planned and provided in partnership with other agencies.

The Quango State

A quango (quasi-autonomous non-governmental organisation) is a semi-independent unit of service provision operating at national or local level. There are models of partnership work where local authorities retain a lead role through a children's trust, including YOT and CAMHS, although these are effectively quangos. Much provision in health (NHS trusts) and education (trust schools) is from quangos, although strategy and some provision in these areas is delivered by children's trusts.

The main issue about quangos is accountability. They are usually managed by a selected board and receive government funding, but unaccountable through the democratic process except to a secretary of state in central government who has overall responsibility but is far removed. The board is often representative

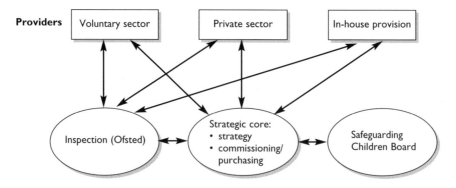

Figure 1.1 The components of the 'mixed economy'

of the partner agencies and there are usually independent members who are meant to be representative of the local community, but concerns can be raised about whether they are disproportionately recruited from the local elite.

The Voluntary Sector

Voluntary organisations are usually registered charities and governed by Charity Commission rules, although some small local groups may not be registered. There is usually a management committee that oversees the work of any paid officers and determines the direction of the work within the aims and objectives set down in their constitution.

The dilemma for voluntary organizations is the extent to which they embrace the 'contract culture' and bid to provide services for the state. By doing so they can expand, but they may lose autonomy and their original mission be undermined.

Despite the Charities Act 2006 which largely addressed matters of governance, debate continues about how to rationalise the legal status of voluntary organisations. First, the extent to which charities can campaign: most try to press for change through running and evaluating exemplar projects. Some voluntary organisations, for example, Shelter, are not charities and see campaigning as their main purpose. Secondly, some charitable bodies, for example many public schools, have tenuous links with 'public benefit', the baseline for charitable status. Miller (2004) discusses the evolving role of the voluntary sector.

The Private Sector

Private companies by definition seek to make profit and the major issue is whether profits and care mix. However, some providers in the private sector have broader motives, perhaps, having decided to leave a statutory service and 'go private' to gain more job satisfaction through the provision of a quality service. There was much rhetoric during the Thatcher years about competition promoting quality, choice and efficiency and this sector has consequently expanded. It appears that particularly with childcare placements, the private sector is often used as a last resort when no local authority resource exists. Although some no doubt provide a good service, regular scandals suggest that some provide very poor services at high prices, exploiting the desperation sometimes faced by social workers looking to place a very demanding young person. If contracts are awarded to private companies largely on cost grounds, it is possible that cheap also means poor quality. There are also questions about the exploitation of workers; with poor pay and conditions, and often poor training, staff of sufficient calibre cannot be recruited or retained.

Owners of private companies often receive no formal supervision unless they arrange consultancy for themselves. Their accountability is through the market system, based upon the assumption that purchasers will make rational purchasing decisions. They are also answerable to Ofsted Inspectors. There is a debate about whether real accountability should be achieved through the marketplace or through inspection (Miller 2004).

'Not for Profit' Organisations

These sit somewhere between charities and private companies. Although they cannot declare a profit, their owners often pay themselves generous remuneration packages, which make them similar to private companies. They are overseen by a management committee although the degree of independence of such committees can often be questioned as the owners have control over the appointments. The most credible organisations will establish a management board of renowned local people able to offer real consultancy; for others the board will be a token gesture to a legal requirement.

Safeguarding Children Boards

Safeguarding children boards hold a strategic overview of the local child protection system. They have wider responsibilities than their predecessors (area child protection committees) and can consider issues beyond the registration categories within the child protection system. They are representative of the agencies constituting the local child protection partnership and can have an independent chair or be chaired by a senior person from a partnership agency, often the director of children's services.

An important role is to investigate unnatural child deaths, not just those where the child was within the child protection system ('Serious Case Reviews', sometimes referred to as 'Part 8 Reviews'). Often such enquires are contracted to voluntary organisations such as the NSPCC, or to independent consultants.

Cafcass

An executive agency of central government administered through regional offices, Cafcass provides a Guardian ad Litem who reports to the courts on the best interests of the child in public law cases, for example care proceedings, and reporting officers who report to the courts in private law cases, for example custody arrangements in a divorce. Their workers are a mixture of employed and sessional social workers. They are therefore independent of case-holding social workers.

Ofsted

Ofsted have broadened their functions from inspecting educational services to inspecting all children's services falling under the remit of the DfCSF. This includes children's social services, but excludes youth justice. A children's rights director (CRD) is located within Ofsted with the main function of consulting with children about their experiences of using a variety of care services. A number of influential reports from the CRD will be discussed later.

Children's Commissioners

Each country in the UK has a children's commissioner. Their function is to represent the views of children to government and elsewhere and to promote policies that benefit children and allow their views to be heard. They can commission research into areas of concern, but cannot investigate individual complaints unless asked to do so by government.

The Context for Practice

It is important to understand the underlying factors that impact upon work with an individual child or family.

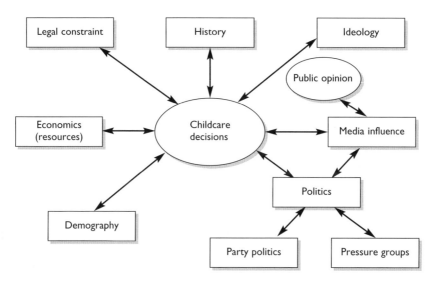

Figure 1.2   The context of childcare decisions

The Law

The legislation quoted in this book relates mainly to England and usually applies in Wales. Each individual chapter will refer to the relevant legislation. Scotland and Northern Ireland have different but usually comparable laws. The three major legal categories for statutory childcare intervention and their numerical significance are shown in Figure 1.3.

The rule of law is a fundamental premise of a civilised, democratic society. Laws should represent the will of the people as expressed through the democratic process, and it is incumbent upon each citizen to stay within the law or face penalties for transgressions.

The law is an important factor in the social construction of childhood (James and James 2004). It defines when childhood ends and sets minimum ages for various forms of behaviour. There are of course contradictions, for example,

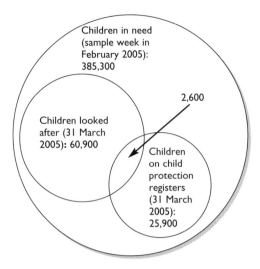

Figure 1.3 Numbers of children in need, children who are looked after, and on child protection registers in England.

Source: Department for Education and Skills 2006c.

sexual intercourse and marriage are allowed at 16 whereas one must be 18 to watch an adult movie or buy an adult magazine. Of more concern is that, although many laws relating to children are designed to promote welfare, most laws seem to restrict and control rather than empower children.

The law impacts directly upon practice through legislation and associated regulations. Central government also interprets the law and issues guidance and ministerial circulars (local authority circulars), that may not strictly hold the force of law, but any authority or worker not adhering to them can face severe criticism if things go wrong. Judicial precedents (case law created in the higher courts) also interpret the law in an increasingly litigious society. The law not only states what a worker must do (duties) and can do (powers), but through the principle of *ultra vires* that they cannot do things not specified in law.

Legislation affects social work through the impact it has on service users. As well as establishing their right to services (such as social security and housing), it also establishes a framework for conduct, determining what is legal and illegal. The role of childcare workers as advocates often derives from questioning the implementation of these laws. Increasingly, overarching legislation such as the Human Rights Act 1998 and freedom of information legislation particularly impact upon childcare workers and service users keen to assert their rights.

The law reflects power imbalances within society. It is largely men from the upper and professional classes who become legislators and judges and there is a complex debate as to what influences those in power. Although there has been a drive towards reducing social differences, ministers, judges and senior civil servants still come disproportionately from privileged backgrounds, often having attended the best public schools and elite universities (Coxall et al. 2003). It is little wonder that they face concerns that they are out of touch with the experiences of ordinary people and tend to pursue policies which favour those in control of the resources in society.

A practitioner can face a professional dilemmas when he or she finds a service user breaking the law, particularly in residential care or a foster home where the premises are being used for illegal activity, including the use of illegal substances. While this is unlawful, the reality is that carers will be reluctant to jeopardise their relationships with young people by involving the police. There are other ethical dimensions to interpreting the law, for example if a worker feels that a service user is being oppressed by it. Examples will be discussed around the concept of the authoritarian state in chapter 8.

An important issue in jurisprudence (the philosophy of law) is the quantity of law. Some argue that society should be highly regulated through legislation while others feel that only minimum controls should exist. Post-war governments have favoured an increasingly regulated society, although a partial retreat could follow from the anti-regulation lobby, which often bases its case on European Union directives.

Practitioners can adopt a creative approach to the law. A good example was the use in the 1980s of pre-court diversion to avoid young offenders being subjected to harsh youth justice legislation. The way to avoid punitive criminal justice legislation was to use the systems approach to keep young offenders out of court (see chapter 8).

Judicial review is an important tool in holding public bodies to account. This High Court action can be used to question any decision of a public body that the complainant considers to be unreasonable in interpreting the law. It is an expensive action and most cases are test cases supported financially by pressure groups.

UN Convention on the Rights of the Child (1989)

The UN Convention on the Rights of the Child was ratified by 177 countries worldwide and by the UK in 1991.

PRACTICE CONTEXT 1.3

Select articles from the UN Convention on the Rights of the Child

Article 2: All rights shall apply to all children without discrimination on any ground.

Article 3: In all actions the child's best interests 'shall be a primary consideration'.

Article 6: Every child has the inherent right to life, and each country should ensure the child's survival and development to the maximum extent possible.

Article 12: The right of the child to express an opinion and to have that opinion taken into account, in any matter or procedure affecting the child.

Article 23: The right of disabled children to enjoy a full and decent life, in conditions which ensure dignity, promote self-reliance, and facilitate the child's active participation in the community. The right of children with disabilities to special care, education, health care, training, rehabilitation, employment preparation and recreation opportunities; conducive to the child achieving 'the fullest possible social integration and individual development, including his or her cultural and spiritual development'.

Article 28: The child's right to education on the basis of equal opportunity.

Article 29: A child's education should be directed at developing the child's personality and talents, and mental and physical abilities to their 'fullest potential', that education shall prepare the child for an active and responsible life as an adult, fostering respect for basic human rights and developing respect for the child's own cultural and national values and those of others.

Source: United Nations Convention on the Rights of the Child (1989).

Sadly, the Children's Rights Alliance which monitors UK compliance with the Convention have regularly identified failings (see chapter 4).

Influencing the Legislators

Childcare practitioners can attempt to influence the law by engaging with political processes both inside and beyond the workplace. Organisations such as trade unions and professional associations, most notably those representing the medical professions, have been successful in influencing policy. The Association of Directors of Social Services had only limited success in raising the political profile of children's work. It is hoped that the successor group, the Association of Directors of Children's Services, by combining the education and social care agendas, will be able to wield more influence, especially upon the minister for children and the children's directorate in the DfCSF. The profile of children will also be promoted by the children's rights commissioners in the constituent countries of the UK.

Pressure groups and children's charities are also important in influencing policy-makers. Most larger groups have policy units and employ lobbyists to influence government. When a new issue arises, it is possible for practitioners, academics and others to come together to form a new pressure group, for example ASBO Concern.

Individuals can also join a political party and seek to influence party policy at local or national levels, for example by attending the annual party conference where, in theory at least, party policy is determined. This should, through the manifesto, set the policy agenda if the party is elected to government.

Working with the Media

Working constructively with the media is another strategy in promoting change. While the media particularly the tabloid press, can be criticized for emphasising and amplifying bad news (which is good news for them), it is possible to develop a more positive relationship that can allow the concerns of professionals and service users to be put before the public, thereby exerting political influence. It is an interesting debate as to whether media reporting reflects public opinion or whether public opinion is influenced by reporting.

Although social work is often invisible to the media, child protection tends to be the focus of negative media stories (Galilee undated report). It is difficult to counter stories about neglect by social workers (when a child is injured or dies), or over-zealous social work actions ('family wrecking'), as confidentiality dictates that social workers cannot justify their side of the case.

Some 'fly-on-the-wall' documentaries have been made that give a realistic 'warts and all' view of social work aimed at challenging the negative media image associated with social work through public education. In agreeing to allow a piece of work to be filmed, it is important to maintain editorial control as it is tempting for producers to edit their material to show the most sensational footage, thus distorting the reality, and thereby potentially showing social work in a bad light.

Demography

Population trends affect the lives of individual children in at least two ways. First, the nature of the family or household in which they live, and secondly the wider social organisation of these domestic living units. Social constructions around 'family' are complex and can fail to embrace the variety of living situations faced by modern children. For example, kinship is often seen as a powerful factor defining a 'family', whereas many children live in households not involving 'kin', for example with foster carers or step-parents. We need another term that describes a household that comprises adults in a caring role and their children. Some demographic statistics from the 2001 census are given below.

> Nearly 1 in 4 dependant children (2.67 million) live in lone-parent families, 3 times higher than in 1971. Of these families, 91.2% are headed by the mother.

Lone parents, especially mothers, are unjustifiably stigmatised in the media as being the cause of childhood problems. These difficulties are probably better explained by the wider circumstances faced by lone parents, for example living on benefits and often in poor neighbourhoods. However, there are some real concerns for children living in lone-parent households, often including the lack of a role model of one gender.

The incidence of step-parenting and children living in a variety of reconstituted households has also markedly increased with more than 1 in 10 children (1.28 million) living in a step family.

The implications of this include problematic relationships between children and step-parents, issues around contact with absent parents and the wider family, and the possibility of step-parent abuse. A particular child might experience several reconstituted 'families' as serial monogamy is the lifestyle choice for many parents.

It has been estimated that 28% of children can be expected to experience parental divorce or separation before age 16.

There is a strong relationship between divorce and emotional problems in childhood and it has been argued that children experiencing parental relationship breakdown should be deemed to be 'children in need', whereas at present problems need to present before help is offered (Douglas 2006).

There are many complexities around being a child in a reconstituted family. Even after a partnership has broken down, significant relationships might survive, for example between the child and the former partner's parents (informal grandparents). While these relationships might not be 'kin', they can provide a fertile source of support for the child. In assessments it is worth asking a child to map their 'significant adult relationships', perhaps around a criterion such as 'people I trust' as well as producing a genogram (similar to a family tree). Such relationships might also provide placement opportunities should the child be unable to live with the parent(s). Kinship care is discussed in Chapter 6.

One in 4 mothers with a child under 18 works full time and a further 4 in 10 work part time. There are nearly 2 million (17.6%) children living in 'workless households'.

Parents are now expected to combine caring with paid work. There is a contradiction here in that the traditional discourse of motherhood suggests that the 'best' parenting is carried out by a mother at home, whereas the Government's 'Welfare to Work' policies are encouraging single parents into the workplace.

Where there is no worker as a role model in a household, there can be concerns that the children will not acquire the 'work ethic' and could face the possibility of long-term social exclusion associated with a life on benefits. Rhetoric from both the Government and in the media tends to demonise such families as being unworthy welfare recipients.

Greater geographical mobility has led to many parents not having their extended family available for assistance. On the other hand, grandparents have become a significant source of childcare for many working parents. Isolated parents, particularly single parents, are particularly susceptible to stress with adverse consequences for their children (DfES 2006a). Community projects, for example Surestart are a valuable way of building alternative networks of support.

> 10% of children come from minority ethnic groups, although there are wide regional variations.

The ethnic mix in a particular neighbourhood will impact upon the lives of individual children and families, whether a child is living in a multi-cultural environment or one heavily dominated by their own or another racial grouping. The issue of belonging, and particularly the concept of 'Britishness' presents major challenges for the 21st century (see chapter 10).

A qualitative study by Beishon et al. (1994) considered the lived experiences, values and attitudes of families of Asian and African-Caribbean origin. Asian families were generally more family-orientated within multi-generational families showing strong support for marriage and traditional family values. African-Caribbeans showed a more flexible approach to families, marriage, cohabitation and divorce, and their strong commitment to children and parenting was not necessarily related to the relationship between the parents.

A major demographic concern is the ageing population that will lead to a worsening of the ratio of workers to dependants and arguably a crisis in funding public services as more demands are made on a diminishing resource base (taxation revenue).

Economics

The economic constraint largely determines the level of resources available to those delivering services. Since practitioners are seldom completely satisfied with the level of resourcing, the concept of rationing is needed to reconcile supply and demand, so that everybody in the organisation from the politicians and directorate who determine departmental budgets, through various levels in the hierarchy, down to front-line workers are involved in deciding who gets what and evaluating competing claims upon resources.

Underlying these resource inadequacies is a retreat from the Seebohm optimism (Seebohm Report 1968), at children's social services would be funded as a universal service. Funding has never been sufficient to deliver that, and instead a culture of rationing and cuts has dominated childcare social work. Central and local politicians tend to blame each other for the insufficiency of funding, but the major issue tends to get lost in the consideration of particular failings such as child deaths.

Resource levels are ultimately determined within the political process, by central government deciding upon the levels of taxation and public expenditure, through to local councillors deciding upon local budgets in the context of setting council tax levels. In reality local councils are severely constrained by complex central government rules in the amount of money they can raise through council tax, and hence their ability to improve local services. The private and voluntary sectors who are service providers within the mixed economy of care experience the knock-on effects of these decisions as budgets within the public sector largely determine funds available for commissioning and purchasing services elsewhere.

As well as these macro-economic factors affecting allocation of resources, we should also look at the economic factors that impact upon the individual household, especially the continuing high incidence of child poverty. Making sure that service users are receiving maximum benefits can make a real difference to the quality of a child's life. Sadly, specialist welfare rights units are now rare within social services, with most welfare rights advice being provided by the voluntary sector (often Citizens' Advice Bureaux). However, it remains good practice for children's service professionals to be able to offer benefits advice.

Organisational Factors Affecting Practice

Although some childcare workers are employed directly by parents themselves, for example child minders, most are employed by an organisation with its own culture and ethos, who will also interact with a number of other organisations each with its own practices and beliefs.

An increasing proportion of services are now delivered through multi-agency and inter-professional work. The compatibility between various organisational cultures is a major area for debate in considering the effectiveness of partnership working, for example the compatibility of education and social service cultures (see chapter 8). Social workers are now employed in a variety of settings in multi-agency teams, and increasingly in the private and voluntary sectors. In the shift from being local government officers, working in relatively large service units, to a greater variety of employment opportunities, there is concern within children's care that there will be a marginalization of social workers.

State social work agencies, children's trusts and their adult counterparts are atypical of a number of other arrangements for employing professionals. First, they are bureaucracies with decisions being made on the basis of policies and procedures, arguably in an administrative rather than a professionally led context. Secondly, they are hierarchies, with typically six or more levels between the top and front-line workers. In contrast, solicitors and accountants, for example, are usually organised in small units under the legal framework for partnerships, allowing decisions to be taken more autonomously by professionals. Benefits resulting from these smaller organisational units include flexibility and the easy accommodation of individual variations and choices.

Children's services have tended to be service-led rather than needs-led, that is, provision is made according to what is available rather than what a service user wants or a professional might feel they really need. Services have tended to be developed on the basis of the vision of officers or councillors rather than in consultation with service users.

Part of the new agenda for social work set out in 'Modernising Social Services' (Department of Health 1998), and for public services in general, is to listen to service users and to tailor services around individual need and choice. The direct payments scheme for adult services users and now extended to children with disabilities is a good example of this. Service users can manage their own care budget and, within the constraints of the budget and the care plan, purchase their own package of care.

An important characteristic of modern social work (and other public sector organisations) is managerialism, whereby practices similar to those used in private industry have been imported into the public services (Clarke et al. 1994). This means that policies are target-led and appraised according to performance indicators. Terms like 'quality' are now defined by accountants and managers rather than being based upon the more subjective views of service users and professionals. Managerialism also involves a shift in power from professionals to managers, with professional discretion deferring to quasi-administrative processes (form-filling).

The 'Quality Protects' initiative which dates from 1998 and was funded for 5 years, set the managerial agenda for children's services. It was the main vehicle for delivering the aims in the broader paper 'Modernising Social Services' (Department of Health 1998) of effective protection, better quality care and improved life chances for children. Children's social services were also charged with providing the right targeted help to ensure that disadvantaged children and young people are able to take maximum advantage of universal services, in particular education and health.

The key elements of the 'Quality Protects' programme were:

- New national government objectives for children's services which for the first time set out clear outcome targets for children, for example to improve the education for 'looked after' children, and to increase the number of children adopted from care.
- Management action plans which set out how local councils intended to improve their services, and the production of league tables and star ratings to promote accountability and comparability.
- New systems were introduced, for example the 'looked after' children's system (LACS) and the national assessment framework designed to achieve quality, accountability and standardisation across the country.
- Partnership between and within central and local government and with the health service and the voluntary sector, leading to the establishment of some new services based upon the partnership model, notably Sure Start, the Children's Fund and Connexions.

There has also been a rise in inspections, based upon both value for money and performance. These two were combined under the remit of the Commission

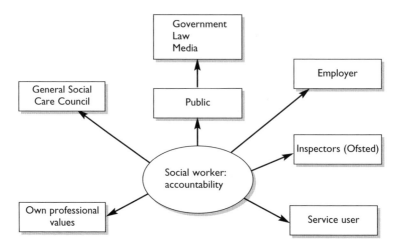

Figure 1.4   Social work and accountability

for Social Care Inspection but all children's inspection work is now carried out by Ofsted.

The question of to whom a social worker is accountable is an interesting one. Despite the activities of the General Social Care Council (GSCC) which, through registration, the three-year degree and code of conduct, has sought to improve the status of social work as a profession, the autonomy of social workers as professionals has diminished. There is an uneasy tension between the accountability a social worker feels to their employing agency, to their professional values and to their service users.

The first cohorts of social workers who obtained a graduate qualification are now in practice. The significance of this is that social work as a profession has now come of age. As well as the new degree bringing increased credibility to the profession, it is now recognised that the initial qualification marks a beginning, not an end, to professional development through certificated study. The revised post-qualification framework will not only prepare social workers for more complex areas of practice, but also provide a route to a qualification at Master's level. This will undoubtedly increase the status and credibility of social work as a profession and bring the academic expectations in line with other caring professions that have taken this route, most notably teaching and nursing, and others to follow, for example youth work. As the children's workforce strategy evolves it is likely that the various professional qualifications for working with children will come together, at least in the provision of a common set of core knowledge and skills.

The Politics of Childcare Social Work

State social services are characterised by the presence and degree of political intervention, ranging from the influence of central government, the activities of local councillors through to the interplay of competing interests that attempt to influence policy. The bedrock of a liberal democracy is the assumption that politicians and public servants should act in the best interests and reflect the views and values of the people (the public service ethic). Modern working practices can undermine this traditional value base (Banks 2004). Political processes are an attempt to reconcile competing values and views for the common good.

In central government there is now a single government department in control of all children's services, the Department for Children, Schools and Families (DfCSF) although responsibility for youth justice is shared with the Ministry of Justice. While it is welcome that one 'super-department' has control over all children's work, under the leadership of a secretary of state and a children's minister, the previous more fragmented system had the benefit that numerous ministers could legitimately represent children's interests, where everything must now be channelled through one super-department. It is possible that the voice of social care could be diminished as the department focuses upon the more costly and politically sensitive schools agenda.

Most children's social care functions are the responsibility of local authorities through children's trusts, although the role is shifting from direct service provision to a more strategic function of commissioning and co-ordinating provision by others.

Local councillors play a significant role in making local policy and holding senior officials to account, although the dynamics of the relationship between councillors and senior managers can undermine this. Managers are paid experts and councillors can find it difficult to gain sufficient good quality information to question their advice.

The political control of a council can markedly impact upon the role of elected members. Where a powerful political group has an overall majority in a Council plus the political will to make a difference, they can be a major force in driving policy change in a similar way to the Government in the House of Commons, which uses party discipline to ensure policies are adopted. However, many councils are often 'hung' (with no overall political majority) and are not highly politicised, which means that there is unlikely to be a clear vision for change from elected members. Reforms to local councils have aimed at increasing the accountablilty of officers to councillors, for example by the election of a full-time mayor or the use of cabinet-style arrangements, similar to Westminster.

It is important to consider the tension between local and national government, often referred to as the centralisation versus decentralisation debate. Many argue the case for local democracy in terms of accountability (to electors rather than bureaucrats) and local politicians being responsive to local needs. The argument for centralisation is often framed in terms of standardisation versus the 'postcode lottery', that it is fairer and more effective if services are provided consistently regardless of locality.

Local democracy has been undermined, by both voter apathy and the inability of local councillors to make a real difference by pursuing distinctive local policies due to the stranglehold of Westminster over local government finance and the prescriptive nature of legislation, regulations and national standards.

Party politics has perhaps become unfashionable, with low turnout rates at elections and the general feeling that politicians cannot be trusted to make decisions in the best interests of the public. However, politics is at the very heart of the world of social care as elsewhere. It is about the mechanisms whereby we influence the things that impact upon us as workers and upon service users. Social care is not an apolitical activity: we can and should have an influence upon resource allocation decisions and the policy decisions that affect us. If we argue that our task is about caring and not politics, we are not maximising our potential benefit to service users through engagement in wider political questions.

A major political issue arises from consideration of the social constructions we place around childhood, parenting and families (discussed more fully in chapter 2); where the state should sit in the triangle of partnership between the state, parents and the child.

There are three issues here. First how legitimate is it for the state to intervene in the private world of the family? Secondly, what is the nature of intervention: should it be helpful or punitive, for example; based on welfare, protection or control? Thirdly, how much power children should have over their own lives?

Following from this is the children's rights approach, which aims to challenge the traditional assumption that intervention should be aimed at parents and suggests that children should be seen as the focus of children's services. Operationally this means that children should be consulted, listened to and provided with mechanisms to participate in their own care planning and overall

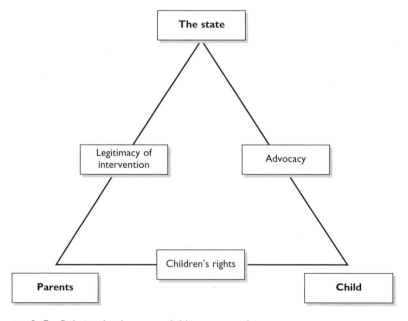

Figure 1.5 Relationship between child, parents and state

service provision. Crucially, they should be empowered and assisted to complain when things go wrong (see chapter 2).

Ideology and Values

Ideologies underlying childcare practice can be found at a number of levels from overarching value positions about the legitimacy and nature of intervention, to matters considered 'good practice' as a result of professional ideologies or research, for example the debate about residential care (see chapter 6). Each individual practitioner will also bring to their practice views and understandings that derive largely from their past experiences and their wider value systems, such as where they stand on the care–control continuum.

Decisions in childcare work are seldom clear-cut – everything is contested. Numerous ideological dilemmas will be raised in this book. A major one concerns the degree of intervention, for example, whether care should be seen as a last resort or one should be more interventionist, especially when the evidence is less than clear and it is difficult to evaluate risk. There is a tendency to err on the side of caution because, although one is damned if you do and damned if you don't when things go wrong, in the current blame culture a safety strategy is likely to be adopted. This can be referred to as *defensive practice*.

Attempts at defining the underlying values of children's work can be found in government documents or more significantly in the codes of practice of the various professional organisations. The General Teaching Council, the Nursing and Midwifery Council and the General Social Care Council have adopted a common code of values for work with children, recognising the multidisciplinary agenda. It has themes covering: respect and communication, partnership working with children and their families and inter-professional work with colleagues (General Social Care Council 2002; GTC 2006).

Fox-Harding (1997) outlines four value positions underlying childcare practice (although in practice elements overlap and converge) and which have a bearing on key principles in the Children Act 1989, in particular, the paramountcy of the welfare of the child and the recurrent theme of parental responsibility. These value positions demonstrate the highly contested nature of childcare work.

PRACTICE CONTEXT 1.4

Value positions in childcare policy and practice

1 Laissez faire/minimalist
   (a)   Belief in a 'minimum state'.
   (b)   Emphasis on the importance of undisturbed family life.
   (c)   Importance of psychological bonding and protection of civil liberties.

2 State paternalism/child protectionism
   (a)   Emphasis on parental duty to provide high standards of care.

(b)   Emphasis on psychological (rather than biological) ties – but more inclined to disrupt those ties if parenting 'unsatisfactory'. Much more benevolent view of 'the state'.

3 Birth family/parents rights

(a)   Amalgamates interests of children and parents, seeing the child as part of family unit, emphasising the centrality/integrity of the 'natural family' and seeing the role of the state as supportive/preventive, rather than as a 'transfer agency' (taking power from parents).

(b)   Resists intrusive, coercive state intervention, but gives a more positive role to the state, for example, where support helps hold natural families together.

(c)   Biological and emotional bonds are interlinked, issues of material deprivation are emphasised. Where children are separated, links with parents (and siblings) should be maintained.

4 Children's rights/child liberation

(a)   Child is seen as a person in their own right (autonomy, choices). This position is concerned with education, employment, etc., as well as social welfare.

(b)   There are different positions on an axis from 'right to be cared for' to 'right to self-determination'. Some of the more extreme 'self-determination' positions tend not to see childhood as a developmental process, but as an oppressed state (oppressed by adults), for example, adults try to deny the sexuality of their children.

Source: adapted from Fox-Harding (1997)

History of Children's Work

The extent to which history is of relevance to modern practice is contested. Learning from the past may ensure one does not make the same mistakes again. On the other hand, a slavish commitment to respecting how things have evolved from the past can stifle innovation and give inadequate recognition to changing circumstances.

Using history requires a consideration of the credibility of a historical account. While much history comes from documentary sources, which themselves usually have a background of contestation and struggle, much recent history, in particular that most relevant to modern social work, comes from qualitative evidence based upon personal accounts. Looking back to our earlier lives, we interpret the past in accordance with our own experiences and ideological stances, we evaluate it with the benefit of hindsight and in the light of modern knowledge. There is a tendency to see our past through rose-tinted spectacles: 'It wasn't like that in my day!'

Parton (2006) discusses the history of child welfare, arguing that the changes within a late modern society (discussed above) are radically altering the relationship between the child, the family, professionals and the state, moving from the post-war period of 'organised modernity' (based on government welfare agencies) to one of 'extended liberal modernity', characterised by individuality and separateness rather than a fixed model of functional families and communities.

In this book history is used in areas where it provides an insight into current practices and dilemmas, for example in considering childcare placements (chapter 6), the failure to learn from the various childcare scandals (chapter 4) and youth justice where we need to reinvent the wheel (chapter 8). It is a sad reflection that many current policies fail to reflect lessons from the past.

Children's Work in a Globalised and Postmodern World

Increasingly social work has to be viewed in a global or internationalist context. Fook (2002) discusses the influence of increasing technological communication and the constraints in promoting change in social work in a world dominated by global capitalism.

Payne (2005) debates whether social work is a modern or postmodern activity. While social work has its roots in a quasi-scientific discourse, and the trend towards evidence-based practice reinforces this commitment, it can be argued that new focuses upon individualism and changes in morality and in consumerist expectations of service diversity are taking the profession into a postmodern world (see chapter 10).

KEY POINTS

- A number of underlying issues have been identified in the structures within which children's work operates, for example whether profit and care mix.
- Interventions are constrained by contextual factors such as demography and resources.
- Social care professionals can impact on change to promote service improvements.
- Practice is carried out within value systems, for example a belief about the legitimacy of state intervention in the private world of the family.

RESOURCES

The context of childcare work
As this is such a broad area, it is impossible to suggest one or a few sources of further information. Textbooks aimed at first-year undergraduates in a chosen area would make a good starting point.

Social policy and social work
Adams, R. (2003), *Social Policy for Social Work*.

Social work law
Brammer, A. (2003), *Social Work Law.*

The media
Galilee, J. (n.d.), *Literature Review on Media Representation of Social Work and Social Workers.*

Professional issues in social work
General Social Care Council website

Inter-professional working
Centre for the Advancement of Interprofessional Education (CAIPE) is a membership organisation promoting inter-professional practice across health and social care: www.caipe.org.uk.

CHAPTER 2

Constructions of Childhood and Youth

This chapter explores social constructions of social work with children and families including the children's rights perspective as an alternative to the dominant social construction which sees children as extensions of their parents. Advocacy, listening to children and families and facilitating their participation, are used as examples of good practice. The murder of Jamie Bulger and the smacking debate illustrate the emergence of dominant social constructions around childhood and parenting. The chapter creates a theoretical and practice framework for working with young people before focusing upon gender-specific work with boys. The practice areas of underachievement by boys in the education system, working with gay youths and adolescent perpetrators are discussed.

Dominant Social Constructions of Childhood and Youth

The main social construction of childhood is dependency. While young children are clearly physically dependent upon their carers, a dependence that lessens with age, and all children have an emotional bond with their adult carers, our society extends the period of dependency into the late teenage years, with, for example, social security policies that make it difficult for 16–18-year-olds to be financially independent. Indeed such policies as student loans and tuition fees are making many young people dependent upon their parents into their twenties. Being dependent creates social positions that have implications throughout society and for the individuals concerned. For example, some young people might not perceive themselves as grown up and fully responsible for their own decisions if they continue to live with parents into their twenties, and hence might be unwilling to accept the responsibilities and social roles associated with adulthood.

We see children almost as the possessions of their parents and assume that parents will make decisions and act in the best interests of their child. Where they fail to do so, it is seen as legitimate for the state to intervene through child protection procedures and other processes.

From the early theories of Postman (1983), which linked the social construction of childhood with the development of knowledge acquisition following the invention of the printing press, our society has continued to emphasise the need to teach children facts and to socialise them into the established mores. Modern educational policies emphasising achievement, both by schools (with league tables, etc.) and individual students, have arguably created a culture of winners and losers. Those who can achieve both in terms of educational outcomes and behavioural expectations (in the 'sit down and shut up' culture in schools) are valued and socially included, whereas those who fall by the wayside in one or both of these areas are demonised and become the subjects of welfare or control, increasingly the latter. Whether some of these interventions are in the best interests of individual children will be revisited later (for example in discussing the authoritarian state in chapter 8).

There are further social constructions around the family and parenting, particularly motherhood. First, we expect carers to be women (Dominelli 2002b). Secondly, pressure group activity from the fathers' rights movement, recognised by the government in legislation (Children (Contact) and Adoption Act 2005), highlighted the issue that fathers were assumed by the courts not to be equally able to have custody of their children (Conrad 2007).

Within our patriarchal society we expect caring to take place in traditional families, with a father who takes responsibility for finances and a mother who stays at home to manage the house and undertake caring – despite the contradictory demographic realities discussed in chapter 1, for example the high proportion of working mothers and single parents. The discourse of the traditional family is deeply conservative and is relied upon to produce compliant and learning children in contrast with single-parent families constructed as producing 'problem children' (James and James 2004).

We experience periodic outrage when the media report cases of lesbians and gay men wishing to foster or adopt, or lesbians seeking IVF treatment. Single mothers are regularly blamed for the wider ills in our society, with rhetoric suggesting that they get pregnant in order to qualify for social housing and benefits, when any observed links between the children of single mothers and problems such as delinquency and truancy are probably better explained by intervening variables such as poverty and the poor social conditions experienced by many single-parent families.

There is a dominant social construction that families should look after their own, with a greater emphasis upon parenting, with increasingly punitive measures against parents whose children truant or commit anti-social behaviour, suggesting that society wishes to place more emphasis upon the family as a site of social control (see chapter 8).

The unclear relationship between the state, parents and children, particularly when attributing blame when things go wrong is illustrated by Case Study 2.1.

CASE STUDY 2.1

Constructing child murderers

The tragic murder of 2-year-old Jamie Bulger by two 10-year-old boys in 1993 brought to the fore the debate about whether delinquency and other forms of anti-social behaviour are a result of inadequacies in individual offenders, whether children are fully to blame for their misdeeds or whether parents and wider society have a responsibility. Those two boys were probably children in need according to the Children Act 1989 and yet they were demonised by the press, which used words such as 'evil' to fuel anger and stoke up public outrage and demands for revenge. An alternative social construction was offered in Norway when in 1994 a 5-year-old girl was murdered by three 6-year-old boys, where the language focused on trying to understand such a dreadful event: 'more sober judgments tried to eschew the need for blame and individual culpability, preferring to investigate the broader social roots of the incident'. (Franklin and Larsen 1995)

The comparison between the two cases highlights the damaging need in our society to blame individual children and young people for complex situations where things go wrong, and the role of the media in promoting this punitive dominant social construction.

There are conflicting views about children, from naughty animals that must be tamed to innocents in need of protection from harm. The latter provides the modern social construction of child abuse and child protection whereas the former informs strategies for working with 'troublesome' young people.

Alternative Ways of Constructing Childhood

Citizenship

Citizenship provides an alternative approach to a construction of childhood. The social constructions of childhood based upon dependency on adults give young people few responsibilities towards themselves, their communities or the wider society; they are constructed as the passive recipients of what adults deliver. The concept of active citizenship gives young people responsibility for their own behaviour and that of those around them as well as those beyond their immediate experience. In practical terms this means giving young people proper information for decision-making and allowing them to participate in making decisions that affect them and wider society. The need for proper information has been recognised by the inclusion of citizenship education for 14–16-year-olds in the national curriculum.

The 'Every Child Matters' agenda promotes the participation of children in planning for their own lives and beyond, for example through schools councils and the youth parliament (Kirby et al., n.d.), although whether this is tokenistic is debatable. The 'responsibilisation' agenda also links with the citizenship approach in arguing that young people should take responsibility for their own anti-social or delinquent behaviour within a 'no excuses' culture (see chapter 8). There are also debates about promoting individual responsibility and participation through volunteering among young people and reducing the voting age to 16.

The Children's Rights Approach

The children's rights approach sees children as having rights of their own which they should be allowed to exercise in accordance with their age and level of understanding. Of course the first problem is who decides, and on what basis, whether a child is sufficiently mature to exercise agency. The issue of underage sex provides a case study of the lack of clarity in this area.

CASE STUDY 2.2

Consent to underage sex

More than a quarter of young people are sexually active before the age of consent, behaviour that is illegal and yet apparently sanctioned as there are very few prosecutions for underage sex between consenting minors (IPPR 2006).

Guidelines from the Department of Health on the provision of confidential contraceptive advice and sexual health treatment to under 16s are valuable in clarifying the apparent contradiction that under 16s are prohibited by law from engaging in sexual relations, whereas the medical and other professions provide sexual health treatments. Parallel to this is the recurrent debate as to whether parents should be told if their child seeks such treatments. The guidance makes it clear that young people under the age of 16 have the same right to treatment and confidentiality as adults unless: 'there is a risk to the health, safety or welfare of a young person so serious as to outweigh the young person's right to privacy, they should follow locally agreed child protection protocols as outlined in '*Working Together to Safeguard Children*' (Department of Health 2004)

There is perhaps still scope for misunderstanding. For example, if a 14-year-old is pregnant, it could be construed that she was the victim of sexual abuse, even if she consented. This hinges upon whether she had the competence to give *informed* consent, which might in part be related to the age of the father.

The children's rights approach questions whether parents can always be relied upon to act in the child's best interests and whether adults are always more competent in evaluating information and arriving at sensible decisions. We cannot assume that parents always put the bests interests of the child before their own, perhaps especially where parents themselves have mental health, drug or alcohol problems, or where the interests of the child are in conflict with those of a new partner, (see chapter 3). Similar concerns can be raised about professionals keen to cover their own backs and not wishing to upset managers by supporting a child with an issue to raise (see chapter 4).

Enquires, especially relating to abuse in children's homes, suggest that young people are often systematically disbelieved, especially when they have learning difficulties (they 'don't know what they're saying') or behavioural problems (they can be branded as liars) (NSPCC 2003c). Prosecutors might not proceed with cases, on this basis that such young people are likely to be unreliable witnesses (see chapter 3). Advocacy services, particularly for 'looked after' children provides a way forward in assisting children to be believed (Children's Rights Officers and Advocates 2000).

Welfare models surrounding childhood are assumed to promote the best interests of the child, but it can be suggested that despite the best intentions of legislation and guidance, other forces are at play, for example organisational factors and power relations between those involved who hold differing perspectives. For example, a child being worked with under the provisions of the Children Act 1989 should be consulted in any decision regarding their care and their views taken into account according to their age and level of understanding (Section 22(4)), however, adults making decisions can disregard a child's views by making the assumption that children lacks competence. If, for example, a 'looked after' child wishes to be placed in residential care, that choice can be overridden by a pro-fostering ideology in the local authority.

The children's rights approach is enshrined in the United Nations Convention on the Rights of the Child 1989 see chapter 1). But even here there is a contradiction in that children's right to protection from various forms of harm may conflict with wider rights, for example the right to privacy. Education is seen as a right whereas for some students compulsory school attendance is seen as oppressive, even as a restriction on their liberty.

The United Kingdom, despite the veneer of being a civilised society, is regularly criticised for policies that breach children's rights. For example, the Children's Rights Alliance for England suggested that the UK government had made little progress to deal with alleged breaches in human rights suffered by children reported in 1995, ranging from child poverty to specific concerns about the rights of children in custody and of unaccompanied asylum seekers (see chapter 4). They did however note a positive change in Government attitude to their concerns (Children's Rights Alliance 2002b). Indeed, a further review in 2003 noted that the government had taken the 2002 report seriously and that progress was being made with the appointment of a minister for children, a children's rights commissioner for England, the repeal of Section 28 of the Local Government Act 1988 (which prohibited the promotion of homosexuality by local authorities) and many other ideas under discussion (such as reducing the voting age to 16 and increasing the level of the minimum wage for 16–18-year-olds). However, the paper pointed to worsening aspects of the youth justice system, including the criminalisation of nuisance behaviour through anti-social behaviour orders (see chapter 8), and ongoing problems with meeting the needs of asylum seekers and eradicating child poverty (Children's Rights Alliance 2003).

It is difficult to envisage applying the children's rights approach in particular settings when as a society the idea of trusting children to make good decisions and listening to them are alien concepts. Even where exercises take place to ascertain the views of service users, it is possible that those who participate are the easiest to reach (perhaps as members of campaigning organisations), raising questions as to how representative they are, especially of the more disaffected groups. Are powerful groups willing to take children's views seriously when they demonstrate against issues that concern them, for example animal welfare or the war in Iraq? How do we handle a decision by a young person to do something that adults believe is harmful (for example, not going to school, wanting to kill themselves or taking drugs)?

In the long term the answer lies in changing the culture in society so as to value children more. In the meantime children being asked to participate need to be given clear information about the boundaries that govern decisions, for example about legal and financial constraints.

Individual projects have operated on principles of children's rights and have demonstrated that children can be trusted to participate and make sensible decisions – see, for example, the case of Countesthorpe College in Leicestershire.

CASE STUDY 2.3

The Children's Rights approach

Countesthorpe College, a state comprehensive school for 1,000 14–18-year-olds, was run on libertarian principles during the 1970s. There were no formal rules and sanctions, students were fully involved in the college management processes and were able to negotiate their own timetable. Social distance between staff and students was minimised, with staff being called by their first names, and there was no staff room or uniform. Interestingly, judged by modern outcome measures (exam results and truancy for example) the results were at least as good as comparable schools and, perhaps more importantly, the college was a 'civilised environment' and young people were contented and productive and arguably entered the adult world better equipped to be rounded citizens.   (Watts 1977)

Sadly, this regime has not survived the education reforms of the 1980s (see chapter 8).

The Importance of Advocacy

There is a power imbalance between professionals and service users, particularly when a service user is faced with several professionals in a meeting. This potentially difficult situation is accentuated when the service user is making a complaint when arguably the primary role of involved workers is to defend their employing agency. 'Looked after' children now have a right to independent advocacy at their review meetings, and all child service users have such a right when making a complaint. Arguably, the need for advocacy services is an indictment of the present system. If, as is assumed, the care authority is acting in the best interests of the child, the child's social worker ought to be able to perform the advocate role.

Children's trusts usually make a fixed-term contract to provide advocacy services with an independent agency, often in the voluntary sector. However, there are still issues about the independence of such advocates in that if they upset the children's trust by advocating too forcefully, their contract may not be renewed. The power of advocates would be enhanced if they were accountable to an independent body, perhaps the Children's Commissioners.

Advocates are expected to support the child or young person whatever their viewpoint, but conflict arises when the advocate feels that the young person is arguing for a course of action detrimental to their own best interests; however, if they try to persuade the child to change their view they are out of role.

It is up to the advocate and the young person to negotiate the advocate's role. In some cases they will ascertain the views and wishes of the young person and speak for them, while in others they will help the young person prepare their arguments and support them while they speak for themselves.

Policy-making

The example of smacking children, which is about the interpretation of the phrase 'reasonable chastisement' (Children and Young Persons Act 1933), will be used as an example of policy-making and the creation of dominant social constructions of parenting and childhood. This is the subject of ongoing debate around what many would argue is an unacceptable and unworkable compromise in the Children Act 2004.

CASE STUDY 2.4

The smacking debate

Whatever our personal views about retaining corporal punishment as the ultimate sanction in disciplining children, in the name of welfare we afford children lesser legal rights to protection from violence than adults. Hitting a fellow adult is assault, yet a parent can legally hit their child if acting 'reasonably', in terms of both the reason for the punishment and the amount of violence used. This derives from our social constructions of children as virtually the property of their parents, in need of protection and guidance, and incompetent to make decisions for themselves.

This becomes more complex when we consider whether the concept of 'reasonable' should be absolute, for example by stating that a smack may be acceptable but a punch isn't (the business of countless child protection conferences), or whether wider social issues come into play. For example, is it more acceptable to hit a male child than a female, a young child than a teenager?

Cultural variations present a difficult challenge. I witnessed a magistrates court case where a father of Asian origin was being prosecuted for hitting his teenage son on the bare backside with a red-hot poker. His defence was that in his culture, taking into account the wrongdoing by the boy, his action was 'reasonable chastisement'. The magistrates did not agree.

Not only do we allow smacking, but libertarian parenting, an approach that maximises the amount of freedom allowed a child, is often misunderstood as offering insufficient boundaries, and most professionals therefore promote 'firm discipline'.

Modern society gives children mixed messages about the legitimacy of violence – for example, we tolerate boxing and war, which are forms of legalised violence.

Although some parents argue that they were beaten as children and came to no harm, or even benefited from the discipline, there is evidence of long-term harm caused by physical chastisement, especially when it is inconsistently administered. For example, Strauss and Kantor (1994) suggest a link between the corporal punishment of adolescents and depression, suicide, alcohol abuse, child abuse and wife-beating.

After considerable debate in parliament and elsewhere, the compromise in the Children Act 2004 moved towards an absolute concept of harm: hitting a child can be acceptable if no visible injury is sustained. Child protection professionals, the paediatricians who have to interpret such injuries, and those who make judgments in the courts and child protection conferences, see this as unworkable. For example, some children bruise more easily than others, so children with sensitive skin will be afforded more protection.
(Stewart-Brown 2004)

Working with Young People

To illustrate how dominant social constructions can impact upon the lives of service users, sometimes adversely, this section aims to create a theoretical framework for understanding the context in which young people operate today, and the social constructions we place upon them and their behaviour, and to apply them to professional practice with young people

Numerous targets have been set (and many missed) for service improvements in working with 'troubled' young people, giving recognition to this particularly complex area of work. The need for service improvements arises from both the immediate difficulties faced by young people and the long-term social exclusion that can result, with adverse consequences for both the affected young people and the wider society (Social Exclusion Unit 2004). For example, improving educational standards for 'looked after' young people has been a priority for the Social Exclusion Unit because of the link between poor educational achievement and long-term social exclusion. Pilots were established, targets set, and yet these young people continue to disappoint in their educational achievements. Statistics show some improvements, noting that 'looked after' children are improving faster in their educational achievements than children in the general population, but they still underachieve (Department for Education and Skills 2005) (see chapter 5).

What is a Young Person?

Age can be considered in absolute terms, or more broadly in terms of age and level of understanding (sometimes referred to as Gillick competence or the Frasier ruling) as a baseline. Although age determines many legal restrictions on young people, arguably many of the problems associated with adolescence derive from the elongation of the life stage, the mismatch between biological maturity at around age 12 or 13 and full adult functioning at 20+.

Theory of Adolescence

The theoretical underpinning of the concept of adolescence will be discussed to consider the development of dominant social constructions of young people and the likelihood that policies relating to young people reflect less than objective factors, for example political rhetoric and media pressure which tend to demonise youths.

The psychology of adolescence

As well as the biological changes associated with puberty, adolescence is characterised as a period of 'storm and stress', when hormones upset mental functioning. However, in reality most adolescents don't have a particularly traumatic time, though clearly some do (Coleman and Hendry 1999).

The politics of adolescence

Young people are a very disempowered group, seen as politically insignificant and so feel that their views are not listened to. Interesting questions present themselves, for example, youths of 16 being denied the vote when they can legally work, have sex and fight for their country. Young people are seen as politically apathetic, perhaps because they don't feel they have a voice or are disillusioned with adult politicians. Young people tend to be more involved in pressure group activity around issues about which they feel strongly than in party politics (Coxall et al. 2003).

The economics of adolescence

Although few young people now have much disposable income due to their dependency, the advertising industry focuses upon them, creating wants and promoting status frustration. There are issues about why young people are economically discriminated against, for example, a lower minimum wage, benefit restrictions, and a greater likelihood of unemployment.

The history/sociology of adolescence

Adolescence is a fairly new social construct. Before the twentieth century children moved swiftly into adulthood, usually when they started work, after leaving school, were married young and had families.

The following themes can be traced from history:

1 Regulation and control: adolescents are seen as a threat to society and in need of control.
2 Changing economic roles from pre-industrial to industrial to postmodern societies now largely deny low-skilled young people access to the labour market.
3 A discourse of protection, from child labour laws to current restrictions on legal activity.

This has led to young people being the age group in society most legislated for – relating mainly to the things they must do (go to school) and can't do. Regulation and surveillance is a major theme of adult behaviour towards young people, which raises the question as to whether it is aimed at care or control.

Modern Moral Panics: The Role of the Media and Deviance Amplification

This section discusses social constructions of young people and the need to demonise them in order to justify highly interventionist policies, including the roles of the media and politicians in 'deviance amplification'.

The following process outlines how the interaction between young people and the adult world leads to a focus on teenage behaviour, which amplifies the concern of adults.

■ Young people tend to exhibit resistance to adult authority in terms of truancy, youth crime, underage sex, problems with parents, 'hanging around', outrageous appearance and other manifestations of youth culture. This causes concern to adults.

■ The term 'moral panics' derives from Cohen's (1973) work on mods and rockers and refers to how a particular behaviour or group culture becomes seen as a threat to society. A stereotyped presentation of youth in the media fuels concern in a 'good news is bad news' culture (they don't tell us that there are young people out there digging old ladies gardens!). A content analysis by *Young People Now* (2004) showed that 71 per cent of press stories about young people were negative and 33 per cent of articles concerned youth crime.

■ The media encourages a belief that today's youths are more depraved than in previous generations, whereas the opposite could well be the case; for example, the rise in reported violent crime could simply reflect a greater willingness to report incidents and as such be indicative of a more civilised society (Pearson 1983). Binge drinking on Friday and Saturday nights is not a new phenomenon; it may just be more visible now.

■ The 'moral barricades' are manned by church people, politicians, the media and 'experts' who want to 'treat' or punish deviant youth. However, it may be agreed that young people's behaviour today is *different* from that of the previous generation rather than being *worse*. For example, there is no doubt greater sexual freedom today, but rather than criticizing that per se, we should encourage more responsible behaviour (for example, safe sex), and consider this freedom as preferable to the sexual repression face[generations. The 'Just say no' approach to sex education doesn with most young people (the UK has the highest rate of teenage in Europe) who respond to more honest and liberal communication. However, critics of a more accepting approach suggest that sex and drugs education tend to encourage promiscuity and drug use rather than allowing young people to make informed choices about safer behaviour. The case study of working with gay youths (below) discusses these issues further.

- Figure 2.1 shows how the latest 'moral panic' gives rise to a sense that something must be done, the tabloid media creating a sense of urgency. Politicians feel pressurized to pass reactive, hasty and often draconian laws, mainly relating to crime, anti-social behaviour and truancy. An interesting question is whether media opinion reflects public opinion or vice versa.

- The irony is that by labelling behaviour, society creates a badge of honour that young people wear with pride within their peer group. They will therefore live up to the label and might even indulge in worse behaviour in a search for ever higher peer status.

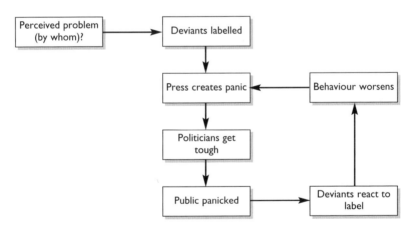

Figure 2.1   Deviance amplification model

Social Constructions of Youth

Although based in biology (puberty), youth is a heavily socially constructed life stage. Most things we know about youth are a result of social constructions.

- *Adultism: an unequal power balance between adults and young people.* What parents and professionals do, repressive laws and law enforcement all impact upon young people. Differential social exclusions exist, for example black young people are demonized and are over-represented in the youth justice system; sexual politics (boys seen as . . . , whereas girls are seen as . . .), and class factors. Housing and employment provide examples of how *all* young people are discriminated against in an adultist world, and disadvantaged young people even more so.

- *Dependency.* Policies based on the assumption that young people will remain financially dependent upon their parents, often into their twenties, place unacceptable pressures on some young people and increase the social exclusion faced by those unable to meet expectations, sometimes due to abuse (for example, having to show 'exceptional hardship' to claim income support).
- *Problematisation.* A focus on particular behaviours by some young people as though they define the norm. There are three discourses of problematisation: dysfunction, leading to therapy, ('treatment'); deficit, requiring education and training; deviance, necessitating control and correction.
- Social constructions of what 'normal' young people are meant to be like: studious, conformist, respectful, asexual and clean living.

Transitions

Being a young person is characterised by the need to make a number of successful *transitions*: from school to work, from living at home to living independently and from a reliance on parents and peers for emotional and practical support to (most commonly) a partner. Other transitions are related to citizenship, and the cognitive and emotional development which allows the young person to become a full participant in the adult world. The adolescent life stage involves more transitions than any other.

Typically, users of children's services are additionally disadvantaged by aspects of their background in achieving successful transitions, often lacking practical and emotional support and financial resources. Workers can assist a young person to compensate for these deficiencies by building alternative networks for gaining resources and by providing advice and support.

Working with Teenagers

In the climate of case management, some practitioners feel they lack the necessary skills and confidence to undertake direct work with young people, but some timely work can avert an escalation of a young person up the 'care tariff'. Focus on Practice 2.1 presents some points questions aimed at promoting effective direct work with young people:

FOCUS ON PRACTICE 2.1

Effective direct work with teenagers

1 Consider who the intervention is for: the young person or the system. There might be pressure from management or an external source to do something, whereas non-intervention might be in the best interest of the young person. I worked with a young man who was a persistent absconder from a children's home, but was not at risk of 'significant harm' while away. The police were pressurizing us to lock him up, as repeated missing

person's reports were wasting their time. Eventually the police and social services agreed to amend missing person's protocols for this young person.

2 Does everyone share the same perception as to whether there is a problem at all, what the problem is and whether anything needs to be done about it? For example, some young people may not perceive drinking or soft drug use as being problematic and will resist attempts at intervention.

3 What needs to be achieved? Set goals and agree a plan with the young person.

4 What are the problems in getting there, for example constraints such as finding employment or housing? If a constraint regularly occurs, consider a more systemic approach, for example, working with a housing provider to establish a specialist housing scheme.

5 What are the resources needed to deliver on a time scale acceptable to the young person? Young people tend to think in shorter time scales than social workers; if they've agreed to something they want it now.

6 Evaluation and review involving the young person fully in determining whether outcomes have been achieved. Do we consider only outcome measures (for example, whether they found appropriate housing or employment) or a wider and more subjective concept of 'progress' as defined by the young person?

7 Contingency planning: sometimes this involves damage limitation rather than best practice. Particularly where the young person doesn't accept a proposed intervention, a compromise based around the least damaging scenario might need to be implemented, for example a child victim of sexual exploitation might reject ceasing 'being on the game'. A package of community support that maximises protection is perhaps preferable to using secure accommodation for their own protection.

Implications for Practice

Direct work with young people requires sensitivity to the special circumstances created by the social constructions around this life stage. One issue is the inevitable worker – service user power imbalance. Often workers feel under pressure to look at behaviours (incidents) rather than feelings. Young people have a very strong sense of justice and injustice and, for example, being wrongly accused of something and feeling that they are not listened to can trigger a behavioral sequence of:

Feeling powerless → Anger → Violence or irrationality

One example I have come across was a mixed race young person who, as one of the few non-white young people in his school, suffered considerable racial bullying. One day he hit out at a fellow student who was taunting him. He was deemed violent and given a fixed-term exclusion. Feeling powerless and not expecting to be listened to, he wouldn't tell the deputy head the reason why he had hit out, preferring to accept the blame.

Below are some suggestions for positive work with teenagers:

FOCUS ON PRACTICE 2.2

Positive work with teenagers
- Everyone is an individual; resist labelling or stereotyping people.
- Be aware of structural factors that impact upon them. For example, is school exclusion about the young person's behaviour or the way schools are run?
- Identify the power relations within which a young person operates. Are they feeling empowered or powerless?
- Take a laid-back non-judgemental view (even if a young person's stance contradicts your own moral position). Avoid the 'generational thing' ('when I was your age . . .').
- Empathise rather than sympathise. Most behaviour is rational; try to understand the rationality felt by the young person, accepting that their concept of rationality may differ from yours.
- Consider the young person's perception of what you say, how you look and how you, behave. The impact of your occupation (authority figure), age, gender, status, race and sexuality.
- Don't patronise. In the eyes of young people, adults tend to exaggerate risk, for example, of clubbing and soft drug use.
- Involve the young person. A plan cannot work without their co-operation and only in the most extreme circumstances can you *make* them do something. The worker should persuade and motivate. Direct or indirect threats are seldom productive as resistance promotes undesirable consequences, for example running away or the need for secure accommodation. Be prepared to back down.
- Consider self-disclosure. Do you admit to things from your own youth? Did you smoke pot but not inhale? Young people see through dishonesty; a 'no comment' response is preferable to a dishonest one.
- Be supportive. Listen and respond positively. You are likely to be rejected if you are perceived as being on the other side.
- Give the person time and space to express themselves in their own way. Are you the best person to facilitate that? Use an advocacy worker, especially if there is a potential conflict between the young person's perception and that of the agency.
- Establish effective forms of communication, especially where the young person doesn't respond well in interview situations. Car journeys allow an intensive conversation without having to make eye contact.
- Create boundaries, explain what confidentiality you are able to offer and define unacceptable behaviour.

- Give the message that you value them as a person even if you have to strongly disapprove of their behaviour.
- Involve others: family and professionals. Exclude others if the young person wishes it.
- Negotiate between competing perspectives, using conciliation and mediation techniques, or family group conferences where the wider family is invited to resolve the problem (see chapter 7).

An idea for longer-term relationships is to set up an 'emotional bank account': after each session discuss what has been paid in and withdrawn and whether the account is in credit or debit.

The overall message is *listen and learn*.

Working with Young Men

One factor behind the emphasis upon work with young men is the gender imbalance in the social care workforce so that, whereas a female service user can request a female worker, of necessity many boys have female workers. Consequently, female workers need to feel comfortable working with boys even when highly personal issues are involved.

This section will introduce the difficult nature of being a young man and then discuss some complex areas of practice. It uses a historical approach, as adolescent identity is heavily influenced by the contradictions between past and present expectations.

A Crisis in Masculinity?

The feminist movement of the 1960s and 1970s shifted the focus of gendered work with young people from boys (who traditionally got more attention because of their behaviour) to girls who were felt to be underachieving in a world of patriarchal masculinity. forty years on, much gender-specific work is again focused on boys (Coleman 1999), partly because of their greater likelihood of being defined as 'problematic' but also because of an apparent crisis in masculinity. Due to changes in families, workplaces and wider social constructions of gender and gender roles, boys are less sure of the meaning of masculinity (Clare 2000). Some argue that, rather than there being a *crisis* in masculinity, boys and men have faced changes in their gender roles but have largely adapted appropriately (Edwards 2006).

During the first half of the twentieth century men knew their roles. There was a strong element of institutionalised violence – not least going to war and being able to fight, and in everyday life being interested in masculine activities such as physical sports and playing with gender-specific toys such as guns. Archer (1979) explores the acquisition of gender roles from a number of psychological perspectives including social learning theory and psychoanalysis.

The male role in both the home and the workplace was based around men in charge, but being protective towards women. Men were breadwinners, often workers in areas associated with masculinity (heavy industry), whereas women were seen as 'natural' carers and homemakers. Feminists suggested that even when women worked, at home men were seldom taking on a fair share of domestic duties and childcare, leaving women working a double shift (Moore 2004). Fathers were seen as disciplinarians for children ('Wait 'til Daddy gets home') and were generally not expected or 'allowed' to show signs of physical or emotional distress or affection.

In terms of the behaviour of young males, there were strong social expectations which provided rites of passage into adulthood. Culturally there was the importance of starting a job (at 15 or 16), which often included initiation ceremonies, and gave the young person an income and social status. Jobs were plentiful and varied and in many cases provided support, for example apprenticeships where a tradesman would take a young person under his wing.

Courtship took place based on the concept of romantic love, but even though personal relationships were probably more defined and straightforward than they are today, there were still confusing messages. Boys sowed wild oats, while women valued virginity and played hard to get. Nice girls did not, while others were labelled as loose (or worse) (Edwards 2004). Young people knew the rules that accompanied being a male or female. They might not always have conformed to them, as evidenced by the various youth cultures, styles and music, but the rules were clear.

During the second half of the twentieth century feminism provided the impetus for changes in roles and attitudes, giving young women permission to do well in school, at work and to take a more equal role in relationships and sex (Osgerby 1998). Men have not enjoyed the same cultural revolution; they still carry the baggage of the past, the culture of masculinity, but have fewer opportunities to express it. In some areas men are seen as inferior, while women are portrayed as more adaptable, able to juggle multiple tasks and to gain emotional support from each other to carry them through change. Social roles at work, domestically (household and childrearing tasks) and general values in society (such as anti-violence attitudes) have become 'feminised'. Traditional masculine values are under threat and yet arguably there has not been an equivalent shift in male attitudes. Males therefore are in a cultural limbo between what they feel they should believe and the reality of what is expected of them in a feminised society.

In the workplace jobs are no longer for life, which emphasises the need to compete with others, including women, in an ever more complex labour market where jobs on offer tend to be in the service sector which have traditionally been occupied largely by women. In a globalised world the proportion of unskilled and semi-skilled jobs is declining in our society, presenting the prospect of low-achieving young people remaining on the margins of the labour market (Social Exclusion Unit 2004).

Not only the feminist movement, but also the gay movement has challenged social constructions of gender roles and sexuality. While it is liberating for individuals be given permission to honestly express their sexuality, this raises contradictions for young men on issues of sexuality and masculinity. Sexuality is now a legitimate concern of the 'caring professions' (Hicks 2005).

At an extreme level, it has been questioned whether men have a role to play at all in modern society, whether in IVF or in reproduction or, at a more general level, when women choose not to enter long-term partnerships and to rear children alone, arguing on the one hand that they are able to function perfectly well as single parents, and on the other that a young male partner is likely to be a drain on their financial and emotional resources.

In this culture young men often see their 'mates' as their social reference group, with women available for relatively casual sexual relationships (Brake 1985). Such young men, disadvantaged in relationships and in the labour market, often have a negative view of their future. As they enter their twenties with few attachments to mainstream societal values there is concern that an underclass of disaffected young men is being created (MacDonald and Marsh 2002). For such individuals, the future is a life of social exclusion, and for society this raises the prospect of the group continuing the crimes and anti-social behaviour associated with adolescents, having perhaps been denied previously available opportunities to form attachments to mainstream society as a means of growing out of problems.

The root causes of the identity crisis faced by young men can be traced to the formative influences at stages in their childhood and adolescence. Earlier influences are normally found in the family, but many young boys grow up in a family without a consistent and positive male role model. As they go through school, especially at the primary stage, they see mainly female professional role models, which reinforces the stereotype that women are carers, while men are elsewhere. For example, in teaching in general the ratio of men to women is around 1 to 3, while in primary schools it is 1 to 7 (Training and Development Agency for Schools 2007).

An interesting question is why, with the growth of feminisation, men continue to display the traditional male trait of being unemotional. Perhaps this is a natural part of male biology, or more likely one of the last bastions of masculinity, something over which boys retain control when so much else seems to be controlled by women. However, the stakes are high, with young men seemingly unable to share their distress with others and resorting to suicide, self-harm or substance use as a means of externalising their anguish and managing negative feelings (Coleman 1999).

Young men are outperformed by young women at every stage in the education system; they predominate in the youth justice system and suffer far more from many adolescent mental health problems. The following practice areas illustrate the pressures faced by some boys in modern society.

Practice Areas

Why Boys Underachieve at School

Underachievement is about gender, class and ethnic inequalities. For example, for achieving 5 GCSE Grades A*–C:

■ In 2004–5 62 per cent of girls and 52 per cent of boys achieved this standard.

■ In 2002 77 per cent of children with parents in higher professional occupations and 32 per cent with parents in routine occupations achieved this

■ In 2004 the best achieving minority ethnic boys were from Chinese backgrounds (70 per cent) and the worst from black Caribbean backgrounds (27 per cent)

Source: Office of National Statistics 2005c.

Possible explanations derive from studies of male subcultures and a consideration of what they are offered in the education system.

Willis (1978) identified an anti-education male subculture in school among working-class youths that was based on 'having a laff' (laugh). A study of 11–14-years-olds by Frosh et al. (2005) attributed this largely to the struggle to meet expectations associated with masculinity, that working-class boys channel energy into:

■ sporting prowess;
■ wearing the right clothes labels;
■ avoiding getting too close to mates in order to avoid bullying and teasing or, worse, being called 'gay';
■ messing around in the classroom, which suggests that they do not take schoolwork or themselves seriously. Work is not 'cool'.

Conversely, middle-class boys in grammar schools or the top streams of comprehensives are motivated by the achievement ethos and do well.

A controversial study by Evans (2006) also considered why white boys fail, suggesting that many working-class boys are driven to leave the family to seek the freedom of the streets. She suggests that this is not a result of poor parenting but a wider phenomenon where boys seek the company of peers to avoid stresses at home.

There are a number of factors relating to schools that explain boys' academic underachievement. The school curriculum largely lacks the practical subjects that boys prefer, and boys do better in the more competitive atmosphere of exams than in course work, which is the basis of much assessment today. Teacher contact with boys tends to be more to do with discipline whereas with girls it is more to do with their work. There is a possible link with puberty in that girls mature earlier, not just physically but also emotionally. Another gender factor could be that girls have more helpful support mechanisms among their peers (Ofsted 2003).

Cassen and Kingdom (2007) confirm that poor educational achievement is disproportionately concentrated in white British boys. They point to the need to reach out to the most disadvantaged groups and to improve their engagement in pre-school, primary and secondary education. They also suggest that 'poor achieving schools' can partly be accounted for by catchment area, but also by how well a school is led and managed.

Gay Youth and Homophobia

Being a young gay man is often 'problematised' because it contradicts traditional concepts of masculinity, especially if the young person is camp. Masculinity in our society is constructed as the rejection of anything feminine: men are seen as powerful and unemotional. However, not all gay men conform to the effeminate media stereotype any more than all lesbians are 'butch'.

Homosexuality itself is a social construct (Edwards 2004). Attempts have been made to identify a gay gene, but even if a biological cause were to be established, we still have considerable control over the expression of our sexuality. Many parents fear their child will turn out to be gay, and hence children are carefully monitored and encouraged to adopt gender-appropriate behaviour, for example boys are told that they shouldn't cry.

The way in which gayness as a social construct is expressed varies between historical periods. In ancient Greece, sexual activity between males was common, usually between an older man and a teenager; it was seen as a higher form of love than that between husband and wife, and was part of the initiation into manhood. Practices also vary across cultures; anthropological studies identify various customs related to homosexuality, often initiation ceremonies around the time of puberty (Williams 1986). There are variations in acceptable male conduct even between Western societies. For example, Italian men can walk arm in arm and kiss on the cheek, whereas in Britain men are allowed to touch each other only in very restricted ways such as handshakes and hugging in sport.

The history of homosexuality accounts for much of the continuing suspicion and discrimination. From 1869 to the 1970s homosexuality was defined as a mental illness and sufferers were offered 'cures', often using aversion therapy (electric shocks would be delivered when a subject was sexually attracted to pictures of someone of the same sex). It was illegal until 1976, and only in 1999 was consent to gay sex reduced to 16 in line with heterosexual sex.

The late 1970's saw the rise in the 'gay movement', a coming together of gay men and lesbians to contest unhelpful labels and negative stereotypes; along with the disability movement and feminism was highly successful in altering dominant social constructions of these oppressed statuses.

FOCUS ON PRACTICE 2.3

Issues for Gay Young People

- Modern society offers few good gay role models, with people like gay teachers being scared to be openly 'out'. Role models in the media tend to play to prejudicial stereotypes, such as being ridiculously camp.
- There is a hidden curriculum that marginalises gay people, and homophobia is particularly rife among young people, although this is slowly changing. A Stonewall study found that 65 per cent of a sample of lesbian, gay or bisexual school students experienced homophobic bullying, and 97 per cent heard insulting homophobic comments in school which were seldom challenged by teachers (Hunt and Jensen 2007). In bullying, the worst thing is being called gay, even if one is 'straight'. Some gay young people counter homophobia by advertising their sexuality, often camping it up.
- Gay adults say they knew they were gay as teenagers, yet few teenagers 'come out' (to themselves, to parents or to their friends), and many become extremely unhappy at living a lie. Evidence of deep unhappiness is seen in higher rates of suicide. Bridget (n.d.) collates the less than adequate evidence in this area which suggests that young lesbians and gay men could be up to six times more likely to attempt suicide than 'straight' teenagers. Advising a young person as to whether and how to 'come out' is extremely difficult because of the likely homophobic reactions and rejections.
- Young gay people who want an active sex life are unlikely to find partners of their own age in their normal social environment due to homophobia. They are therefore likely to drift into the adult gay scene of bars and clubs where they can become involved with older people who are attracted to their youth.
- Given a lack of role models and peer support, it is important to assist a gay teenager to establish a positive gay identity. Telephone and face-to-face advice services, websites and gay youth groups can assist in this. Many local areas now have groups for young lesbian, gay or bisexual people which provide mutual support and social activities, often run by voluntary organisations with sponsorship from statutory agencies, commonly the youth service.
- A major challenge is to assist young people to engage in safe sex, especially given a tendency within the gay community to be promiscuous.

Adolescent Perpetrators of Sexual Abuse

The complex area of work with adolescent perpetrators of sexual abuse provides an example of the unclear divide between victim and perpetrator which informs practice in a culture where assessing and managing risk is important in balancing the rights of an individual against those of the wider society.

There are a number of ways to construct young people who are apparently engaged in inappropriate sexual contact with another child or young person.

First, we can see the behaviour as a criminal act, a sexual offence that should be dealt with through the youth justice system. Secondly, we can see the behaviour as evidence that the young person is a child in need who requires support and assistance from children's services. And thirdly, we can see the behaviour as evidence of emotional or behavioural difficulties that require therapeutic intervention.

The first question is whether the sexual behaviour is 'normal', 'deviant' or even 'dangerous' because, while some adults might feel uncomfortable about it, sexual experimentation is a normal and usually harmless aspect of teenage life. Another concern arises from the tendency of professionals to see wayward sexual behaviour in terms of victim and perpetrator, even where both parties are consenting. The issue here centres on the concept of informed consent. Age difference is often important: where one party is two or more years older than the other some degree of coercion may perhaps be involved. The Sexual Offences Act 2003 creates a clear boundary by stating that in no circumstances is sex with a child under 13 acceptable, but between 13 and 16 the position remains unclear. The issue of consent centres on competence, but there are contradictions in the law; a 15-year-old might be deemed competent to consent, but sex with a 15-year-old remains illegal.

We should also be wary because young people exhibiting sexually inappropriate behaviour might themselves have been victims of sexual or physical abuse (NSPCC 2002), but it is suggested that a majority of abused adolescent abusers do not go on to become adult abusers (paedophiles) (Department of Health 2006).

Inappropriate sexual conduct can be more an abuse of power, an aspect of bullying, than for sexual gratification. That is one reason why men in all male establishments who consider themselves 'straight' might engage in homosexual activity, or alternatively such behaviour can be considered a phase that some young men go though en route to a heterosexual identity.

Hackett et al. (2005) suggest that 17% of all cautions and convictions for sexual offences in England and Wales in 2001 involved under-18s. This is likely to be an under-recording, since many young perpetrators are dealt with outside the criminal justice system. Indeed, best practice would suggest that prosecution should be used as a last resort, probably following a risk assessment suggesting a risk to other children and the need for inclusion on the sex offenders register.

The Department of Health (2006) review of research literature and service provision in this area suggests that services for adolescent perpetrators remain patchy and that more research needs to be done to establish the effectiveness of various existing programmes. Existing research suggests that children with learning difficulties are over-represented as perpetrators, and that many perpetrators have other psycho-social needs and may suffer from conduct disorders, post-traumatic stress disorder and wider educational problems, showing high impulsiveness, emotional loneliness and low scores on self-esteem and assertiveness. This suggests that treatment should be based on sexual awareness and social skills training and that in the majority of cases criminalisation is not necessary. However, the report argues for the development of a robust assessment tool to determine who are likely to develop into dangerous adult offenders and to devise a national strategy to address the issue.

KEY POINTS

- Dominant social constructions govern the way we view children, the main one being dependency upon parents who are in control.
- Alternative social constructions such as citizenship and children's rights cast children in more powerful roles in society, giving them more agency.
- Young people are striving to be seen as adults and yet the negative stereotyping and the social constructions around this life stage (problematisation, adultism and dependency) create frustration with their status, and calls for young people to be controlled.
- Teenage difficulties are gender- and class-related, with working-class boys being defined as particularly problematic.
- Gender issues are illustrated by a crisis in masculinity, and the confusion between gender roles and stereotypes illustrated by the problems faced by gay young people.
- The need to attribute blame to young people when things go wrong is illustrated by the murder of Jamie Bulger and the way we view adolescent perpetrators of sexual abuse, often failing to appreciate the wider factors that inform such behaviour.

RESOURCES

Social constructions of childhood and adolescence

Roche J. and Tucker S. (2004), *Youth in Society*. A reader with numerous relevant chapters.

Research Briefings from the Trust for the Study of Adolescence: numerous summaries covering a wide variety of transitions are available at www.regard. ac.uk.

Websites of children's charities.

Citizenship

The National Youth Agency has a participation team and a gateway website: www. participationworks.org.

The 'Every Child Matters' website contains material on involving children in decision making: www.everychildmatters.gov.uk/participation.

The Teachernet website provides information on citizenship education: www. teachernet.gov.uk.

Children's rights
The Children's Rights Alliance for England brings together 380 voluntary organisations to campaign for the implementation of the UN Convention for the Rights of the Child: www.crae.org.uk.
Action on Rights for Children is a web-based campaigning group: www.arch-ed.org.

Work with boys
The National Youth Agency provides a good starting point in this area. www.nya.org.uk.

Male sexuality
A few specific Projects work on male sexuality. For example, Survivors Swindon: www.survivorsswindon.com
Websites offer information and chat-rooms. One suggested on the Channel 4 schools programme 'Coming Out to Class' (Feb. 2007) is the Gay Youth Corner: www.thegyc.com.

Adolescent perpetrators
Department of Health (2006). *The Needs and Effective Treatment of Young People who Sexually Abuse: Current Evidence.*
Hackett, S., Masson, H., and Phillips, S. (2005). *Mapping and Exploring Services for Young People who Have Sexually Abused Others.*
Lovell, E. (2002), *Children and Young People who Display Sexually Harmful Behaviour.*

CHAPTER 3

Child Protection: A Social Constructionist Perspective

> This chapter describes and critically assesses the procedural model underlying childcare assessments and child protection interventions and considers how definitions of abusive behaviour reflect current dominant social constructions of childhood, family and caring. It discusses wider concepts of childhood misery, especially bullying, and the bottom line issue of child deaths. It introduces the complex areas of practice with families where there is domestic violence or where parents have drug or alcohol problems as examples of what is meant by 'good enough parenting', and of assessing the best interests of a child. Marxist and feminist perspectives are used to discuss how child protection systems reflect underlying power imbalances within modern society.

Some writers use the phrase 'safeguarding children' as an alternative to 'child protection'. This reflects the 'Every Child Matters' policy agenda which seeks to broaden children's services from child protection to meeting the needs of a wider group of children 'in need of protection'. Munroe and Calder (2005) caution that this shift should not be at the expense of children who continue to suffer 'significant harm'. In this book I use the term 'safeguarding' to discuss wider policy issues only.

Social Constructions around the Procedural Model

Child protection practice aims to keep abused children safely at home in their own families rather than removing them to 'accommodation' for their own safety. I shall call the current multi-agency model of childcare assessments, including those involving child protection, the 'procedural model'. It is the basis for the dominant social construction of child abuse and protection and is based on the registration categories of:

- physical abuse (16 per cent)
- sexual abuse (20 per cent)
- emotional abuse (21 per cent)
- neglect (43 per cent).

Numerical significance of the categories is given in parenthese (Department for Education and Skills 2006c).

To be registered on the child protection register, in addition to a multi-agency child protection conference finding sufficient evidence of past or future abuse, the child or young person must be under 18 and the alleged act should be as a result of an act of commission or omission by a parent or other carer. Even something as seemingly incontestable as the maximum age is not clear; for example, it difficult to register cases of sexual abuse when the alleged 'victim' consented and is over 16. Child protection conference decisions are based on the *balance of probabilities test*, rather than the criminal test of *beyond reasonable doubt*, which sets a higher threshold of evidence. While this is appropriate for protecting children, it can lead to confusion when an alleged perpetrator is not prosecuted, or a prosecution fails for lack of evidence. I once disarmed someone threatening to kill their alleged perpetrator of sexual abuse because the Crown Prosecution Service felt that there was insufficient evidence to prosecute.

Even within these registration categories there is contestation, and most child protection enquires are not headline-grabbing stuff but on the margins of current definitions. For example, technically it is an act of abuse to allow young people to view adult pornographic material, but a child protection investigation (Section 47, Children Act 1989) would be unlikely in the face of other priorities unless the child was very young, or had been compelled to do so. Most child protection social workers, mercifully, have never been involved in a child death or other serious matters.

Included or Excluded?

What is legitimately included within the procedural model varies over time, hence child protection is not an absolute concept but a social construction.

- Intra-familial (within family) sexual abuse has evolved as a category over the last 30 years, but there is still contestation about the nature and incidence of it. For example, we tend to think that males are almost exclusively the perpetrators, whereas female abuse is now more commonly identified; it is said to be around 5 per cent of sexual abuse for girl victims and 20 per cent for boys (Finkehlor 1986). Caution should be exercised in interpreting these figures, largely due to taboos in reporting female abusers, especially by boys, as it might contradict the traditional concept of masculinity, and they may perhaps feel flattered by being offered sex by an older woman. This blindness to the possibility of female sexual abuse suggests unease at questioning social constructions of women, particularly mothers, as caring and nurturing. Many adolescents are now recognised as perpetrators, said to be responsible for around 25 per cent of sexual abuse (NSPCC 2002). A thin line exists between 'normal' adolescent sexual exploration and abusive behaviour, especially when the sexual contact was consensual (see chapter 2).
- Some extra-familial (outside the family) practices are outside the remit of current procedures. Unless the parent or other carer can be accused of

'failure to protect', for example, by allowing children to mix with known child sex abusers (paedophiles) or play in known dangerous places, it would be a matter for criminal investigation rather than social services intervention, although social workers will be involved in joint interviews of the victim with the police and in wider planning for the investigation of adult perpetrators, for the future safety of other children.

■ The definition is constantly being widened. Professional abuse came to the fore following scandals, particularly involving residential workers, for example, Frank Beck in Leicestershire (Leicestershire County Council 1993), 'Pindown' in Staffordshire (Staffordshire County Council 1991) and the abuse in north Wales children's homes (Waterhouse 2000). Abuse by teachers and foster carers is also relatively commonplace, but less often hits the headlines. New categories are evolving, for example, domestic violence (discussed later in this chapter).

■ There is no such thing as 'corporate abuse'; only individuals are apparently capable of perpetrating abuse. If, for example, social services place a child inappropriately due to lack of resources or available alternatives that is not deemed abusive.

■ There are still taboos, for example, not accepting that ritual abuse exists. Scott (2001) suggests that despite a number of high profile but failed investigations of satanic and other organized occult abuse rings, even the definition of ritual abuse has been associated with being 'beyond belief'. She suggests that media reporting of the more sensational aspects of such cases have made it more difficult for credible stories of victims to be believed, and thus for them to receive proper therapeutic support.

■ Other recent examples where abuse exists but has not been constructed as such include concern about deaths and bullying among young recruits in the armed forces and among young people in custody (Stuart and Baines 2004). The lack of joined-up thinking regarding the problem of young runaways and the dire adverse consequences of prostitution and drug addiction are also causes for concern (see chapter 4).

A feminist perspective on child protection suggests that whereas legislation and practice guidance use the term 'parent' in dealing with concepts like 'failure to protect', in reality it is mothers who tend to get the blame. Conferences debate whether the mother was negligent in not knowing that abuse was happening or, worse, did know and colluded in it (Macleod and Saraga 1994). This applies equally to other children's policies that focus upon parenting, for example, few fathers are seen by education welfare officers investigating truancy (see chapter 8).

A Marxist would note that child abuse is seen as a largely working-class phenomenon. Although most social services investigations do still involve working-class allegations, this could reflect better policing of the poor, or that middle-class families, being more private, are better at covering up their wrongdoings, that is what goes on behind closed doors is less visible (Thorpe 1995). Certain practices in upper-class families that could arguably be constructed as abusive are positively encouraged, for example, sending children to boarding schools from as young as 8, and meeting out cruel and degrading punishments in the name of character building. A Marxist perspective would debate the unequal power relationships within a capitalist society that tend to accuse the poor and protect the rich for it is the powerful who decide who and what is socially constructed as problematic (Corrigan and Leonard 1977).

Making Sense of Assessments in Childcare: Critical Perspectives

Assessment is:

1   part of a *process* of intervention or care management;
2   a means of rationing resources by effectively prioritising tasks;
3   deciding how identified needs can be met within available resources;
4   an opportunity to assess risk to the service user, others and the agency.

There are two kinds of assessment:

1   general assessment under the National Assessment Framework and the Common Assessment Framework;
2   specific assessments, for example, of prospective foster carers, ASSET assessments for young offenders and pathway plans for care leavers.

The Common Assessment Framework (CAF)

Implemented nationally from 2008, the CAF brings together previous assessments for special educational needs, social services interventions and medical issues into one standardised assessment package to promote a joined-up approach to meeting additional needs. It is designed to promote early identification of additional needs and a holistic approach to interventions devised in partnership between children, parents and professionals.

The national framework for assessment is based on the triangle in Figure 3.1 which outlines factors about the child, the parents and the general environment in which they live. It is based upon the ecological approach which attempts to take an assessor beyond the presenting problem towards an analysis of causes and a consideration of all the complex and interacting systems that impact upon the lives of individuals and families. Garrett (2003) welcomes the inclusion of the Family and Environmental Factors axis, as these wider structural factors were not explicitly included in previous policies and reflect the New Labour project of acknowledging poverty as a factor in childhood difficulties. However, critics have suggested that wider structural factors impacting upon a child and family are often under-represented in the outcome of assessments since the assessment model is based upon individual case work. For example, unemployment in the family might be considered, but causal factors, national and local economics and the impact of the neigh-

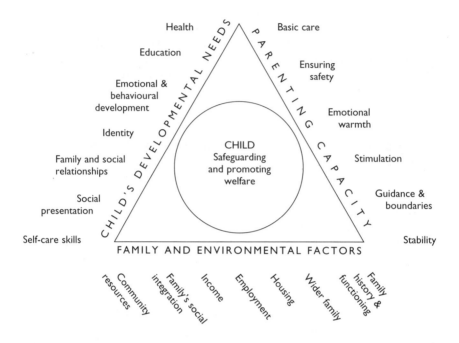

Figure 3.1   A framework for assessing children in need (Department of Health 2000)

bourhood are unlikely to be included. In such cases the individualization of problems through case work places blame unduly upon the parents. Garrett (2003) links this to the interventions that might flow from the assessment in the 'new politics of conduct', 'micro-engagements' such as parenting orders and the range of tutors and mentors aimed at assisting with perceived poor parenting.

Important Themes in Assessment

Probably the most important and most complex theme is working in partnership with children, parents and other professionals/agencies. The Children Act 1989 makes this a requirement, although the practice issues present numerous challenges, the greatest of which is that, however much professionals might aim to work alongside and assist a family, in the end it is they who decide whether the parenting is 'good enough' and whether or not the children should be removed.

The partnership approach derives from service users being the experts in their own situation, and to gain the best information and to implement a workable plan, service users must be an integral part of the assessment process.

A worker carrying out an assessment needs to be aware of their own impact on the situation; power imbalances, use of authority, the expectation of expert knowledge and many personal factors impact upon service users' perceptions of the worker. Allied to this is the importance of listening to children and parents. A danger with the 'tick box' approach is that gathering information becomes an end in itself, whereas people should be allowed to tell their story in their own way without the forms taking over. While many practitioners criticise the structured 'tick box' nature of assessment and many other aspects of children's work, forms are designed only to obtain relevant information systematically, they do not replace professional judgement as to the nature of the problem and what to do about it.

In an era of evidence-based practice, it is important to make judgements based on both the evidence collected in the particular case and the research that can inform decisions in interpreting this unique situation. The use of evidence is a complex issue. The most sophisticated evidence comes from predictive models: if a person has a number of predisposing factors, there is a certain probability of their being an abuser. The problem is that, even if we know that a person with these characteristics has an 80 per cent probability of being an abuser, we don't know whether the person before us is one of the 80 per cent who is, or more importantly, one of the 20 per cent who isn't, an abuser; that decision is a professional judgement.

Risk assessment is a major theme in child protection work. An accurate assessment of risk allows safe decisions to be made at a time when resources are severely limited. When starting an assessment it is easy to become overwhelmed by the negatives of the situation: the house is filthy, there are a lot of empties around, the child has dirty clothes and so on. The skill is to keep a cool head when evaluating risk, not only the immediate risk but also the longer-term situation, particularly the potential for change. Immediate risk can often be managed through a package of support, perhaps utilising family aides or children's centre resources.

It should not be assumed that intervention will make things better, the likely outcomes of possible forms of intervention and non-intervention should all be evaluated. Sometimes damage limitation is necessary, the realisation that a preferred plan will not work, and that the least damaging alternative is the best one to pursue, especially in the face of non-cooperation from an older child or parents. 'Cascades of intervention' is a cautionary term suggesting that one intervention leads to another, and in the end the combined interventions prove more damaging than the original problem. A current example is the punitive approach to truancy discussed in chapter 8.

The exercise in Focus in Practice 3.1 invites consideration of the realities of childcare assessment work: rationing resources and reconciling supply and demand in a manner that keeps children safe and maximises the benefit of available resources. There is an important difference between reality and best practice, and practitioners need to appreciate both. In making decisions the manager is likely to consider urgency (how quickly something should be done) and importance (whether it needs to be done at all and where it ranks in relation to other priorities). Risk management is about prioritising tasks that are highly important and urgent.

Inbox Rationing Exercise
Prioritise the following referrals and decide what action to take on each.

You are a team manager responsible for childcare assessment and today you have one duty social worker. Here are today's referrals. How would you prioritise the work?

1 Neighbour phones to express concerns about children who live in the flat above. She thinks they're aged about 2 and 3. Single teenaged mum, with men 'always coming and going'. She often hears the children crying in a very distressed way and last night she could hear the mother screaming at one of the children because they wouldn't eat their food. Mother seems 'at the end of her tether'.

2 Mother of 14-year-old son phones to say she's worried about him. He's seldom at home and when he comes back late at night she thinks he's 'on drugs'. He's angry and uncommunicative and just goes to bed. She tries to talk to him but gets told to 'f— off'.

3 School teacher worried about an 8-year-old child. Seems very tearful, scruffy and often doesn't have proper food for lunch. Has only been in the school for six weeks having recently moved to the area.

4 School teacher worried about 13-year-old girl. Used to be a good and reliable student, but in the last few months her work has deteriorated, she's often late and lacks concentration. There have been a few unexplained absences.

5 Grandparent phones, worried about 12-year-old grandson. She thinks he's been hit by her daughter's new partner. Boy denies this but says he 'hates Jim' and thinks he should 'bog off'. Her daughter tells Gran to mind her own business.

6 Health visitor phones to say that a family with a newborn child and a 2-year-old are struggling. The place is a mess, often cold, and the parents are often arguing when she goes around. She thinks they drink a lot as there are often empties around when she visits early in the morning.

7 YOT worker is concerned about the parenting of a 12-year-old facing his first court appearance for shoplifting and other minor theft. The family are chaotic and seem to have few routines – for example, nobody wakes him up for school so he's usually late or takes days off. Can we help?

8 Police phone to ask you to collect a 15-year-old runaway found sleeping on a park bench they took to the police station in the early hours. She says she's from Manchester and ran away because her step-dad 'keeps coming on to her'.

Other situations that require urgent attention:

1 A physical or sexual abuse referral.

2 The emergency duty team accommodated a teenager who was thrown out of home. No proper paperwork done. Must be moved from the emergency bed as only available for 24 hours.

3 A placement breakdown.

See end of chapter for suggestions.

Using the Procedural Model of Assessment and Intervention

This section discusses in detail the process of carrying out a childcare assessment thought to warrant child protection. The National Assessment Framework (Department of Health 2000) and Safeguarding Children (Department for Education and Skills 2006a) detail how social services should respond to new referrals, including those considered to be child protection cases.

Recognition and reporting of child protection concerns is the responsibility of all agencies working with children, and indeed all members of the public. The issue goes beyond the training of childcare professionals to recognise and act appropriately in matters of suspected abuse. What needs to change is the culture in society that permits ordinary people to ignore adult behaviour towards children that they consider unacceptable. Have we been in a public place, a supermarket or beach for instance, and witnessed what we felt to be excessive chastisement, and done nothing about it? Worrying research suggests that a quarter of a million adults would do nothing if they had a child protection concern, the most common reasons being not wanting to get involved or not knowing what to do (NSPCC 2006a).

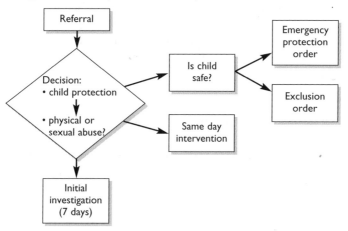

Figure 3.2 Child protection process: early stages

Referrals

Who makes them?

Health visitors are the main source of referrals for younger children while teachers are the main source for school-aged children. Under multi-agency procedures social services is the lead agency for child protection and should receive all referrals. Years of interprofessional struggle have established an acknowledgement that individual professionals and their agencies cannot decide to handle a child protection concern outside the system, although many child protection workers can relate cases of unacceptable maverick behaviour. One example was a head teacher who unacceptably decided not to invoke the professional abuse procedure when a senior teacher attacked a student: she rationalised that he was an 'excellent teacher' and the young man 'very demanding'. She excluded the student and closed the matter as a one-off incident in no need of further investigation.

There is a structural clash between the confidentiality that professionals, including doctors and clergy, offer their service users and the expectation that any suspected child abuse must be reported. We are concerned that the public are generally unaware that the usual rules of confidentiality are over-ridden in child protection cases, a complex debate, even given that the primary goal must be the protection of abused children. Social workers now tend to make their confidentiality contract explicit at the start of an intervention, and other professional need to find ways to achieve this. The danger is that people aware of abuse might not disclose it to a trusted professional if they know that the matter will be formally reported, and so the abuse goes unrecognised and the adult, often the primary carer, remains unsupported. It is of concern that many clerics, especially Catholic priests, feel that their pastoral relationship, especially within the confessional, gives them permission to over-ride the protocols.

Particular ethical dilemmas present themselves when an older child or young person discloses abuse and asks the professional to 'keep it to themselves'. While the young person might feel that the professional is violating their trust by insisting that the matter is properly referred, it is an uncomfortable price to pay for protecting that child and other potential victims. Best practice is that the confidentiality rules are made clear from the outset and that professionals use their skills in communicating with the young person to persuade them that referral is necessary.

Main subjects of referrals

Statistics suggest that in the year ending 31 March 2006:

> Of the total of 569,300 referrals to social services 23 per cent were repeat referrals that had previously been made in the last year. (Department for Education and Skills 2006c)

Although good practice suggests that a child should remain on the child protection register for the minimum time consistent with their safety, there is concern about the 'revolving door syndrome' whereby children join and leave the register repeatedly. Deregistration can reflect an over-reliance on short-term evidence of safety rather than a longer-term view of the child's needs, often exacerbated where cases are closed on deregistration rather than being reclassified as a child in need.

> The mean referral rate is 515 per 10,000 children, but local areas vary from 3 per cent of councils reporting a referral rate of less than 200 per 10,000 to 6 per cent reporting a referral rate of 1,000 per 10,000. (Department for Education and Skills 2006c).

It is unsatisfactory that massive local variations exist in the rates of conferences and registrations which cannot be fully explained by local factors such as the degree of deprivation.

Managing referrals

Among professionals as well as the public, blindness to abuse can result from a fear of making trouble or making a fool of oneself if the referral is not substantiated, to fearing the time and emotional energy that a referral will involve, or being accused of making a malicious allegation. Some professionals try to cover their backs by referring every little concern, while others seemingly turn a blind eye to even serious matters. Simple logistics can affect referrals. For example, PE teachers used to commonly identify physical injuries, but now that children seldom shower in school this is less likely.

It is difficult to achieve a balance between a number of referrals made and the ability of social services and other child protection specialists to process seemingly endless referrals. It is a question of priorities, picking out the children suffering *significant harm* from those *in need* (Children Act 1989) in the context of resource limitations. The level of functioning of any childcare team relates to supply and demand, not need. The task is to ration resources safely by prioritising the most dangerous referrals.

The resources issue can be acute, with a particular department or team able to process effectively only the most severe physical and sexual abuse referrals. While few team managers feel comfortable noting 'no further action' on any child protection referral after only the most basic enquiries, to try to investigate everything can lead to a failure to identify the most serious cases and to concentrate limited resources on them. It is difficult to prove and achieve successful legal action in cases of low-key sexual or physical abuse, particularly emotional abuse and neglect, so it is likely that these will attract low priority. It is politicians and managers who through the allocation of resources decide what can and cannot be done.

Resource shortages can be about funding or, increasingly commonly, a failure to recruit appropriate staff to work in child protection. Often the blame culture deters people from child protection careers, or workers choose more comfortable and less stressful areas of practice.

The way to minimise rationing problems is through gatekeeping. For example, rather than individual teachers making a decision as to whether to make a child protection referral, the designated child protection co-ordinator in the school (often a deputy head) gatekeeps the decision, having attended the appropriate multi-agency training and gained the knowledge and experience to make that important initial judgement. Individual teachers and other professionals should, however, retain the right to make a referral should they feel concerned about a gatekeeping decision.

At a systems level, from a children's services perspective, the key to avoiding bombardment lies in liaising with potential referrals, perhaps through termly meetings with families of schools and their associated professionals, and regular meetings with health visitors and other professionals working with young children. At these meetings rapport can be established between the various professionals, and boundaries discussed as to what is an appropriate childcare referral. Such meetings can also look creatively at ways of solving wider problems, such as problematic drug use in the area, rather than individualising the concern to particular young people.

The Social Work Process

This section outlines the progress of a child protection referral, including key decisions (centred and displayed) and time scales (in italics) and discusses some of the issues raised at each stage.

Potential child protection referral received
First decision (team manager/duty social worker)
Same day as referral
Is it a child protection case?

There is a debate about who should take referrals. Some argue that it is a task for a well-trained administrator, others feel that only the most skilled social workers should handle these important initial discussions. It can be difficult to determine the seriousness of a referral from a short discussion with a referrer, usually over the phone.

Games can be played around 'up-tariffing' referrals. For example, in one authority the principal officer, for resource reasons, decreed that family aides could be deployed only in child protection cases. Not surprisingly, the proportion of cases defined as child protection increased dramatically. There is a perverse incentive to justify requests to management for additional resources by inflating workload statistics.

Is it physical or sexual abuse?
Requires same day intervention

One of the most crucial decisions is the need to balance the immediate safety of the child and the need to preserve evidence against the temptation to be too reactive.

I remember the case of a duty social worker going out on a medium priority referral and coming back to the office in a state of panic, saying that parents had barricaded themselves in their flat with two young children whom the original referrer had felt to be at risk of physical abuse. The police had been called but, rather than using heavy tactics to enter the flat, had sensibly asked for advice from social services. The bottom line was that strong arm tactics could put the children at more risk while a delay of an hour or two was unlikely to. The outcome was that a phone call to a health visitor established that she had been visiting the family until a few months before and had a good relationship with them. She managed to persuade them to let her in, and after some discussion they accepted that social services were not the enemy, and working in partnership the family agreed to accept a package of support. Risk-taking led to a successful outcome.

Immediate protection; legal measures: emergency protection order (Children Act 1989, Section 44) or exclusion order (Family Law Act 1996)

Exploring the Threshold of Care

One of the most important but controversial decisions is whether to apply to a court or magistrate for an order to remove the alleged abusing parent or the child from home pending the child protection investigation under the Children Act (Section 47, often referred to as a 'Section 47 investigation'). There are civil liberties issues here, especially since the initial application is *ex parte* (those subject to the application are not heard).

This decision should be informed by a risk assessment of the immediate danger to the child, including the ability of the non-abusing parent to protect, and possible effects on the investigation, especially the impact upon working in partnership with parents and children. Good practice suggests that wherever possible the child should remain in the home and the alleged perpetrator move out, even if an order is required to achieve this and social services has to pay for alternative accommodation.

Some areas operate an interventionist approach, arguing that having a court order gives power to control the investigation and gain the compliance of the parents; others argue that orders indicate an adversarial approach and should be used only as a last resort. The views of the child should be sought and taken into account in accordance with their age and level of understanding. The reality for child protection workers is that they are damned if they do and damned if they don't. If they adopt the strategy 'If in doubt whip them out', they are likely to be accused of wrecking families, but if they fail to remove a child who subsequently dies or is seriously injured they can be blamed. Although it is a highly skilled professional judgement, a major factor in the judgement remains the predisposition of the front-line decision-takers to be interventionist and to play safe, rather than risk trusting in the family. Within the current blame culture the safety strategy, defensive practice, is likely to predominate. Munro (2002) discusses this complex area of decision-making, evaluating risk in the context of the complex interaction between intuitive and analytical thinking.

It is ironic that in such cases as the tragic death of Victoria Climbie, it was the carers who neglected and eventually killed Victoria, but the social worker was blamed, both in the media and by her own employers in disciplinary procedures that led to her dismissal and inclusion on the register of adults unsuitable to work with children. This was successfully appealed and the Care Standards Tribunal interestingly both praised the social worker and strongly criticised her management for insufficiently supporting her (Care Standards Tribunal 2004 (268PC)).

In making decisions the social worker and their manager can seek legal, medical and other professional advice, but the Cleveland Enquiry (Butler-Sloss 1998) gave weight to the view that advice is just that: Social Services do not have to act on it. However, within the blame culture, social workers need to be wary of not acting on authoritative advice from other, higher-status professionals.

Preserving evidence

Child protection investigations suggest an uneasy balance between the 'best interests of the child' and the need to preserve potential evidence for prosecuting a perpetrator. A successful prosecution might help to protect that child from further abuse, and future potential victims. It is an interesting aside that child protection uses the language of criminal law rather than social work, for example, 'investigation' rather than 'assessment'.

Initial investigation (intake social worker/other agencies)
Within 7 working days

Enquires of other Agencies

At an early stage the investigating social worker will contact other agencies known to the child to share concerns and ascertain whether they have relevant information or views. Often at this stage a clear picture emerges as to whether the referral is likely to develop into a Section 47 investigation.

There are civil liberties implications about sharing highly confidential information without the consent of the subject, which are overridden by the need to protect children. It is good practice to seek consent wherever possible.

The national children's database (Contact Point) will promote the easier identification of professionals involved with a child, especially in cases where the child has moved to another area. There are, however, debates about the security of data held on the national database, particularly who has access to it and in what circumstances, and about consent for confidential information to be stored (see the Action on Rights for Children website: www.arch-ed.org). A report from the Foundation for Information Policy Research alerts us to wider potential problems with how electronic data could be abused, for example by collecting negative information about certain groups of disadvantaged children that could then be used to discriminate against them, perhaps by using fallible models to predict potential delinquency (FIPR 2006).

Joint interview with child

Interviews are now conducted by specially trained social workers and police officers. It requires skill to gain information from the child in a supportive way, which minimises the trauma to the victim while at the same time preserves evidence that can be used in court, for example, not asking leading questions. Skills in communicating with children have to be age-appropriate and take into account the emotional state of the child and their level of understanding. For example, play or art can be used as communication tools with younger children. In order to minimise the number of times the child must tell their story and for evidential purposes, the interview is usually videotaped.

Discussion with non-abusing parent

The crucial question here is when to conduct the interview with the parent thought to be non-abusing. In making this decision protection of the child should be the paramount consideration, although working in partnership means that the parent should be kept fully informed of developments and their views sought as early as possible. There is a risk that evidence could be destroyed if the non-abusing parent is colluding with the abuser.

Statement from alleged abuser

The police will take a formal statement from the alleged abuser if it appears that criminal charges could be brought. It is good practice for the decision as to if and when this statement should be sought is taken jointly with social services in the best interests of the child (see Figure 3.3 for details of the protection process).

Figure 3.3 Child protection process: later stages

Strategy discussion

As a result of the initial assessment, a formal decision is made about whether there are sufficient concerns to proceed to a full Section 47 investigation. Guidance suggests that this can be a strategy meeting, or relevant professionals can be consulted over the telephone, with the eventual decision being taken by the investigating social worker and their manager (DfES 2006a). It is unlikely that parents or the child will be involved in this important decision, which arguably undermines the concept of 'working in partnership'.

The discussion should consider:

- whether or not to call a child protection conference;
- how to plan the full core assessment;
- the immediate needs of the child and family and the safety of the child.
- what information to share with parents, and how and when.

This is a crucial stage in the process. Collating and weighing up the evidence collected is a highly skilled task, which can put a child at risk if not conducted professionally.

Core assessment
within 35 working days

(This was discussed earlier in the chapter).

'Child Protection case' conference
within 15 days of the strategy discussion

It is the role of Social Services in consultation with other participants in an investigation to convene the **Child Protection Conference** if necessary. Key tasks include the following issues:

Provide chair, venue and administration

The role of the chair is crucial for the conference to be managed effectively. Chairs, whether or not full-time specialists, should be given extensive training and opportunities to meet together and to give feedback to management on the working of the child protection system. For example, they might wish to express a view as to the appropriateness of the number and nature of conferences called. Chairs should particularly ensure that everybody present is empowered to contribute. This might mean controlling some of the more powerful professionals who tend to dominate meetings to create space, where appropriate, for front-line workers and the child and family to contribute, since they are more likely to know the situation best.

Decide on attendance

An assumption that families and children should attend conferences about them is now good practice, assessed according to the 'best interests of the child' test. The child's attendance should be decided according to their age and level of understanding and their views. Even if an older child does not attend the meeting it is good practice for them to be available to meet the chair who will explain the process beforehand and check that someone is briefed to express their view. It is currently not a requirement that independent advocates be available to children at child protection conferences, although as good practice this is offered in some areas. During the meeting the child might need to be consulted and the meeting will be adjourned to allow this. The chair should explain the outcome of the conference to the child and any family members not present throughout.

There are some cases where it is not possible for the child and/or parent(s) to attend all of the meeting, for examples where:

- the child expresses a reasonable wish that someone shouldn't be allowed to attend;
- parties have different interests which it is felt should be heard separately; each party will attend for part of the meeting;
- the confidentiality of a third party might be undermined (such situations should be minimised as they compromise partnership working and can lead to unaccountable decisions based upon unsubstantiated information);
- there is a threat of violence;
- attendance could undermine the police investigation.

Prepare the child and family

The conference should be a mechanism for sharing information already known to the child and family. It is poor practice to expose the child or family to distressing information or opinions of which they were previously unaware.

Social workers and other professionals preparing reports for the conference should share the contents of these with the child and family in advance of the conference. The social worker should take the lead role in explaining the child protection process to the child and family and the conference chair should check their understanding.

Produce a report on core assessment/investigation

The social worker should summarise the content and outcome of the Section 47 investigation. This will normally collate the input from other participants, although other agencies might choose to present their own written submissions.

Within the time scale it might not be possible to fully complete the investigation but sufficient information should be available to inform the decisions of the conference. It is clearly crucial in managing workloads that sufficient time is allowed for intensive assessments.

The conference decides

The following decisions can then be made:

- whether to register and which category;
- who to nominate as a key worker (key workers are almost invariably social workers);
- how to formulate a multi-agency protection plan.

The decision to register is based upon a consensus as to whether the child has been abused or is at risk of abuse and can be made safe by a child protection plan.

The protection plan will specify what multi-agency action needs to be taken to keep the child safe. Almost invariably this will involve regular contact with the child by one or more professionals. As is known from enquiries following deaths, it is crucial that the child is the focus of the intervention, that social workers do not collude with potentially abusing parents and that the child is actually seen and spoken to on every visit in accordance with the protection plan. If there are logistical difficulties they need to be overcome, for example, finding an interpreter for a non-English speaker.

FOCUS ON PRACTICE 3.2

The role of the key worker

1 **Acts as centre of communication between all involved.** Enquires following deaths of children on the child protection register often point to a lack of communication between the various professionals involved in the protection plan. While each person has a duty to communicate any issues or concerns to the key worker, the key worker should also be pro-active in contacting the other workers to check on the progress of the plan.

2 **Sets up a core group to co-ordinate work on protection plan.** Increasingly, communication between front-line professionals is facilitated by regular face-to-face meetings of a core group convened by the key worker within 10 days of the conference.

3 **Ensures recommendations of protection plan are actioned, particularly that the child is seen.** As well as ensuring the safety of the child, the key worker should be proactive in ensuring that recommendations within the protection plan aimed at achieving longer-term improvements are implemented with a view to a future conference having sufficient confidence in the safety of the child to remove them from the register.

4 **Responds to changes in circumstances.** The key worker should respond to changes in the child's circumstances. A serious deterioration requires urgent consultation with colleagues to consider further action, including removing the child. In less urgent situations, the key worker should consider reconvening the conference early to consider amending the child protection plan in the light of changed circumstances.

5 **Works with child and family.** As an experienced professional, the key worker may be the right person to undertake some direct work with the child or family, or it may be appropriate for this to be contracted from other agencies with the key worker concentrating upon managing the plan. Therapeutic work with the victim may be constrained by the injunction against contaminating evidence if a prosecution is pending.

> **6 Involvement with care proceedings or other civil court action such as a child assessment order; involvement with police and Crown Prosecution Service (CPS) in criminal proceedings.** The key worker is likely to be the main person to link with the police and the CPS in ensuring that the child's best interests are taken into account in any decisions about criminal prosecutions.

Review child protection conference
First review within three months, then at least six-monthly

Review conferences consider developments since the last conference and decide:

- whether the child should remain on the child protection register;
- on revisions to the child protection plan, particularly focusing on the safety of the child.

Evaluating the 'Procedural Model'

It is difficult to evaluate the success of the procedural model as there is a built-in tendency to highlight failures, most notably when a child dies. Undoubtedly thousands of children have been enabled to remain at home safely following abuse allegations, and countless social workers and other professionals have been dedicated to making that happen. On the other hand, the overall rate of child homicide has, with some fluctuations, remained constant for 28 years (NSPCC 2003a), so either the procedural model is not identifying the right children, or it is failing to protect some of them.

The biggest indictment of the procedural model is the obsession with the categories and circumstances as presently defined to the exclusion of a wider concept of childhood misery. Large proportions of children's services budgets are devoted to unsubstantiated abuse allegations at the expense of other child-care functions, not least prevention (see chapter 7).

The tragic death of Victoria Climbie and the subsequent enquiry report (Laming 2003) again focused attention on continuing failures to protect those children defined as being at risk of significant harm and therefore within the procedural system. We therefore continue down the road of trying to refine the systems to work more effectively.

Managing Child Protection: Messages from Research

In investigating child abuse we need to be aware of the 'iceberg phenomenon'. We research known allegations and known perpetrators and make the dubious assumption that the one-fifth above the surface is the same as the four fifths below.

A further difficulty arises from basing research upon known incidents. In using criminal and other statistics, we have to be aware that a rise in reported incidents of sexual abuse might not indicate that there are more incidents of sexual abuse, but simply that more victims have been willing to come forward, or even be a logistical consequence of changes in reporting procedures. We live in a more open society where sexual matters are less taboo, a wider range of options for disclosure and support exist (for example, Childline), professionals and the general public are more alert to the possibility of abuse and it is now recognised that welfare agencies and the police are better trained to conduct investigations in a professional and humane way. Similar arguments could be made for domestic violence and other sexual crimes such as rape.

Research by Childline (part of the NSPCC) provides a mixture of valuable case studies and analysis of the reasons why children have contacted them over the last 18 years and the support they have offered, often over a sustained period. Bullying has now replaced sexual abuse as the major reason for calls. It is significant that many children feel more able to contact an anonymous helpline than to talk to apparently trusted adults in their life (Easton and Carpentieri 2004).

The investigation of child abuse based upon the procedural model of referral, investigation, conference, registration, protection plan, deregistration and closure, has limitations even in terms of protecting the children within that system. For example, we often fail to recognise the following factors:

- The investigation itself can be damaging, particularly in the case of sexual abuse, for example, having to submit to an intimate medical examination and to relive the experience when telling one's story, often several times.
- The current system provides little opportunity for therapeutic work. The long-term damaging effects of child abuse are seldom recognised. Adult psychiatrists often testify that a common reason for breakdown in middle age is previously undisclosed abuse in childhood, or disclosed abuse where the victim has not been provided with proper post-abuse therapy.
- After the closure of a child abuse incident, it is likely that the child remains a 'child in need' under the Children Act 1989, and yet ongoing provision is seldom offered as team allocation constraints dictate that closure is needed to allow new investigations.
- Most child protection referrals come to nothing and yet consume a high proportion of childcare budgets (Thorpe et al 1995).

Following from 'Child Protection: Messages from Research' (Department of Health 1995) the government launched the 'refocusing debate' urging social services to divert resources from child protection to wider preventative services. This initiative was undermined, partly because the resources were inadequate and the emphasis upon 'performance' meant that things that work (like community work) could not be justified as cost-effective, but largely because in the 'cover your back' culture, no team manager was going to write 'No further action' on a child protection referral in order to release resources for prevention. The refocusing policy did, however, inform future policy developments, for example the emphasis upon meeting the needs of disadvantaged young children through Sure Start and the wider concept of 'safeguarding' children (Department for Education and Skills 2006) (see chapter 7).

However, the greatest scandal is that the structural factors that blight children's lives such as poverty, poor housing and lack of opportunities, are underrated. There are at least two ways in which these contribute to abuse. First, in our materialistic society such things are arguably abusive in themselves in that they exclude people from full participation in modern society. Secondly, there is a link between such factors and parental stress, which is linked to abuse (Department for Education and Skills 2006).

The 'achievement culture' which is based upon a very narrow definition of success is also to blame in contributing to the worrying increase in incidence of child and adolescent mental health problems and suicide. The current government aims to increase 'social inclusion', whereas mainstream systems like schools, the youth justice system and the increasing inequalities within our society actually increase it. Although the government has taken valuable steps in the taxation and benefits systems to reduce child poverty, these seem minimal within the bigger picture, and fail to impact upon those families who are the most disadvantaged, often referred to as 'hard to reach' families. Poverty is not just about money, but about life chances. For example, the teenage pregnancy strategy seems to fail to recognise that young women sometimes get pregnant, not because thet are ignorant of contraception or suffer from moral weakness, but out of a rational choice, given a perceived lack of other opportunities.

Child Maltreatment and Wider Unhappiness

The NSPCC report, 'Child Maltreatment in the UK' (2000), based upon a large sample survey of children, aimed to move the focus from the present social constructions of abuse to wider issues of childhood misery. Bullying was a major focus of the report, being a feature of the childhood experience of almost a third of the sample, and 43 per cent of young people had experienced 'aggression'.

Our society is starting to realise the importance of bullying in destroying childhoods. The Anti-Bullying Alliance, funded by the Department for Children, Schools and Families, spearheaded by the National Children's Bureau and the NSPCC and involving around 50 voluntary organisations, co-ordinates support to schools and promotes effective approaches to reducing and managing bullying and creating a safe environment for learning (Spotlight 2004). Best practice suggests that not only should adults listen to children and take their concerns seriously, but peers have a valuable role to play in creating an anti-bullying culture and in supporting victims.

Working against Protection and the Risk Culture

Our society has gone to considerable lengths to protect children from exploitation, but some argue that increasing concern about child abuse has led to children being 'protected' to the point that their childhood is threatened. For example, the concept of 'stranger danger' is being used to frighten children from interacting with adults and vice versa. We are scared to let our children go out to play, depriving them of sociable interaction with peers, exercise and fresh air.

The issue of child deaths illustrates the confusion in society about the inflated sense of risk faced by our children. However, we should not fall into the trap of arguing that the danger posed by child sex abusers is a pure 'moral panic'; there are dangerous people from whom children need protection. Many are now being monitored through MAPPA (multi-agency public protection arrangements) designed to plan for, monitor and review potentially dangerous violent and sexual offenders, including registration on the Sex Offenders Register. Concerns continue about inadequate resources for such strategies, and in some cases the inability to force subjects to comply with plans.

Debate continues as to the wisdom of allowing parents and others to know the whereabouts of child sex abusers in their communities. A more structuralist perspective would advocate shifting the focus from perpetrators of abuse to making communities safer with, for example, more supervised play opportunities.

The following case study considers the emotive issue of non-accidental child deaths (see Case Study 3.1).

CASE STUDY 3.1

Child deaths

The ultimate concern within any civilised society, and particularly in relation to its child protection systems, is children who lose their lives non-accidentally at the hands of adults. For example, 70 under-16s in 2003/4: of these, 30 victims were killed by parents, 11 by suspects known to them and only 10 by strangers. In 19 cases there was no known suspect. Children under 1 year old were most at risk of homicide with a rate of 45 per million compared with 16 per million for the total population (Office of National Statistics 2005).

Cases of mothers acquitted on appeal after having been convicted of killing their infants warn of the complexities in this area, not only in the use of 'expert witnesses' but especially perhaps in distinguishing between a cot death and an infant murder or infanticide.

We might also wish to include some children who die 'accidentally', especially as the largest cause of death among children is road accidents. Each month more than 200 children under 15 are killed or seriously injured by traffic. Deaths on the road are over 20 times more frequent than extra-familial killings and although they are deemed to be 'accidents', arguably many are preventable (Pritchard 2004). Controversy exists as to why those who kill by dangerous, even drunk, driving seem to be treated more leniently than other killers.

Although stranger killings are relatively rare, it is usually these cases that hit the headlines. Pritchard and Sayer (2006) suggest that there are relatively few 'very dangerous' people in society with previous convictions for violence and sexual offences who remain dangerous to children upon their release from custody. The authors question whether, in the name of protecting children, it would be acceptable to use preventative detention to detain this small group long term. Of course no predictive model can ever be certain as to who will and who won't commit such heinous crimes, and such a proposal therefore seems unacceptable in our society. Thus it seems that accidents waiting to happen must actually happen before action can be taken.

Preventing Deaths in the Child Protection System: Near Misses

SCIE (Bostock et al. 2005) have argued that rather than concentrating upon child protection incidents that go seriously wrong (when children have been hurt or killed), organisations should shift the focus to learning from mistakes made in less dramatic circumstances or 'near misses'. There is clearly a difficulty here in that individuals and organisations have a vested interest within the blame culture and litigious society, to attempt to cover up rather than to learn from mistakes (see chapter 4).

SCIE argue that the 'risk management' approach developed elsewhere in the public sector, notably in healthcare, can allow 'learning organisations' to adopt the systems approach to analysing mistakes to avoid repetition, situations where something could have gone wrong but was prevented, or where something did go wrong but no serious harm resulted. In a pilot study, 60 near misses were identified and analysed, most commonly reported by front-line practitioners, situations where potential significant harm was either overlooked or misjudged, or where resources were not available. These tended to result from poor prioritisation of work, inaccurate or incomplete information, or poor decisions by other teams or agencies.

Supervision provides the immediate opportunity for identifying near misses, but there has to be a relationship of trust between worker and supervisor and a 'no blame' culture for errors to be disclosed. The next line of defence against mistakes is to establish a reporting system, as happens in the aviation industry. The ability to learn from reported incidents is dependent upon a positive organisational culture, and leadership (see chapter 4). A significant number of near misses are uncovered during complaints investigations and it is crucial that, rather than covering up such incidents mistakes are admitted and apologies offered so that service users are fully empowered to contribute to the investigation (Bostock et al. 2005).

The Bostock et al. (2005) study was unable to consider latent failures beyond front-line staff involving actions by other players, including senior managers and politicians, which is clearly an area for further research, perhaps especially where senior people fail to take responsibility, as was identified in the case of the death of Victoria Climbie (Laming 2003), or where resource shortages promote risky practice.

Practice Areas: Good Enough Parenting

Child protection workers apply the concept of 'good enough parenting' when assessing whether a child is suffering 'significant harm'. In many cases the quality of parenting is largely determined by the ability of the parent(s) to put the child's needs before their own, for example where there are issues of parental substance abuse, mental health problems or learning difficulties, or where there is domestic violence. This section will examine situations where adverse adult behaviour affects the quality of parenting.

Such cases can become particularly complex where the emotional bonds between child and parent(s) are good and yet physical or other aspects of parenting are poor, even dangerous. Parents may be well intentioned, rather than actively abusing their child, but the environment may still be abusive, the abuse lying in acts of omission rather than commission. Children with a strong bond with their parent(s) are likely to resist being removed for their own safety.

This section develops a model to explore the complexities of assessments in these practice areas. Practitioners carrying out assessments need to evaluate the strengths and weaknesses of the parenting in the context of risk and compared to the possible strengths and weaknesses of removing the child. An assessment might uncover a child 'in need', or suffering 'significant harm', and requiring a child protection risk assessment.

Dimensions of Complexity

Child dimensions

There is a need to distinguish between the immediate issues, possible physical or emotional abuse or neglect for example, and the long-term effects. Immediate dangers might include: substances or paraphernalia left around, behaviour when the parent is 'out of it' and the possible influences of parents' associates (who might, for example, be sex abusers).

In considering the longer-term issues, the possible harm caused by remaining in such a household versus the possible outcome of being 'looked after' needs evaluating. The long-term consequences of emotional abuse or neglect need to be considered, plus the possibility of the child being sucked into the lifestyle of the parents. It is known that children who drink excessively disproportionately have drinking parents, but some children can react to parental problems in the opposite way, for example by becoming very anti-alcohol (Robinson and Dunne 1999).

Another dimension is that the young person could be a young carer in need of support. If emotional or practical needs cannot be met by parents, other support mechanisms are needed to protect the young person from a damaged childhood. Further, young people in these situations could suffer mental health issues related to stress. On the other hand, coping with adversity can be an important factor in building resilience and coping mechanisms (see chapter 9).

Adult/parent Issues

Children's services will be concerned about the child, adult services are likely to be involved with the parents. Links with adult services (social services and health) are likely to be crucial in achieving a successful outcome for child and parents (Kearney et al. 2003).

Childcare social workers concentrating upon the best interest of the child are likely to be concerned with the willingness and ability of the parents to change their lifestyle in response to the identified concerns. Adult services will focus on the needs of the parents. There can be a clash in objectives, for example, where adult services feel that the threat of removing the child is impeding the recovery of substance-using parents.

Organisational issues

Reder and Duncan (1997) in their study of serious case reviews (often following child deaths) noted poor participation by adult psychiatric services in child protection and a lack of awareness among child protection workers of parental mental health difficulties. With the split between adult and children's social services and the move towards more multi-agency working, we can envisage further potential conflicts between child and adult workers at all levels as practitioners and managers will no longer be part of the same agencies.

Practice Area

Domestic Violence

Domestic violence, which can combine physical and sexual elements (rape in marriage is now illegal), always involves an element of emotional abuse and is largely about the misuse of power. Power has to be seen in the context of the social constructions we place around male–female relationships (patriarchy) and between parents and their children (the smacking issue, for example). Historically, attitudes of the police and other professions have often been based on the assumption that a man should be left to run his household as he sees fit. The police often failed to investigate 'domestics' as assault until recent changes in attitude, especially the establishment of specialist police domestic violence units. Further social constructions around family privacy often make it difficult for the police to investigate incidents adequately, especially if the victim declines to make a complaint.

Domestic violence occurs between partners in an intimate relationship, usually perpetrated by men on women, but it may be women over men (contradicting gender stereotypes) or between gay partners. It also includes elder abuse and abuse by carers. Domestic violence occurs across the class spectrum, although, as with child abuse, it is more likely to be visible in the working classes.

There are special issues relating to the abuse of women from minority ethnic groups, especially perhaps in Asian communities where gender politics are different, generally in favour of men.

- 23 per cent of women and 15 per cent of men aged 16 to 59 reported that they have been physically assaulted by a current or former partner at some time in their lives. Of those victims who had children in the household, 29 per cent said the children had been aware of the last assault they had experienced.
- Domestic violence accounts for 23 per cent of all violent crime.
- 26 per cent of young adults reported that physical violence sometimes took place between those caring for them during childhood. For 5 per cent this violence was constant or frequent.
- There is a strong overlap between physical, sexual and emotional abuse of children and domestic violence, and high proportions of those experiencing abuse from parents also witnessed frequent violence between them.

Source: NSPCC Key Child Protection Statistics (2006b)

The Law

Until 1976 the only legal protection to victims of domestic violence was under the common law offence of assault. The Domestic Violence and Matrimonial Proceedings Act 1976 gave more protection to victims and the Family Law Act 1996 strengthened the law by introducing a non-molestation order which can apply to partners or children. The Domestic Violence, Crime and Victims Act 2004 gave more powers to the Police to arrest for breaches of a non-molestation order, and civil courts can now issue a restraining order even where there is no criminal finding of guilt. It also extends protection to same sex couples and introduces a new offence of familial homicide which closes the loophole whereby parents could escape justice if it was not clear which of them actually killed their child.

In terms of protecting children, the provisions of the Children Act 1989 were strengthened by Section 120 of the Adoption and Children Act 2002 which extended the definition of harming children to include harm suffered by hearing or seeing violence against others. Until recently social workers had little involvement in domestic violence unless it was thought that the child was also a physical victim. Now it is recognised that witnessing the abuse of others is itself abusive, child protection procedures should be followed.

Much of the work in this area has been carried out in the voluntary sector (by Women's Aid refuges and others) and this remains the case. Housing legislation has been strengthened to give rights to housing for victims of domestic violence, so now there ought to be no purely logistic barriers to leaving an abusing partner.

For reasons of simplicity only, the following largely assumes a male perpetrator and female victim. Students might consider applying the concepts to female on male abuse and same sex abusive partnerships.

Countering Domestic Violence

Work with women

A feminist approach suggests counselling based around 'consciousness raising', contesting what victims often say, that they feel they contributed to the abuse. They need to understand their situation in terms of structural issues around patriarchy. Mutual support and information sharing through group work can be of value in identifying that each victim is not alone in their suffering, to suggest survival tactics and give information for change (how to leave the abuser). Work to increase self-esteem can empower the victim to proceed with criminal proceedings against the perpetrator.

Strategies for protecting the children and making the mother aware of likely long-term consequences for them will be based around empowering her. The big issue is why victims stay with abusing partners even today when the resources to leave are available. Around 40 per cent of prosecutions have to be dropped when victims withdraw their statement, although the CPS are now showing a greater willingness to proceed when victims retract if there is suffi-cient alternative evidence. Advocacy services can be invaluable in supporting victims reluctant to prosecute (Home Office 2005)

Serial victimisation can be a pattern for some victims, where one violent partner is replaced by another. This suggests learned destructive behaviour and poor self-esteem in the victim. In terms of protecting a child, there needs to be a careful assessment of each new partner. Child sex abusers can make relation-ships with vulnerable women to gain access to their children.

Work with children

In conducting interviews with child victims it is important to give 'permission' to the child to break the secret that often masks domestic abuse. This means explaining to the child the purpose of the involvement and the possible courses of action that could result. It is important to avoid an over-zealous child protection response; after all, the child has probably lived this life for some time. An immediate risk assessment is necessary as is a consideration of the effects on the longer-term future of the child, such as their schooling. If the child seems immediately safe, try to examine the dynamics of the family and the position of the child within it (do they, for example have a role in protecting the mother?). How do they feel? (Fear for their mother, fear of going into care, fear of making things worse if the abuse comes out).

Work with perpetrators

Most work on violence and anger management is currently undertaken by Probation, though it is sometimes contracted out to the voluntary sector.

Work with male abusers usually involves considering issues of masculinity and how to express manliness without resorting to violence. It is often based on cognitive behavioural techniques, requiring perpetrators to take responsibility for their actions and to propose alternative behaviours when stress factors are present. It is important to ensure that perpetrators really want to change, and are not just conforming to a programme to avoid an undesirable alternative, such as prison. This work usually explores the personal history of the perpetrator to try to explain how and why they became violent. Consideration will be given to the pattern of the abuse, whether it is premeditated or spontaneous and whether there are external triggers, for example being drunk. Research in the US (Gondolf 1998) suggests that altering gender attitudes is the key to change, for example teaching men to talk rather than hit out, teaching them positive views of women and seeking to change their attitudes rather than just helping them to manage violent impulses.

Group work is often used to get men to confront their denial, rationalisation and minimisation.

Work with families

Sometimes work with the family unit seems appropriate. Options range from conciliation to family therapy. Although in any victim–perpetrator situation there is always an interaction between the two parties, the family approach is perhaps most effective when the dynamics within the family unit, rather than the failings of one party are disproportionately causing the problems.

Where a violent partner leaves the home, issues of contact between abusers and separated children need consideration (Joseph Rowntree Foundation 1996). As with other contact scenarios, the best interests of the child should be paramount and their views taken into account according to their age and level of understanding. Beyond that, there might be evidential issues that require the interaction at contact to be witnessed. The role of contact centres is important in making safe contact possible, especially as custodial parents can feel that they are being forced into an unsafe arrangement. On the other hand, the views of fathers also need to be heard; mothers and courts can block viable contact by overstating the danger.

While there is a presumption that contact is normally in a child's best interests, we should not be blind to the possibility of abuse, even death, during contact. Saunders (2004) examined the deaths of 29 children in 1994–2004 as a result of contact and residence arrangements, five of which were as a result of court-ordered contact, highlighting the need for proper risk assessments of contact arrangements.

Substance Use by Parents

Substance use can be a major barrier to a parent's ability to put the interests of their children before their own. However, we should not assume that all serious substance users are inadequate parents; some have stable habits and can function quite well. Thus, we cannot make blanket judgemental statements such as 'Children of heroin addicts should be in care'. Every case needs to be assessed on its merits in the context of the age and wishes of the child. Although young people often recognise the inadequacy of parenting, they can become resilient and recognise that their parents do care about them, even if physical care is poor (Joseph Rowntree Foundation 2004).

Some parents with addiction problems will lead chaotic lives with poor routines (so, for example, there might be nobody to prepare the child for school and groceries might not be purchased), spend most of their money on substances (a cause of neglect) and indulge in dangerous behaviour, for example leaving needles or substances around. In the case of alcohol there is an association with violence, memory lapses and perhaps prolonged absence from the home (possible neglect). Lower-key but longer-term concerns are likely to centre around emotional abuse, whether the parents are meeting the emotional needs of the child or leaving them to their own devices, and whether the lifestyle of the parents will impact on the future of the child.

The stigma felt by children will vary depending on such factors as the neighbourhood. It is likely that the greater the stigma will be felt where the abuse relates to illegal substances, or where parental misconduct is public, such as drunkenness.

There are special areas of concern, such as when a woman continues substance use during pregnancy, where the child may be born addicted and hence be difficult to manage during the withdrawal period; there is also a link with long-term childhood behavioural problems. There is a case to be made for conferencing an unborn child for neglect if a pregnant user fails to heed advice to give up substances during pregnancy. (Then again, what about a woman who smokes during pregnancy?)

Parents with Mental Health Problems

It is estimated that around 16 per cent of parents may suffer mental health problems, ranging from short-term depression through to long-term psychosis which might involve periodic hospitalisation. The impact upon a child will depend upon the length and severity of the illness, and crucially the availability or otherwise of a well parent or other secondary carers. It is estimated that around one-third of young carers are caring for parents with mental health difficulties (Green 2002).

Green (2002) suggests that parents with mental health problems have impaired social performance and have disproportionately conflictual relationships which can adversely affect parenting; in the longer term this can lead to behavioural problems in the affected children. There is also a greater probability of child protection concerns.

Fictitious Illness by Proxy (Munchausen's) Syndrome

This syndrome involves the fabrication or induction of illness in a child, most commonly to get attention from medical professionals. It particularly challenges traditional constructions of parents and childcare professionals as being caring and promoting the best interests of the child. It is thought that mothers are the perpetrators in around 85 per cent of cases, and in rare cases medical or other professionals (Horwath 1999). Detection is particularly difficult because many perpetrators present as credible and particularly caring. In some cases the fictitious symptoms are merely described, in others they are created by the carer interfering with the child to induce symptoms. In extreme cases covert clinical observation (hidden cameras) establishes that the carer is harming the child.

Parents with Learning Difficulties

Regular media coverage focuses attention on whether parents with moderate learning difficulties should be allowed to parent their children. In most cases it is appropriate to offer support to such families, but sometimes parents are unlikely to be able to offer long-term adequate care for their child, and 'permanence' elsewhere is necessary. Is it appropriate for a child to remain in an intellectually impoverished environment, or should the be placed with nice middle-class adopters? Should this decision be made at birth to minimise the harm to and delay for a child if the parents are allowed to attempt parenting, often with several care episodes? The 'families torn apart' headlines and the possibility of a legal challenge under Section 8 of the Human Rights Act (the right to privacy and a family life) can make such a decision especially challenging for practitioners (Roberts 2005).

A potential problem arises as the child grows older and, especially if they are more intellectually able than their parents, issues can exist around creating boundaries. In one case I encountered, a well-meaning and caring father used to hit out at his young teenaged son, not understanding more subtle parenting techniques, which resulted in a physical abuse registration, a care order and a 'revolving door' between home and care placements for the child.

Considering whether parents with moderate learning difficulties should be allowed to have children and parent them is a hangover from the eugenics (science of controlled breeding) movement of the early twentieth century which supported the segregation of the 'feeble-minded' to prevent them from breeding. Arguments for the sterilization of people with learning difficulties are still made, but many would argue that advocating selective breeding is a dangerous road for a liberal democracy, especially as the issue becomes one relating to who decides who can breed and who cannot.

KEY POINTS

- Child protection is a social construct; some maltreatment is included in and some excluded from what is currently defined as abuse.
- Decisions taken as part of assessment are about rationing resources and meeting need.
- Interventions are disproportionately targeted at the poor and women.
- Assessments and interventions tend to focus upon personal inadequacies in a child or family rather than the wider societal factors underlying problems, thus blaming the victim.
- In determining 'good enough parenting' there is often a complex interaction between the needs of the child and parental problems that inhibit parenting.

RESOURCES

General child protection
What To do if You're Worried a Child is Being Abused (2003, DfES). A summary of processes, including flowcharts designed for professionals other than social workers. Can be confusing and fails to focus on the issue of identifying abuse and assessing immediate risk.

A good starting point for child protection research is the NSPCC Inform website. You can register for free weekly email updates on a wide variety of childcare and child protection issues (CASPAR) and access research reports and their library which offers reading lists, and a search facility: www.nspcc.org.uk/inform.

Parents with issues
Kierney, P., Levin, E., and Rosen, G. (2000), *Alcohol, Drug and Mental Health Problems: Working with Families*.

Kierney, P., Levin, E., Rosen, G. and Sainsbury, M. (2003), *Families that Have Alcohol and Mental Health Problems: A Template for Partnership Working*.

Government Reports
Hester, M. and Westmarland, N. (2005), *Tackling Domestic Violence: Effective Interventions and Approaches*.

Home Office (2005), *Tackling Domestic Violence: Providing Advocacy and Support to Survivors of Domestic Violence*.

Parmer, A. et al. (2005), *Tackling Domestic Violence: Providing Support to Survivors from Black and Other Ethnic Minority Communities*.

Walby, S. and Allen, J. (2004), *Domestic Violence, Sexual Assault and Stalking: Findings from the British Crime Survey*.

Downloaded from: www.ecm.gov.uk

NSPCC (2002), *Mentally Ill Parents and Children's Welfare*.
NSPCC (2003a), *Domestic Violence and Children: A Resource List*.

Joseph Rowntree Foundation: Findings series
(1996), *Domestic Violence and Child Contact Arrangements*.
(1998), *Domestic Violence in Work with Abused Children*.
(2000), *Working with Families where There is Domestic Violence*.
(2004a), *The Effect of Parental Substance Abuse on Young People*.
(2004b), *Understanding What Children Say about Living with Domestic Violence, Parental Substance Misuse or Parental Health Problems*.
(2005), *Drugs in the Family: The Impact on Parents and Siblings*.
Downloadable from: www.jrf.org.uk

Young-voice.org publish a number of booklets about young people's experiences of a number of problems in their lives including:
Mullender, A. (2003), *Stop Hitting Mum!* Gives an insight into young survivor's views of domestic violence.

Young carers

Website set up by the Princess Royal Trust for Carers. www.youngcarers.net. Barnardo's also have an interest in this area: www.barnardos.org.uk.

Suggestions for Focus on Practice 3.1   Inbox Exercise

1   There could be concerns largely because of the age of these children. The children appear to be in need under Section 17. There is no real evidence of physical or sexual abuse and as such is unlikely to warrant urgent investigation. However, checks should be made of other agencies to clarify the level of concern. It could be a malicious neighbour scenario.

   Urgency: medium   *Importance*: medium

2   Sadly this is typical of parents of teenagers seeking help and is likely to be written up as 'no further action' and the mother advised to seek help elsewhere, maybe a local project in the voluntary sector. There is a need to monitor referrals on this boy in case a pattern of concern suggests that he's on the threshold of 'accommodation', which would markedly increase the level of priority.

   Urgency: low   *Importance*: low

3   Again the basics for a neglect investigation are present but no factors indicate urgency. Ideally a common assessment should be started, but this is unlikely to be prioritised. Would check the child protection register (prior to the national database) in the former home area and see if there are concerns from other agencies, and advise the teacher to see the parent(s), express the concerns and observe the response. Would make a further decision based on this information. Could be that the child is simply unsettled after the move.

   Urgency: low   *Importance*: medium

4   Out-of-character behaviour is of concern in a teenager; it could be indicative of sexual abuse, or more likely a lower-key personal or family problem. If time allows, would make checks of other agencies, but would advise teacher to have a discussion with the girl and report back any concerns. Perhaps the EWO could become involved.

   Urgency: low   *Importance*: low

5   This could be indicative of physical and/or emotional abuse or just resentment by a child of mother's new partner. Telling Gran to mind her own business could indicate a cover-up. Would check with other agencies and ask the head of year to talk to the boy and report back.

   Urgency: medium   *Importance*: medium

6   The two young children might be suffering neglect or their level of parenting is adequate while not being excellent. Ideally they should be defined as

children in need and a common assessment commenced. Would ask the health visitor for more detailed information and ask her to monitor the situation. Might offer a resource, for example a family aide.

Urgency: low   *Importance*: medium

7   This is symptomatic of a boundary dispute between your team and the YOT. They feel they're not resourced to do 'family work', but unless there are more specific concerns, the referral is unlikely to be seen as a priority by you either. Since there will be a referral panel (see chapter 8) involving the child and parents, these issues could be discussed further and perhaps supervision, activities or a family group conference could address them. Perhaps the YOT has a mentoring scheme or the EWO could address the school attendance and lateness issues. A systemic approach would suggest some negotiations with the YOT, and maybe other agencies such as CAMHS to clarify boundaries.

Urgency: low   *Importance*: low

8   You will need to respond to this. Your duty worker will interview the child with a view to getting her back home, to avoid 'accommodating' her and probably incurring the cost. You would inform the home authority of the situation, particularly any disclosure of abuse, suggest putting her on a train and hand it over to them. They might be concerned about her absconding again, so you might negotiate a car journey and escort (at their expense).

Urgency: high   *Importance*: low

In reflecting on these decisions, little Social Services intervention was offered either to help the individual children, each of whom could have been deemed to be at least a 'child in need', or to give positive messages about our services to the referrers or referees. Some situations were deferred until another time, matters of potential safety were checked and action stimulated by other agencies, which made it possible to cope with the demands of the day. If a physical or sexual abuse referral had come in, the team manager would have been creative to find additional resources.

CHAPTER 4

Safeguarding Children Living Away from Home

Enquiry reports considering child abuse deaths and professional abuse have identified similar concerns about management and organisational failures. The chapter considers first similarities between the Laming Report into the death of Victoria Climbie (Laming 2003) and the Kirkwood Report into the abuse of children in Leicestershire children's homes in the 1980s (Leicestershire County Council 1993), and then considers what makes the organisational cultures of social services agencies potentially dangerous, examining factors related to healthy cultures and whistleblowing to uncover serious concerns. Systems failure is discussed using as examples the safeguarding of those living away from home in residential care and prisons, children who run away and child asylum seekers.

Failures to Learn

It is unrealistic to suppose that further scandals relating to child abuse will never happen because the services and the individuals who provide and consume them are all too complex. However, it is disappointing that lessons have not been learned from earlier reports into the deaths or sexual abuse of children in the public care system. Whatever the failings of individual practitioners, one of the most worrying issues is the failure of organisational and managerial arrangements that should have promoted safe practice.

The Laming Report (2003) investigated the tragic death of Victoria Climbie, whose parents had hoped for a better life for her in Europe. She was privately fostered by her aunt and her partner, having recently entered Great Britain from her African home via France. She was horribly neglected, physically abused and eventually killed. As with many earlier reports following child deaths, the report noted a failure in communication and co-operation between the numerous agencies involved, and much of the blame fell on the allocated social worker and her supervisor. Less media attention was paid to the failings of the organisations in which these individuals operated, to which attention is drawn in the Laming Report (2003):

> . . . the principle failure to protect her was the result of widespread organisational malaise. (p. 5)

> . . . the greatest failure rests with the managers and senior managers of the authorities whose task it was to ensure that services for children, like Victoria, were properly financed, staffed, and able to deliver good quality support to children and families. (p. 5)

While few practitioners would argue that their service is adequately funded, there is little doubt that resource shortages have seriously undermined the capacity of social services departments to deliver adequate services. Tough and sometimes risky decisions have been taken to ration available resources. The report commented:

> Sadly many of those from Social Services who gave evidence seemed to spend a lot of time and energy devising ways of limiting access to services, and adopting mechanisms designed to reduce service demand. (p. 13)

A lack of accountability was identified, that is who was actually responsible and could be held to account for a particular piece of work. The report suggested:

> The single most important change in the future must be the drawing of a clear line of accountability, from top to bottom, without doubt or ambiguity about who is responsible at every level for the welfare of vulnerable children. (p. 6)

This is one of the major disadvantages of the hierarchical structure of children's services. Practitioners and line managers are apparently held to account by their superior, but it is seldom clear who actually holds the responsibility when things go wrong. Supervision of middle managers by senior managers tends to be about resources and strategy rather than accountability for individual cases.

The report even suggested that managers can lose sight of their major objective – to provide quality services to children – in their struggle to meet organisational needs through unhelpful policies and procedures.

Laming thought that elected members should be kept informed of potentially troublesome cases and that while the job of senior management is strategy, they cannot be absolved of responsibility for what goes on at the grass roots of their department. The report suggested:

> What is needed are managers with a clear set of values about the role of public services . . . together with the ability to 'lead from the front'. The Enquiry saw too many examples of those in senior positions attempting to justify their work in terms of bureaucratic activity, rather than in outcomes for people. (p. 6)

The Kirkwood Report (Leicestershire County Council 1993) examined the widespread physical and sexual abuse of children over a 13-year period in a number of Leicestershire children's homes where Frank Beck was officer in charge. It identified a 'management vacuum' which allowed the abuse to continue despite numerous complaints to staff and the police. Beck was seen as 'good with difficult kids', a status that seemed to make him unchallengeable within an extremely weak and complacent management structure (Kahan 1994).

New areas of concern are evolving, for example, the Laming Report (Laming 2003) highlighted the dangers to children living under private fostering arrangements and there is regular media coverage about the nature and quality of services provided to unaccompanied asylum seekers. The challenge to those in authority is to act now rather than awaiting another tragedy.

How Care Agencies Can Allow Abuse

This section explores a model that seeks to explain why organisations that are established to care and protect can become dysfunctional and abusive, examining some issues relating to participants within caring organisations and then the wider concept of organisational culture.

Vulnerable Children

First, not all children living away from home are equally vulnerable to abuse. It is estimated that children with disabilities are between three and four times more likely to suffer child abuse, and that overall 31 per cent of disabled children are likely to suffer abuse compared to 9 per cent of non-disabled children (NSPCC 2003c). This increased vulnerability relates in part to disabled children being more likely to be living away from home and to specific vulnerabilities, for example a child with learning difficulties being particularly vulnerable to sexual exploitation.

However, there are factors that make the whole group of children living away from home vulnerable to abuse.

- Young people, especially those living in residential situations might be scared to disclose abuse, either because they fear retaliation (especially if several staff are involved) or because they fear they will lose the placement and be in an even worse situation.
- The child may have no trusted person to whom they can disclose their problems and from whom to seek support. A professional to whom a disclosure is made might not take the matter further because the allegation contradicts their view of the alleged perpetrator (for example, Frank Beck was seen as an excellent childcare worker), they are scared of being labelled a whistleblower, or worse, they might not believe the young person. In the latter case rationalisations can include an expectation that a 'difficult' child is likely to lie, or that a child with learning difficulties has misunderstood a situation.

Even if after disclosure the concern is taken forward, there is an inbuilt tendency for one or more organisations to cover it up. This might be to protect the organisation's reputation and the position of senior managers who fear for their own futures if things get out, or just because of incompetence, as in the case of Frank Beck. Further problems can arise even if the young person is believed, because of insufficient evidence or the young person is an unreliable witness.

Although professionals are now more willing to listen to and believe a young person, there are counter-tendencies. For example, it is said that children know how to cause trouble for carers by making allegations. They might be attention seeking, vindictive, or hoping to gain favours or even compensation. On the other hand, they could be telling the truth.

A difficult situation results from allegations where there is no evidence (just a young person's word against a carer's). Good practice suggests that we should believe the child, but although a carer is in law deemed innocent until proved guilty, in professional abuse investigations they can have their reputation and career ruined even if the investigation concludes that the allegation is 'not proven' (an intermediate stage between guilty and not guilty). This implies that although there has been no finding of guilt, doubt remains. This is unsatisfactory from an innocent carer's perspective, especially as it is almost impossible to prove one is innocent of something one has not done, and yet in these professional cases one seems to be guilty until proved innocent.

Adult Perpetrators

Given the vulnerability of children living away from home, it is inevitable that adults who aim to abuse children will seek involvement in this sector.

Since the Warner Report (1992), following the various abuse scandals in residential care in the 1980s, numerous changes have been made to the checks on adults seeking to work with children. The murders of two schoolgirls in Soham by Ian Huntley in August 2002 reopened the issue, and the Bichard Enquiry (2004) suggested even tighter checks, especially around the sensitive issue of whether police intelligence information, often not supported by a charge, prosecution or conviction, should be released to potential employers. Here we have to balance the need to protect children against the possibility that a completely innocent person, perhaps the victim of a malicious allegation, can be prevented from doing a job they love and children deprived of an excellent worker. The Safeguarding Vulnerable Groups Act 2006 set up a new Barring Board to adjudicate on contentious cases, streamlined checking systems and made it a criminal offence for an organisation to allow a person to work with children, in a voluntary or paid capacity, without the correct checks.

It is worrying if a culture of fear among children makes them mistrust all adults on the one hand, and on the other if there are shortages of skilled and motivated childcare workers because of fears of allegations and the effect these can have on individual careers. However, because the care industry provides a potential abuser with a fertile hunting ground for vulnerable victims, the balance is almost impossible to achieve.

Child Perpetrators

Children need protection not only from adults inclined to abuse them but also from other children who might be bullies or perpetrators of sexual abuse (see chapter 2).

Organisational Cultures

It is difficult to define the term 'culture' particularly as it is sometimes applied to aesthetic activities or to ethnicity. 'Organisational culture' refers to the norms and values, which are often not formally articulated and often below the level of an individual's consciousness, that apply within an organisation. Connolly et al. (2006) who apply the concept to child protection suggest that:

> culture is understood to relate to some shared elements which connect people in a common way of experiencing the world, and determine what is perceived to be appropriate and inappropriate behaviour in any particular context. (Connolly et al. 2006: 17)

An individual joining an organisation is likely to quickly perceive whether they are 'one of us' or hold values contrary to the dominant organisational culture. The cultural values they experience might be markedly different from the organisation's formal statement of values, as published in recruitment material, for example.

An organisation's culture has its roots in its history. Some organisations with long histories can be resistant to change if members adopt the attitude that 'we always do it like that here'. This can be deeply embodied in the underlying beliefs of the organisation, for example, a religious group struggling to adapt to a secular society, deciding how to meet the needs of children from other faiths.

At an organisational level it is interesting to see whether the formal organisational structure (hierarchy) matches who really has the power to make decisions. In some organisations interest groups, perhaps a trade union, seem to have more power than those occupying senior positions. Some individuals seem to acquire a status above their position in the hierarchy, which makes them almost 'fireproof'. It is not always clear how such a status is achieved, but it often reflects membership of informal alliances or formal groups inside or beyond the organisation. Gosling and D'Arcy (1998), when examining Frank Beck's abuse, discuss his networks of other abusers, a common characteristic of child sex abusers. There is a debate about whether membership of various secret societies is compatible with public service ethics, or whether there may be a conflict of loyalties and unaccountable decisions.

Wardhaugh and Wilding (1993) suggested eight elements in organisations that can contribute to what they describe as the 'corruption of care'. This analysis relates to various forms of institutional care:

■ The corruption of care depends upon the neutralisation of normal moral concerns. For example, the 'Pindown' regime in Staffordshire saw normal civil liberties subjugated to a strategy for managing 'difficult' behaviour (Staffordshire County Council 1991).

- The corruption of care is closely connected with imbalances of power in organisations. In dysfunctional organisations not only service users but often front line carers are stripped of powers that would be taken for granted in a healthy organisation. For example, people are not consulted about their care or working life and can be subjected to repressive forms of control.

- Particular pressures and kinds of work are associated with the corruption of power. Those most at risk are those with little status in society, for example young offenders or children with learning difficulties as opposed to children attending public schools who arguably enjoy the protection offered by high-status parents, but are still at risk as they are relatively isolated which can make reporting difficult.

- Management failures, particularly not setting clear aims, objectives and structures for supervision and monitoring. Staff are likely to feel professionally isolated and this increases the possibility of their turning a blind eye when something goes wrong, fearing they will not get the support of superiors (see the section on whistleblowing below).

- The corruption of care is more likely in enclosed institutions. That is why a range of options now aim to give outside contact to those who lack them. There is perhaps more scope for abuse in large institutions for young offenders as is discussed later.

- The absence of clear lines of accountability. This is most likely in small private establishments without an external manager. The issue is whether the child's social worker (often a long distance from the placement) or the Inspectorate (Ofsted), or both, should enforce accountability.

- Particular models of work and organisation are conducive to the corruption of care. An example of this was the use of regression therapy by Frank Beck whereby older children and teenagers were required to wear nappies and bounce on his knee in the name of therapy (Leicestershire County Council 1993).

- The nature of certain service user groups promotes the corruption of care, with very 'difficult' young people seen as a danger to themselves or others. This is evident in the debate as to what constitutes reasonable force when restraining a child in a children's home.

Significant Developments

In 1997 the incoming Labour government received a comprehensive 'Review of Safeguards for Children Living Away from Home' (Utting 1997), which audited children's policies and services in England and Wales. This influential report acknowledged that the care system itself, as well as individual abusers, was responsible for failing to protect children within it. In making a number of recommendations about running residential establishments, working with parents, vetting staff and listening to children, it influenced the 'looked after' children initiative and the Quality Protects agenda (see chapter 5).

A follow-up report noted a number of improvements but expressed concern about continuing deficiencies relating to the need to define parental rights and responsibilities, to meet the needs of children with emotional and behavioural problems and to properly register private foster carers (Stuart and Baines 2004a).

A further critique is offered by the joint inspectors' reports on Arrangements to Safeguard Children (CSCI 2002; 2005). While again noting progress, they suggest that insufficient priority is given to safeguarding particular groups of children: those in the youth justice system, children with disabilities, 16–18-year-olds with mental health difficulties, and those with mental health problems placed in secure settings. They express concern about the monitoring of some placements, and of unregulated places where children live, including the armed forces and private foster homes. They also felt that there is a greater need to listen to children.

The Children's Rights Alliance, an alliance of the major children's charities, grassroots organisations and local authorities, monitors implementation of the UN Convention on the Rights of the Child in England. Their report (2002b) is highly critical of many aspects of compliance with the Convention. In particular they point to concerns about the number of children in custody and policies towards those who truant or commit anti-social behaviour, which do little to address the causes of the behaviour (see chapter 8). They point to poor progress towards eradicating child poverty and to the inadequacy of services for asylum seekers.

Preventing Abuse in Residential Care

It is difficult to establish the amount of abuse in residential care, which includes not just children's homes, but other residential establishments such as boarding schools and adolescent psychiatric units. One reason is the focus on enquiry reports following well-publicised scandals where staff have committed physical and/or sexual abuse against residents, rather than on a broader consideration of abuse of a child by another child and lower-level actions such as bullying, whether by staff or other residents.

Following 'Pindown' in Staffordshire, Frank Beck in Leicestershire and the north Wales children's homes abuse (among others), the Children Act 1989 introduced a number of measures designed to improve the protection of children in social services care:

- *Independent visitors.* Each child without significant contact with a parent or other supportive adults should be appointed a visitor who can ensure that they have an independent outside voice.
- *Complaints procedures.* Every child and significant stakeholder in the care process has the right to make a complaint. There is a three-stage process:
  1 *Informal stage*: a manager reviews the situation that caused concern.
  2 *Formal stage*: a manager in no way connected with the case and an independent person investigate the complaint.
  3 An independent panel hears the complaint.

More recent legislation has further tightened the framework for protecting children:

- *Independent advocates* for children complaining and attending 'looked after' reviews and meetings (Adoption and Children Act 2002).
- *Independent inspections* (Care Standards Act 2000). Set up the independent inspectorate (now Ofsted) and closed a number of loopholes where care services had previously escaped inspection.
- *Vetting of staff/carers* (Protection of Children Act 1999 and Safeguarding Vulnerable Groups Act 2006).
- *National standards* state what can be expected of care services and can therefore be used to hold practitioners to account for failings.

The effectiveness of these safeguards should be evaluated in the context of the wider concerns about the manageability of residential care (see chapter 6).

Promoting Healthy Organisations

Care organisations should operate within a concept of the public service ethic, an assumption that services are there to meet need, and that those involved in provision are properly motivated towards achieving that objective. However, not only do some children's workers have ulterior motives, including the abuse of children, but some organisational arrangements themselves work against this. For example, the debate raised in chapter 1 as to whether profit and care mix, and the retreat from professionalism (where clear values can be found) towards managerialism (were values can be subordinated to pragmatic concerns such as rationing resources and meeting targets).

Freedom to Care (n.d.) suggest that integrity is a crucial element of a healthy organisation:

> integrity is the ability to perform the duties required of one's role without sacrificing personal, professional or corporate integrity; but rather allowing that integrity to inform and mould the means and objectives of performance.

There is no magic formula for creating a healthy organisation, but there are a number of characteristics that tend to distinguish a healthy from a dysfunctional organisation: communication, leadership and vision, staff morale and motivation, strategy and clear roles and responsibilities for all participants.

Communication: clear structures and organisational arrangements that promote communication are essential to a healthy organisation. Communication should be both top-down (managers raising organisational issues with subordinates) and bottom-up (subordinates giving feedback to those at higher levels). Without effective forms of communication an organisation cannot respond to change, and tends to become oblivious to its own problems. Since knowledge is power, weak managers will seek to restrict information that could be used to contest decisions and practices.

Good communication requires both effective systems (staff bulletins, 'quality circles', focus groups, regular meetings of co-interested workers and the like) and, probably most importantly, creating a culture that gives staff and service users permission to communicate issues and concerns.

Freedom to Care (n.d.) suggests that open management is:

> that which facilitates honesty, transparency, timely and effective communication and sharing in decision-making and the avoidance of unnecessary secrecy, defensiveness and exclusion.

Leadership: being an effective leader is not just about organisation, it is also about being able to create a clear mission and vision for workers and to inspire them to achieve it. Weak leaders will often hide in their office adopting strategies like 'never say yes if no or maybe will do' (the safety strategy), 'never decide today what can be left until tomorrow' (the assumption that if left, problems will go away). In such cases subordinates often receive the message that it is their job to protect the boss from bad news.

Weak leadership can disempower front-line workers who become unclear of expectations of them, which can promote massive variations in practice across the organisation. It creates a void of decision-making which is often filled by informal systems lower down, which are largely unaccountable and inconsistent.

Staff morale and motivation: are crucial factors in a successful organisation, especially in the care sector where staff are the major cost and where services are mainly delivered through personal interactions between staff and service users. In dysfunctional organisations a disempowered service user might well be linked with an equally disempowered front-line worker. Managerialism is often associated with control: giving staff instructions, and mechanisms to achieve compliance, ranging from performance-related pay (the carrot) to the use of disciplinary procedures (the stick).

An alternative approach to motivation seeks to trust, reward and stimulate staff, recognising their strengths and weaknesses and being supportive and empowering. This approach is more likely to promote openness and honesty and a culture in which people can put service users first, thereby minimising the potential for abuse.

Vision, strategy and clear roles and responsibilities: for all participants to promote clarity of purpose and individual accountability.

> Accountability is the preparedness to explain and justify individual and corporate acts and omissions to relevant stakeholders at appropriate times, and mechanisms by which this preparedness may be effected. (Freedom to Care, n.d.).

In an accountable organisation failings can easily be identified and rectified as structures provide checks and balances that hold individuals to account, question decisions and limit the power of individuals and small groups. In local government the role of elected councillors is meant to constraint the power of officials, and supervision holds individuals to account within the line management structure.

Whistleblowing

The first line of defence against abuse in organisations is listening to children and other stakeholders who make allegations, and investigating those allegations fully. In some cases staff will become aware that abuse is present, or might suspect it. In such circumstances they have a clear duty to inform their superiors, which is known as 'whistleblowing'. However, there are numerous high-profile cases where staff have attempted to 'whistleblow' and, instead of being listened to, have been marginalised, often labelled troublemakers, disciplined and dismissed, or feel so oppressed and demoralised that they can no longer function. Knowing this, others are deterred from disclosing abuse, fearing for their own career and livelihood. Although colleagues might also know of the abuse and offer personal support, they are unlikely to do so officially, leaving the whistleblower isolated and vulnerable. A straw poll of final year social work students by the author suggested that a large majority, when confronted with knowledge of abuse, would attempt to move jobs rather than risk whistleblowing. While concern for one's own future is understandable, this is a recipe for continuing abuse in a dysfunctional organisation.

One of the many cases where social services staff attempted to whistleblow was that of Alison Taylor who on several occasions attempted to report the abuse of children in various children's homes in north Wales, both to managers and to a councillor who informed the police. No significant action was taken. fifteen years later, the Waterhouse Enquiry (2000) into the abuse vindicated Ms Taylor and recommended that each local authority establish clear whistleblowing procedures. However, by then she had lost her job, and suffered so much emotionally that she felt unable to return to care work (Community Care 1996).

The Public Interest Disclosure Act 1999 aims to safeguard workers with genuine concerns at work who blow the whistle. Whistleblowers cannot be discriminated against for taking action beyond the organisation if the concern is covered by the Act, the action of the whistleblower is 'reasonable' and they have exhausted the normal processes of informing managers of their concerns. However, if an employer wishes to dismiss a whistleblower it is possible to base action on some other minor allegation of misconduct.

While it is likely that dysfunctional organisations will attempt to cover up concerns of abuse or other serious allegations, it is not inevitable. A healthy organisation will be a learning organisation and will wish to learn lessons from complaints and concerns raised by staff and others.

Positive action when there are serious concerns

When attempts to report concerns through the line management structure have failed, it is legitimate under the Whistleblowing legislation, and arguably a moral duty, to take the concerns elsewhere. The following diagram summarises the options open to a 'whistleblower':

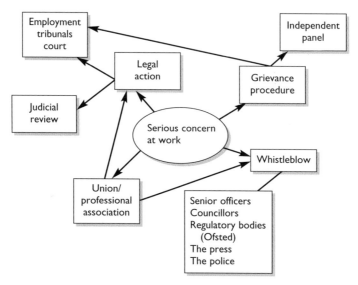

Figure 4.1 Getting redress when things go wrong for an employee

It is important that whistleblowers gain the support of an external agency, most commonly a trade union or professional association, and advice about tactics that work from pressure groups such as Freedom to Care or Public Concern at Work. Whistleblowing can be a lonely, isolating and highly stressful experience as managers try to protect themselves against allegations of wrongdoing or incompetence. Gaining information is often the first task, using the freedom of information legislation to gain records pertaining to the issue in question and maybe wider decision-making in the authority. Clearly management will be reluctant to provide evidence to be used against them and numerous loopholes are employed to deny access to particular documents, but refusals can be appealed to the information commissioner.

The first avenue for raising issues is using employment rights, most commonly commencing with the grievance procedure. However, if it is clear that the organisation is in cover-up mode, this is unlikely to be effective. If a grievance fails, this can either be appealed to an independent panel established by the employer and/or to an employment tribunal.

The other approach is to contact those outside the management structure. Clearly, the police are a good starting point if criminal allegations are involved, and Ofsted should be informed. Care needs to be taken about confidentiality as management can commence capability procedures against an employee who breaches professional practice rules.

Approaching politicians may be effective depending upon the individual politician and wider political factors, for example the relationship between the senior managers and their supervising politicians.

Using the press can be a productive way of moving matters forward, but the press can twist facts in order to construct dramatic headline stories. Once a story is in the public domain via the press, any news medium can use it and place their own spin upon it, perhaps questioning the integrity of the whistle-blower rather than publicising the concerns.

Workers can also be involved in supporting service users who have complaints or concerns. Clearly there is a potential conflict of interest here, in representing the management position versus supporting the service user in pursuing their grievance. It is therefore preferable for the service user to obtain independent advocacy and advice from such agencies as the Citizen's Advice Bureau, an advocacy service or a solicitor.

Practice Areas

The following practice areas illustrate continuing failures to protect or fully meet the needs of children living away from home.

Children in Prison

Young offenders' institutions housed 2,495 under-18s in September 2005. There were a further 251 placed in secure training establishments and 249 offenders in local authority secure units, which means that nearly 3,000 young offenders were locked up in 2005. (Home Office 2006b)

Custody is meant to be the sentence of last resort, and yet many young people in custody are not a serious threat and could receive alternative community sentences (NACRO 2006).

Campaigners are concerned about not only the ineffectiveness of custody, but also the inhuman and degrading way in which so many young people are incarcerated, which is summarised in the report 'Rethinking Child Imprisonment':

> Throughout the late 1990s, reports from the Chief Inspector [of prisons] became increasingly critical. At times, it seemed there were not enough words in the English language to communicate the horror and disgust of Inspectors who entered those closed institutions to meet and talk to some of the country's most vulnerable and troubled children. (Children's Rights Alliance 2002a: preface)

Those in custody not only are convicted offenders but are themselves very needy. The CRA interviewed 755 young offenders and found that:

37 per cent had been in care, 33 per cent had drugs and 21 per cent alcohol problems upon entering custody and yet 53 per cent received no help with these problems while detained; 84 per cent had been excluded from school and 9 per cent said they last went to school when they were under 12. They noted that the Social Exclusion Unit (2002) found that of children in custody, nearly half had literacy levels below that of the average 11-year-old, around 85 per cent of those in custody showed signs of a personality disorder, and one in ten showed signs of a psychotic illness. (Children's Rights Alliance 2002a)

As well as successive reports from the Prison Service Inspectorate discussing dirty, overcrowded conditions in a number of young offenders' institutions and upon regimes that cannot promote much purposive activity, there are several more serious issues. First, the report into the racist murder of Zahid Mubarek in Feltham YOI in 2000 identified 186 failings and was severely critical of both the practice of enforced cell-sharing and the poor availability of mental health services in custody.

A further concern is the high rate of suicide and self-harm among young inmates:

Between January 1998 and January 2002 there were 1,111 reported incidents of self-harm by young people under the age of 18 in YOIs, and 12 self-inflicted deaths (January 98–August 2002), all by hanging and all males.   (Children's Rights Aliance 2002a)

While it is inevitable that prison will not be a pleasant experience, it is unacceptable that these children must have been intolerably unhappy to contemplate taking their own lives, and that the prison staff failed in their primary duty – to protect the young people in their charge from harm.

It is difficult to prevent bullying in any institution, but the closed nature of custodial settings and the problematic backgrounds of the inmates make custody a fertile site for particularly brutal bullying.

An Inspectorate questionnaire on personal safety in custody showed that 26 per cent of respondents had been assaulted by other juveniles and 39 per cent said they would not feel safe to tell staff. The inspectorate described bullying as 'endemic' and particularly a problem for new arrivals, younger boys, those in custody for the first time and those from rural areas. (Children's Rights Aliance 2002a)

In 2002, the High Court ruled that the Home Office was wrong to argue that child protection provision in the Children Act 1989 did not apply in custody (*Howard League for Penal Reform* v *Secretary of State for the Home Department*). The YJB now employs social workers in YOIs and local authorities can investigate a range of child protection concerns in custody including the disclosure of historic abuse and allegations of current abuse by staff or other young people. Another problem has been that 'accommodated' children have been deemed to lose their 'looked after' status while in custody, suggesting a lack of welfare concern for them and planning for their future.

The use of control and restraint and strip-searching in custody has raised concerns. Carlile (2006) investigated the death of Gareth Myatt, a resident in a secure training centre who died in 2004 after a restraint involving three staff, and found that across the secure estate pain was used to enforce compliance. Carlile suggested that this was unacceptable and could be illegal. There were over 15,000 incidents where physical force was used against youngsters in a 21-month period. The report commented that much of the treatment witnessed could, had it occurred elsewhere, be seen as abusive and could trigger child protection investigations.

We shall now consider two areas where it is not a particular institution that has failed to protect young people, but the wider system whose failure has caused childhood misery.

Systems Failure: Young Runaways

Around 100,000 children per year run away, many absent for just a few hours. More worry are those who are absent for several nights with no indication of their whereabouts. The Social Exclusion Unit defines a runaway as under 18 years old and spending one or more nights away from the family home without permission. On that definition it is estimated that around 20,000 children run away annually and around a quarter of these are under 11. (Social Exclusion Unit 2002a)

The Children's Society (2004) suggest that the reasons for running away include family breakdown (23 per cent didn't get on with parents), violence (13 per cent said that parents 'hit them a lot') and rejection (12 per cent felt that parents didn't care).

For many years the Children's Society and others have been campaigning for the problem of young runaways to be taken seriously and yet, despite official recognition in the Social Exclusion Unit (2002a) report that running away is a severe problem both for the individual and for society, there is still no nation-wide strategy. In 2002 the government issued guidance to local authorities suggesting a local strategy to prevent and deal with running away (Department of Health 2002), but by 2004 only 43 out of 150 local authorities had implemented these protocols (Children's Society 2005).

The Children's Society report 'Safe and Sound' (2005) was their second national survey of runaways. Sadly, the overall figures seem to have changed little since the original report in 1999.

'Safe and Sound' (2005) estimates that around 12 per cent run away because of 'maltreatment' (physical or emotional abuse) and that up to 7.5 per cent of 14-year-olds (the peak age) run away each year. About half stayed with friends, 35 per cent with relatives and 16 per cent slept rough. Worryingly, one in eight had resorted to survival tactics including begging and stealing and 1 in 12 reported being hurt or harmed. Only 4 per cent approached official agencies for help.

The suggestion is that the power wielded by the statutory agencies makes them badly placed to assist runaways, and that some form of national agency managed by the voluntary sector is the way forward.

An important sub group of those running away are those who abscond from local authority accommodation. Although they make up only 2.1 per cent of the overnight runaways in the Children's Society research (2005), 'looked after' young people are around three times more likely to run than children in the general population. Many young people who run from care have a previous history of running from elsewhere so it is difficult to demonstrate a link between running and the quality of care services.

In some cases it is argued that secure accommodation should be used to prevent persistent absconding from care. Under the Children Act 1989 (Section 25) one of the criteria for using secure accommodation is a double test:

1   he (*sic*) has a history of absconding and is likely to abscond from any other description of accommodation; and
2   if he absconds he is likely to suffer significant harm.

Thus absconding itself is not sufficient to detain a child. Professional judgements must be made about what harm the child is likely to suffer, and whether a relatively short period in security is likely to repair a lifestyle that puts the child at risk, for example, prostitution or drug abuse. Indeed, it is likely that a child committed to such a lifestyle will simply run again when released, and arguably will have become more alienated from the care system through being detained. On the other hand, for some young people a period in security can provide time to reflect and gain a commitment to change their lifestyle.

A further Children's Society study (Smeaton 2005) looked at young people who are missing longer term, for continuous periods of 4 weeks or more. The study focused upon 23 'detached' (from carers) 13–21 year olds. It examined what happened before the young person became detached, what happened to them while detached, the support they were able to access and what happened to them subsequently. An important finding about lives prior to running was that although there were often high levels of family conflict and other warning signs, for example truancy, in almost half the cases there was no prior agency intervention. Many of the young people who survived used informal support networks of peers and adults, but few turned to formal agencies for help. In some cases there was a firm decision to avoid formal agencies for fear of being made to go home.

The problem for runaways is that they run the risk of being recruited for the sex or drugs trade or drifting into crime as they often have no funds or legitimate means of getting any, and can be in immediate need of food and shelter. This scenario is made worse by there being few dedicated safe beds for the group and, depending upon age, they often fall between the cracks in the statutory services.

Under-16s must be accommodated in placements registered for 'looked after' children, but in the case of those who run away out of their home area this is unlikely to be made available; they are likely to be told to go home and assisted to that end. Over-16s are in a slightly better position as they can legally seek independent accommodation, but as with other homeless youngsters they are often caught in the 'no money, no home' situation. Claiming benefits under the exceptional hardship rules is difficult, much more so without an address, so they are often forced to accept hospitality with strings attached from those who prey on vulnerable young people.

A strategic approach to the problem would start with a nationwide programme to prevent running away. This would include education as to the dangers involved, family support work to prevent breakdown, and local accommodation for those who must leave, since they are less likely to have to resort to desperate action where they have social networks. The problem is that if a young person approaches children's services saying that they are unhappy at home, but are not being physically or sexually abused, they are unlikely to be prioritised to receive a service. What is needed are 'crash pads', basic hostel-type accommodation that can be used as a temporary safe environment from which to plan for the future.

For those who have run away outside their locality there needs to be a network of safe places where they can stay, tell their story without fear of being arbitrarily sent back, and make proper plans for their future. As children in need, they require proper support to implement those plans to prevent their running away again. There used to be a small network of safe houses but all except one have closed due to lack of funding.

Systems Failure: Child Asylum Seekers

Children who come to this country to seek asylum are caught up in the moral panic fuelled by the tabloid press that seems to suggest that the country is being overrun by immigrants many of whom are undesirable. What is often forgotten is the extreme trauma suffered by the individual child, both in their home nation which caused them to flee in the first place, and on the journey to the UK.

There are two categories of asylum-seeking children, those who are with their families and those who are unaccompanied. In 2004 local councils were supporting some 7,800 unaccompanied children of whom 76 per cent were over 16 (Joint Chief Inspectors' Report 2005).

A major issue with unaccompanied asylum seekers is the difficulty in establishing their age without appropriate documentation. Clearly a young person has a vested interest in trying to convince the authorities that they are a child in order to receive better services. A test, which can involve a medical opinion and X-rays, is being developed to establish age.

Those who are accepted as children are deemed by some local authorities to be 'accommodated', while others have given assistance under Section 17 (preventative monies). A High Court judgement established that Section 20 (accommodation) should be used and established an entitlement to leaving care services (*R. Behre and others* v *Hillingdon* 2003).

There have been concerns that these young people receive inadequate care services. For example, Mitchell (2003) cites an Audit Commission Report (1999) suggesting that 50 per cent of over-16s and 12 per cent of those under 16 were placed in bed-and-breakfast accommodation. Clearly there are very real problems in finding appropriate placements that reflect the cultural and language backgrounds of the young people, especially as they are largely concentrated in the local authorities that have points of entry to the UK (ports or airports). Similarly, there are enormous challenges in ensuring that the educational and cultural needs of this diverse group are met and that they have access to appropriate therapeutic interventions that can address the trauma they have suffered. The Refugee Council (2005) suggests that more than a quarter of refugee children had significant psychological disturbance, which is three times the national average. However, Kohli and Mather (2003) suggest that this group are remarkably resilient and are less likely to be 'psychologically dishevelled' than indigenous children who have been harmed by their parents.

For those who are with their families concern has been expressed about the use of detention in asylum centres, especially for those in the fast track to deportation scheme. It seems that the requirements of the Immigration Service override the best interests of the child (Refugee Council 2003). Crawley and Lester (2005) discuss the impact of detention upon an estimated 2,000 children per year and a campaign has been established to close these asylum centres.

Further concerns have been raised about Section 9 of the Asylum and Immigration Act 2004, which allows benefits to be withdrawn to unsuccessful asylum seekers in the hope that they will leave the country (Refugee Council and Refugee Action 2006). This could mean that children are 'accommodated' as their parents have no means of supporting them. It is clearly not acceptable to remove a child from a loving, caring family in these circumstances and, following some pilots, the government are unlikely to implement this section.

KEY POINTS

- A major indictment of children's social work has been the inability of professionals and organisations to learn from the 'scandals' following child deaths and abuse within the 'care' systems.
- The concept of 'organisational culture' is crucial to understanding the tendency of organisations to cover-up abuse.
- Children in residential institutions are particularly vulnerable to abuse by adults and peers.
- Many children living away from home are at risk but not protected because

they are outside mainstream childcare systems – e.g. runaways, children in custody and child asylum seekers.

■ Healthy organisations are ones with open communication, good leadership and a culture that values both service users and staff.

■ Despite legislation to protect 'whistleblowers' it remains difficult to gain redress when things are seriously wrong in an organisation.

RESOURCES

Regular updates on progress in this area published by the Joint Inspectors' Group. www.safeguardingchildren.org.uk.

The Children's Rights Alliance (England) produces regular reports, especially about the overuse of custody: www.crae.org.uk.

Public service ethics

Banks, S. (2004), *Ethics, Accountability and the Social Professional* explores the issues of ethics and accountability in the public services.

Residential care

NSPCC (2003d), *It Doesn't Happen to Disabled Children.*

Barter, C. (2003), *Abuse of Children in Residential Care.*

Miller, D. (2002), *Disabled Children and Abuse.*

Asylum seekers

Save the Children have a special interest in this area: www.savethechildren.org.uk.

Home Office website for those working in this field: www.nrif.org.uk.

European Social Network (2005), 'Promoting Inclusion for Unaccompanied Young Asylum Seekers and Immigrants'.

Research in Practice (2005), *On New Ground: Supporting Unaccompanied Asylum Seeking and Refugee Children and Young People.*

Young people in custody

Resources can be found on the websites of penal reform organisations such as NACRO, the Howard League and others, on the sites of children's charities interested in this area and organisations in the children's rights movement, e.g. www.nacro.org.uk; www.howardleague.org.uk; www.childrenssociety.org.uk; www.crae.org.uk.

Whistleblowing

There are two voluntary organisations offering support and help in this area:

Public Concern at Work: www.pcaw.co.uk.

Freedom to Care: www.freedomtocare.org.

Hunt, G. (ed.) (1998), *Whistleblowing in the Social Services*, provides a good introduction to this area.

CHAPTER 5

The Looked-after Children's System

This chapter discusses and reviews the procedural approach to looked-after children and the Quality Protects agenda based around national standards and performance, and considers whether, in the name of efficiency, consistency and standards we have moved too far from caring and relationships. It considers what young people say about their social workers and other carers and the implications for effective practice. It questions whether managerialist interventions have deskilled social workers from effective communication with service users, and the effects of 'professionalisation' on service delivery.

The effectiveness of current policies aimed at improving standards is discussed in relation to the practice areas of the education of looked-after children and leaving care.

Looked-after Children: The State as Corporate Parent

It is a sad reality that the state acts as corporate parent to around 60,000 children at any one time who are looked after (still popularly referred to as 'in care') either by voluntary arrangements with parents ('accommodated') or under care orders. The state shares parental responsibility with those who had it prior to admission and there is therefore a crucial partnership relationship between the State, parents and the child. The looked after children's service is expensive, with the average Looked-after child costing £675 and receiving 3.4 hours of service per week (ONS 2005b). It is therefore crucial from care and cost effectiveness perspectives that the service delivers good outcomes for its service users.

The critical question about work with looked-after children is how well equipped the state is to act in a parenting capacity and how it can most effectively perform this role. The last 30 years has seen a shift in both the type of young person cared for by the state and the nature of services offered. Gone are the group of young people cared for by state or by voluntary organisations for all or most of their childhood, sometimes even orphans. Now children spend relatively short periods being looked after and are then restored home, or for those needing long-term substitute care, permanence is normally provided through adoption, residence orders or special guardianship (Adoption and Children Act 2002). A smaller group of young people leave the care system to live independently.

Looked-after Children's System: The Practicalities

The Looked-after children's (LAC) system is the main planning mechanism for looked-after children currently in use in England. From January 2006 it merged with the Framework for the Assessment of Children in Need and their Families to form the Integrated Children's System. This is designed to provide a seamless information gathering and planning system from first referral of a child through to rehabilitation, permanency or independent living. Although young people often resent the formality and lack of normality in these processes, given the numbers of people involved in parenting a looked-after child or young person, there needs to be a formalised approach to developing and monitoring care packages.

FOCUS ON PRACTICE 5.1

Summary of the components of the LAC system

Essential information record
Part 1 (the 'front sheet') provides basic information about the child and family.
Part 2 provides more comprehensive information about background including legal and placement history.

Placement plan
Part 1: *Placement agreement* includes the information and agreements, which must be completed before a child is placed.
Part 2: *Day-to-day arrangements* provides detailed information about a child's everyday routines including health, education and identity and arrangements for contact.

Care plan
The care plan ensures that all looked-after children have clearly stated objectives for their care and a strategy for achieving them to avoid 'drift' (where the child remains in care due to a lack of activity to move them on). Most plans are designed to enable the child to return home as soon as possible, or to be prepared for a permanent placement or independence.

Review of arrangements
The review of arrangements, following proper consultation, informs the review process and ensures that the overall care plan is still appropriate, that the placement and its agreed objectives continue to meet the child's needs, and that work identified via the assessment and action records has been undertaken.

Assessment and action records

Assessment and action records are intended to help those professionally responsible for someone else's child to measure progress, assess the standard of care and plan improvements. They are not normally used before the child has been looked after for four months.

Six age-related assessment and action records exist to record progress across seven dimensions: health, education, identity, family and social relationships, social presentation, emotional and behavioural development, and self-care skills. Questions about younger children are directed towards the carer; both the 10–14-year-olds and those aged 15 and above answer for themselves.

In terms of working practices, gone are the days when the child's social worker was sometimes the nearest thing they had to a functioning 'parent'. In the present managerialist culture promoted by Quality Protects (see chapter1) and the looked-after children's system the social worker is a case manager, an auditor of a package of care commissioned by the department. Proper relationships are provided elsewhere, through contact with birth parents or other significant family members, by foster carers or other carers, for example befrienders, independent visitors or mentors.

In the past social workers might have evaluated their interventions with a child in terms of the quality of the relationship, but now 'success' is evaluated through performance indicators and targets. It is interesting to question whether there is a clash between what the agency expects of a social worker and what would meet the real emotional and personal needs of the child. This is often articulated in terms of the 'little things' such as remembering a child's birthday, or acts of human kindness, for example having the time to help a young person to settle into a new placement, not just delivering them with their possessions in a bin bag. Young people commenting upon their social workers often suggest that the *process* has taken over, that social workers do not have the time or inclination to engage with them as a person, or to listen to and try to understand their story.

The 'tick box' approach promoted by the LACS largely denies individuality in favour of a fixed view of childhood into which the child should fit, for example school achievement. Whereas a social worker might have a task for a time-limited visit, such as completing an assessment and action record, the young person might want to talk about something personal. It is unlikely that the worker will provide 'permission' for more personal interactions, in contradiction of the professional rhetoric about listening to children and empowerment. Arguably, because social workers are unable to get these things right, we need the range of complaints procedures, advocacy services and independent reviewers.

Professionalism as well as managerialism has hijacked the traditional concept of a relationship between a social worker and a looked-after young person. The language now speaks of roles and tasks. The culture of child protection makes it difficult for workers to show small acts of human kindness in case these are misinterpreted, and the need to protect oneself from the threat of allegations as well as the child from potential abuse has led to working practices that can be unhelpful in building relationships, for example not being alone with a child without a witness. Showing kindness can be labelled as being 'over-involved'.

Effective social workers need to be conscious of the power imbalances between themselves as adults and professionals and the children they serve. These can be reflected in the image the worker projects to the child, the way they dress and speak for example. Power relationships are also apparent in the procedures employed within the agency, for example, how to conduct planning meetings and reviews in a manner which allows the young person to feel comfortable attending and participating. Young people themselves often want to question the abnormality of having to have meetings, annual medicals and such like, which they often deeply resent.

Power imbalances can be accentuated by factors such as class, race, culture, sexuality and gender. Teams need to reflect on these issues when recruiting workers and allocating work. For example, should a black boy have a black male worker? What is important is that he should have access to one or more appropriate role models who will facilitate the development of his identities as a man and a black person. Where team composition does not reflect the characteristics of service users, particular issues arise as to how to use the skills and experiences of minority group team members. This is particularly important as the term 'ethnic minority' disguises the cultural and religious background of each individual child or worker.

Packman (1986) characterises looked-after young people according to the role they play:

- *volunteers*, who want to be helpful and co-operative;
- *victims*, who are in need of reassurance and support; and
- *villains*, who are often felt to require control.

However, there is a tendency to stereotype looked-after young people negatively as 'sad' or 'bad', which can encourage professionals to deny the individuality of the child and their unique personal story. Children's workers should contest such unhelpful stereotypes.

A case manager needs to be able to balance the welfare of the child against the need to ration resources. Perhaps the move towards quantitative outcome measures is more about meeting the needs of managers than of the service user.

Of all the workers involved in the care of a looked-after young person the field social worker, the case holder, is crucial in implementing the care package. The field worker's role comprises the following components.

> ### FOCUS ON PRACTICE 5.2
>
> **The role of the field worker**
> 1 To manage statutory requirements:
>
> - provide a placement plan and the other statutory documentation in the LACS
> - organise contact;
> - inform parties of care plan;
> - initial and annual medical;
> - initial review (within 28 days of being looked after);
> - statutory reviews (first after three months, six-monthly thereafter);
> - statutory visits, including assessment and action records.
>
> 2 To provide continuity, especially across placement moves
> 3 To troubleshoot any problems (key worker role)
> 4 To develop a professional relationship with the young person, especially looking out for any abuse.
> 5 To promote open recording and the participation of the young person in the care plan

Promoting Contact

The Children Act 1989 includes a duty to promote contact between a looked-after child and their parents and other significant adults or siblings. Even in cases where the child is unlikely to be restored home, contact is a crucial part in maintaining identity, a sense of self. Triseliotis et al. (1995) suggest that contact sends important messages of reassurance to the child who might be suffering the stress of loss and separation, self-blame and conflicts of loyalty to family members. Contact enables the child to develop their personal identity through keeping in touch with their roots.

Under Section 34 of the Children Act 1989 a court can make a contact order to resolve disputes about contact. Such an order can terminate contact. It is hotly debated whether contact should be enforced against the child's wishes, for example when an abusive parent argues that they have a right to contact. The child's wishes should be taken into account in accordance with their age and level of understanding, and should inform decisions. The best interests of the child override parental wishes in cases such as that illustrated in Case Study 5.1

Contact arrangements can be informal and extensive, or limited and highly controlled. Where contact might be felt to be potentially damaging to the child, it can be supervised and most areas now have contact centres where such sessions can take place. Sometimes supervision is just to ensure the safety of the child, in others it can be part of an assessment process, to observe the interaction between adult and child.

CASE STUDY 5.1

Contact

Two sisters aged 11 and 12 had been sexually abused by their father. On his release from prison he requested contact with his daughters. The girls were adamant that they did not want any contact with him and the social worker felt that contact could be damaging, even dangerous. The social worker and the reviewing officer agreed that they were 'Gillick competent' and their views should be respected. The father made an application to the Family Court for a contact order, which was granted. The local authority appealed and the High Court overturned the ruling, accepting that the children's views, in the circumstances of the case, took precedence over the presumption of contact in the Children Act 1989.

The current legislative framework, with its emphasis upon maintaining contact, reflects previous concerns that children entering care quickly lost significant contact with their family (Bullock et al. 1998). This may have been for logistic reasons such as the distance of the placement from the home area, or may have reflected the complex relationship difficulties between parent and child which could have been a factor in the care episode, or even complex dynamics and rivalries between natural parents, carers and the department. The local authority can facilitate contact by paying travel expenses to parents or other significant relatives.

Some parents seem nervous about contact, perhaps especially if it is in the home of the carers. It is important in planning contact arrangements to go beyond practical arrangements and consider the human factors. However, contact is valuable in itself – it doesn't have to be about treats.

What Children Say about Care Services

The Commission for Social Care Inspection studied what looked-after children think of their care services. The report suggests a generally high level of satisfaction of children with their social workers and draws up a profile of an effective social worker. Valued qualities include trustworthiness, availability and reliability. The children felt that social workers should listen to them as individuals and allow them to make their own decisions. Changes were disliked, especially multiple placements and changes of social worker. Poor social workers were often felt to be focused towards adults (carers) or their employers (Morgan 2006).

A survey of 22,000 'children receiving personal social services aged 10–17' again indicates a good degree of satisfaction with services, although half didn't know how to complain and, worryingly, 25 per cent said that they were never offered choices about their care (Office of National Statistics 2005b).

Voice (2004) have developed a blueprint for a child-centred approach to children and young people in public care. Key areas include:

- respecting and valuing children, not seeing them as victims or in need of control, but as individuals in their own right;
- allowing children to express their individuality, and understanding their perspectives;
- putting the needs and interest of children before those of adults and organisations;
- respecting their human rights;
- respecting the competence of children to make decisions for themselves.

An Evaluation

It seems fashionable to portray the LACS as failing many of the children in it. For example, in the foreword to the Green Paper on LACS 'Care Matters' (Department for Education and Skills 2006b), the Education Secretary describes the LACS system in terms of promoting 'insecurity', 'ill health', 'lack of fulfilment' and educational underachievement. Stein (2006) outlines reasons why we should be more positive about the 'care' system. First, as most care episodes are relatively short (with 40 per cent of children returning to their parents within six months, a relatively short episode in a child's life) the care system should not be blamed for poor outcomes. Secondly, in relation to suggested poor outcomes for care leavers, many of those who leave care between 16 and 18 have entered the system in their mid-teenage years having already suffered a number of deprivations, and often come from a very low starting point, being behind in their schooling or suffering from a variety of emotional problems. Outcome measures may not recognise that some young people do use opportunities within the care system to move on, though they may not catch up by their leaving care age, but might have by their early twenties.

Stein (2006), sceptical of outcome indicators, suggests much broader measures of 'success' using a subjective evaluation of how young people themselves judge their well-being and progress. He estimates that around three-quarters of care leavers had achieved or were making good progress towards positive outcomes.

Future Policy

To support the LAC is not to say that the proposals in the Green Paper 'Care Matters' (2006) and the subsequent White Paper 'Care Matters: Time for Change' (Department for Children, Schools and Families 2007b) to improve the status of and rewards to carers and the stability and quality of the care experience are not required. Clearly services can be improved, but we should not expect wonder solutions to overcome the suffering already experienced by most children in the LACS.

The proposals sit well with the systemic approach. They start by arguing for more preventative measures aimed at keeping young people out of the care system, for example, by the greater use of intensive family therapy and family group conferences. One of the most radical proposals in the Green Paper is to establish GP-style social work practices to manage services for looked-after children. By owning their own practice, groups of social workers and other professionals would have the incentive to make their career in this field, thereby improving consistency and reducing changes for the young people. The practice would manage its own budget, spending it in consultation with the young people and promoting creativity in the way the funds are spent.

Proposals place a greater emphasis on the health and education of young people and include the suggestion that young people make a slower transition to independence by remaining with foster carers until the age of 21. Increased funding, including university bursaries, will support young people in education (DfCSF 2006).

Practice Areas: Raising Standards

This section explores two overlapping areas where the government has promoted considerable changes in policy and practice but where outcomes remain questionable.

The Education of Looked-after Children

The educational underachievement of looked-after children provides an interesting case study of where admirable policies aimed at avoiding the long-term effects of social exclusion through raising educational attainment have not fully achieved their objectives. A comprehensive report by the Social Exclusion Unit (2003) highlighted the poor achievements of looked-after children; targets were set to improve outcomes and resources deployed to achieve them.

> In 2003 a standard was set for at least 15 per cent of young people in care in Year 11 to achieve five GCSEs at grades A*–C by 2006, but figures to September 2005 suggest that only 11 per cent achieved this. (Social Exclusion Unit 2003)

However, from a systems perspective it is questionable whether, given the inputs to the system – in many cases very damaged children, these targets were viable or achievable.

Young people in the care system want to do well in school but feel that they have been disadvantaged by poor liaison between schools and care services, and that in some cases schools do not understand their difficulties or special needs (Department for Education and Skills 2006). In some cases it is practical difficulties that inhibit achievement, for example multiple school moves.

The 'Care Matters' (2006) Green Paper suggests some further policy developments to address these issues, including expending more resources and

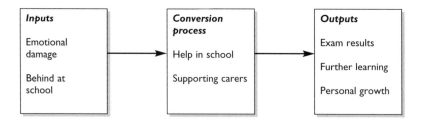

Figure 5.1 Systems approach to the education of looked-after children

giving more powers to local authorities to prevent school moves, providing additional funding to schools and social workers to finance personal educational plans, and providing a 'virtual head teacher' in each local authority to promote these policies and support the professionals involved.

Leaving Care Services

There are many ways of leaving care, most commonly returning to a child's birth family. This section focuses upon meeting the needs of the estimated 7,000–8,000 16–18-year-olds who leave care annually, those being prepared for and moving to independent accommodation (Research in Practice 2003).

The transition to independence, or more fashionably 'interdependence', is a major goal for the relatively small group of older looked-after teenagers who are unable to return home. Numbers without decent support networks have declined in recent years with the demise of the large institutions, and many now leave with at least the informal support of natural family or former foster carers. For many such young people the transitions they face happen in quick succession and at a faster rate than for other young people, and coupled with their other disadvantages (lack of money, poor educational achievements, poor job prospects) these processes can be quite daunting (Research in Practice 2003).

Until the Children (Leaving Care) Act 2000, social services departments had a power rather than a duty to support care leavers. Practice was patchy, and in many areas an authority that had spent hundreds of thousands of pounds on a care career would dump a care leaver at 18 (often 16), in bed-and-breakfast accommodation, and close the case.

The current legislation makes it the duty of children's trusts to provide a proper service to care leavers. The key to success is planning. All 16–21-year-olds who are 'eligible' or 'relevant' (looked after prior to 16 and still looked after at 16) should have a 'pathway plan' which addresses their needs through the various transitions. This can be based on the normal care planning process and might use assessment and action records. Each care leaver should have a personal adviser to steer them through the plan (which might be combined with other roles, for example, a Connexions personal adviser). The other major change is that eligible young people aged 16–18 are the financial responsibility of the children's trust and are no longer eligible for income support. Financial and personal support normally lasts until 21, and may last until 25 if the young person remains in education.

Many children's trusts have now established specialist leaving care teams, or have contracted this to the voluntary sector. It is important to negotiate the availability of appropriate housing resources leading to a permanent tenancy, and housing associations (registered social landlords) are often partners in this. Figure 5.2 shows this triangular model of partnership.

Care leavers are now deemed to be in 'priority need' for housing (Homelessness Act 2002). However, it is clear that physical resources alone are insufficient without appropriate support. Young people in particular struggle to manage their usually very limited financial resources and to keep control of their front door, making sure that their accommodation isn't used as a doss house by other young people seeking to hang out in premises not controlled by adults, with all the associated problems that can bring.

Figure 5.2   Triangular partnership for leaving care services

Support should not just be from professionals but aim to enhance the young person's ordinary social network. Drawing a network diagram can help to identify the significant support people for an individual (see Figure 5.2). In my career I've been amazed at the goodwill shown to young people trying to establish themselves, for example the next-door neighbour who insisted on providing meals and doing the washing for two care leavers placed in a Housing Association terraced house, the boss who took a care leaver under his wing and arranged assistance to settle him into his Housing Association flat. But there are also the moaners!

Another crucial factor is the neighbourhood. Where care leavers are offered 'difficult to let' council accommodation it is often located in problematic areas where they might feel unsafe or where they could get sucked into local problems.

Former foster carers can be a valuable source of support, although they currently work on a voluntary basis and are often exploited by the system. Current proposals to improve services for looked-after children aim to address this (DfES 2006).

The major challenge for those managing leaving care services is the young people who don't have the motivation or ability to make a successful transition to adulthood. There is no easy answer as to how to care for this small but significant group. From a children's services perspective the aim is often to refer the young people to adult services for long-term support, but there are many young people who don't fit into any of the established adult categories, and hence will not be offered a service. For them it seems that the aftercare service has to struggle day by day to provide whatever they can. For a few individuals institutional care in prisons or psychiatric hospitals might become the reality.

Dixon and Stein (2005) undertook research on leaving care systems in Scotland where legislation similar to the 2000 Act in England was enacted in 1995. This suggested that the whole care experience, especially placement and educational stability, is the crucial factor in determining outcomes for care leavers. Many of the young people with the most successful outcomes had ongoing relationships with former foster carers. Sadly, despite improvements in the legislation many of the respondents believed that they had been moved from supportive placements too early and felt pushed out, only a few had been allowed to remain in successful residential or foster placements after they turned 18, with 73 per cent leaving these placements at 15 or 16. The study found that there was a significant link between the quality of preparation for leaving care and successful outcomes, although sadly, despite the requirement for pathway planning, fewer than half the respondents felt that they had experienced a proper planning process. Good preparation needs to include practical, emotional and interpersonal skills and to be tailored to the diverse need of each individual.

In terms of after-care, the most important indicator of successful outcomes in education, employment and training, and in accommodation and personal well-being, was the availability of informal or formal support networks. Formal support was often provided by a partnership between the local authority, a voluntary agency and a housing provider. The study suggests that specialist leaving care workers provide more accessible and valued support. About half of their sample had some contact with former carers and many received support from family members, although in some cases negative family links and unhelpful peer influences caused difficulties (Dixon and Stein 2005).

For those without adequate informal support networks, the use of a mentor, usually a volunteer, can fill the gap. Fourteen mentoring schemes in England were evaluated by Clayden and Stein (2005), who suggested that in an increasingly formalized and task-driven care system, mentors can provide a crucial and more personal relationship to young care leavers.

Broad (2005) suggests that despite the impact of the 2000 Act, there are still substantial challenges: the provision of services is still patchy, and the educational and health needs of young people leaving care are not being adequately addressed within target driven services, for example, the target to improve the number of care leavers achieving at least one GCSE is meaningless in terms of improving job prospects. However, the news is not all bad. Despite the national figure of only 1 per cent of care leavers entering university, there are success stories. By considerable investment of time and money Ealing has achieved a figure of 12 per cent (Valios 2006).

KEY POINTS

- The state current struggles to corporately parent some 60,000 children at any one time
- The looked-after children's system might be efficient but largely fails to address the human needs of the young people within it.
- Policy-makers set targets for improvements but there has been a lack of recognition of the complexity of working with this group of young people.

RESOURCES

Education of looked-after children

Barnado's (2006), *Failed by The System: The Views of Young Care Leavers on their Educational Experiences*. 2006. Downloadable from www.barnardos.org.uk/resources

Leaving care

For facts and figures a good start is Research in Practice (2003). *Leaving Care.*
A number of other research reports have been published by the Joseph Rowntree Foundation:
Allen, M. (2003), *Into the Mainstream: Care Leavers Entering Work, Education and Training.*
Barn, R. et al. (2005), *Life after Care: The Experiences of Young People from Different Ethnic Groups.*
Downloadable from: www.jrf.org.uk

For young people

The Care Leavers Association: wwwcareleavers.com.
The Who Cares? Trust publishes a magazine for young people (*Who Cares?*) and advice for young people, some for younger children: www.the whocarestrust. org.
A National Voice is a campaigning group run by care-experienced people: www.anationalvoice.org.
Voice (for the Child in Care) is a campaigning organisation that aims to make a difference by asking young people in care what they want. Together with the National Children's Bureau they run the Blueprint project (Voice 2004), listening to what children want in order to improve the care system. Voice services such as independent visitors and independent people (complaints procedures):www.voiceyp.org.

CHAPTER 6

Placements for Looked-after Children

Despite best intentions and ideology, many placements are made in crisis and are often not ideal in meeting a child's needs. This chapter deploys the systems approach to 'looked after' children aiming at minimising their number, and the use of inappropriate, unplanned and distance placements. It examines outcomes for young people leaving 'the system' and a number of dilemmas around placements; for example, the role of Residential Care and the trend towards adoption and permanence.

Childcare Placements

Placements for looked-after young people are one of the most hotly contested areas of childcare practice, especially the debate between fostering and residential care ('Res Care'). Some practitioners argue that res care is potentially damaging, unmanageable and expensive while others see it as a 'positive choice' (Wagner 1988), with many occupying the middle ground, arguing that it is a necessary option for the most difficult young people considered 'unfosterable'.

Of the approximately 60,300 looked-after children in 2006, 70 per cent were placed with foster carers and only 7,700 in residential care. These figures included 2,800 unaccompanied asylum seekers. (Department for Education and Skills 2006d)

The terms 'residential care' and 'foster care' cover a wide range of options. Res care can mean a small local children's home, a large establishment in the country that will probably also provide education (community home with education (CHE) or special boarding school), through to secure accommodation.

Fostering covers a spectrum from emergency to long-term placement. There are also a variety of roles, from those who care for less damaged children and receive only the basic costs of care, to those who are professional carers and receive a salary for caring for the most challenging children. Beyond that are the 'permanency' options: residence orders, special guardianship and adoption. (see Figure 6.1).

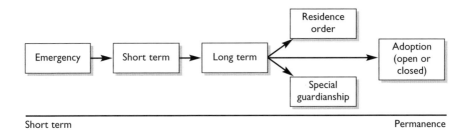

Short term   Permanence

Figure 6.1   Continuum of substitute-parenting placements

An important issue highlighted by a government target and performance standard is the high number of placement moves experienced by many looked-after children. Even planned moves can be numerous. Perhaps a young person will enter the system as an emergency and be placed in a residential unit or an emergency foster home for the first 72 hours. They might then be moved to a short-term foster home while the core assessment is carried out (there is often a limit of around six weeks on these placements). If they are identified in the assessment as needing longer-term care, they will be moved to a long-stay foster home. If they require permanence, another move is likely. Add to this scenario placement disruptions caused by behaviour problems, personal issues faced by the carers and often inadequate matching when the placement was made, and it is easy to see how 6–8 placement moves is a common experience faced by young people who spend longer periods in the care system.

While it can be difficult for workers and managers constantly to identify new placements and orchestrate moves, a lack of emphasis is often placed on the practical disruption faced by the young person and the feelings evoked. Changes of school, problems in maintaining contact with friends and family and getting to know a new area add to the trauma of having to adapt to new people and their domestic situation.

When making placement moves there is a need to concentrate upon the 'little things' such as packing possessions in proper luggage rather than bin liners and to ensure that the worker involved is the one most appropriate for the child and has sufficient time to ensure that the young person is enabled to settle into their new environment rather than just being dropped off.

At the sharp end of the debate about placement moves is the increasing practice of placing young people out of their home area. This is often as a result of the need to purchase a resource from the private or voluntary sector, often due to the lack of local resources or vacancies, although sometimes it is because of a care plan that suggests the need for a highly specialist resource.

One factor in placement decisions is the developmental needs of the child. It is now generally felt that young children cannot have their need for nurture met in a residential unit and hence many local authorities have a policy of not placing (say) under-10s in residential care. For younger children requiring a long-term placement, whose emotional needs need to be met, the main deciding factor in making a placement is the likelihood of the child bonding with the carers (Howe 2005).

Some older children neither want nor need a family environment, perhaps because of earlier damaging experiences, and require some broader concept of substitute parenting or an alternative living experience. For these individuals, 'unusual carers', (including single people) might be an appropriate resource.

Placement Decisions

On a bad day a childcare team manager will find that a child, most likely a teenager, needs a placement and nothing is available. That need is likely to be as a result of a placement breakdown or an emergency admission to care. Hours of staff time can be consumed in seeking a placement, which sometimes involves calling in senior managers to unstick situations (perhaps instructing a residential unit to take someone). Often what is offered is less than ideal, for example, the resource might be a long distance from the child's home, or is very expensive if purchased from the private sector. (This can promote a placement move to a cheaper resource at a later date even if the child has settled in that placement.)

Many other placements are made on a planned basis. There are a wider range of factors to be considered in making planned moves. Many are covered by the term 'matching', which means seeking a good fit between what a carer is offering and what the child needs. Much professional debate regards how much weight should be given to ethnicity, religious and cultural factors, for example, placing black children with white carers or vice versa. Problems arise, for example, when a carer from a similar ethnic background is of a different religion from the child, and there is debate as to whether class should be a factor, for example, should working-class children be placed with middle-class carers?

Planning should incorporate time-scales that are realistic, bearing in mind that children often resent excessive delay, their concept of time being shorter than ours. Thus, for example, introductory visits should be as concentrated as possible, but allow time for reflection and discussion.

The most important point is to listen to the child. What might seem a textbook placement to the worker might present real issues for the child. For example, a young person might be unhappy that a potential carer resembles an abuser.

We should consider the concept of a 'placement tariff', that children be placed at the lowest level possible when placements are ranked from the most ordinary to the most complex. For example, a child entering the system should not normally be placed in res care but in an 'ordinary' foster home. This approach is contested, with some feeling that all placements should be available to all children, and that the concept of a tariff means that res care is used only as a last resort which promotes the problems discussed below.

Residential Care

History

The history of childcare social work is largely one of institutional care, initially in workhouses (see Dickens's (1839) *Oliver Twist* for a literary portrayal of life for an orphan in the early Victorian age) and then in large institutions, usually run by charities. Inner city refuges for homeless children rescued from the streets were largely replaced by massive institutions in the country offering accommodation and all other facilities for children from birth to adulthood (often known as village complexes) so that they seldom related to their local community. Such places often attempted to prepare children for work, for example, Barnardo's had a sea training school and a print school for boys, while girls were largely prepared for domestic service. Some children were sent abroad to start a new life in the colonies, especially Australia and Canada. Some children did leave the institutions to be 'boarded out' (fostered), having almost invariably been chosen by well-off families, and sometimes lived almost as servants. Those chosen were predominantly girls, younger children and 'perfect white boys', leaving others, disproportionately black boys, to endure a childhood of institutional care.

The Second World War saw the mass evacuation of children into the country from cities vulnerable to bombing. This both awakened interest in the concept of substitute families and led to caution as scandals emerged about the mistreatment of evacuees. In particular, the death of an evacuee, Dennis O'Neill, at the hands of his carers led to a government enquiry (Curtis Committee 1946) and early attempts to regulate fostering, the Boarding Out Regulations of 1955.

Academic discourses around attachment theory also evolved from the 1950s, for example, the work of Bowlby (1971), which cast doubts on whether the emotional needs of children could be adequately met by institutional care. The term 'institutionalised' was used to describe young people who had been brought up in children's homes and lacked the necessary life skills. These children suffered lifetime problems, such as difficulties with practical skills and problems in forming and sustaining relationships, often labelled attachment disorders (Howe 2005).

The 1960s saw a response to these concerns with developments in the residential care concept with many of the larger cottage complexes being run down and closed. The residential care industry developed around assessment centres where children were initially placed, through small community-based homes with minimal staffing where children were typically integrated into normal schools and communities, to the relatively well-staffed larger institutions referred to as community homes with education (CHE). The latter saw their role as containing and correcting difficult behaviour. Many CHEs, often former prison service establishments known as 'approved schools' (one below Borstals in the then hierarchy of provision for young offenders) became associated with young offenders while the smaller and more locally based establishments were seen as for the 'needy' children. Not surprisingly, residential assessment centres tended to recommend residential placements, thus perpetuating the residential system.

Parallel systems were developed by education departments as 'special boarding schools', although the users, poor children from deprived backgrounds, were broadly similar to those placed in CHEs, and placement depended on which department had identified the problem. Labels like 'maladjusted' were applied to the children, but what struck me then was how well adjusted such young people really were to adverse conditions.

A significant piece of childcare legislation, the Children and Young Persons Act 1969, made a major policy leap by arguing that offending behaviour was evidence of wider social need and therefore offenders should be integrated into wider care systems. So CHEs and smaller children's homes started to integrate their children, although the stigma attached to the large country establishments remained. Sadly, much of the 1969 Act with its more liberal stance was never implemented.

Many teenagers who went through approved schools and CHEs in the 1960s and 1970s will remember their harshness. They were often largely male establishments, staffed by macho males, often ex-military. Bullying was rife and the weaker boys (there were a few girls' establishments) had a particularly rough time within a residents' culture that reinforced the authoritarian regime. Rules were strict, regimes regimented and there was little time to talk, except to a few attached 'therapists'. By modern standards care was often degrading with, for example, communal showers often associated with personal remarks about one's body.

Abusive regimes were often justified in the name of cure or therapy. For example, in one establishment operating along behaviourist lines, the negative reinforcers were so strong that the ultimate sanction was regularly used, where young people were denied their clothes and covered only in a bedsheet. In one of Frank Beck's establishments in Leicestershire, 'regression therapy' was used, whereby teenagers were made to wear nappies, sat on Beck's lap and bounced like babies. Beck was eventually convicted of numerous counts of sexual abuse (see chapter 4).

Many of these concerns came to a head in the 1980s and 90s with scandals about residential care. Many of these involved sexual abuse of residents by staff, in Leicestershire, north Wales and Northern Ireland, for example. Others, notably Pindown in Staffordshire centred on the use of control. The saddest observation is that abused children were placed in res care as a place of safety only to be further abused.

The late 1970s saw a massive decline in the use of children's residential care for a number of reasons: professional and academic discourses about both their lack of effectiveness and the degrading nature of some regimes, and not least their cost. As the heyday of social services expansion of the 1970s was transformed into the cuts of the 1980s, the days of mass residential care became numbered.

As the places in residential homes declined, new challenges emerged. Specialist units could seldom be justified in any locality and therefore the few surviving local units became generalist, and were required to take anybody who needed a placement, which created concerns about unmanageability.

At the same time, parallel developments saw an expansion of alternatives to residential care, particularly a greater emphasis on keeping children in their natural families and in foster care.

In conclusion, there are historical parallels with current practice, for example that punitive policies towards young offenders are ineffective (see chapter 8). Another common factor is that interventions apparently in a child's best interests can be damaging, for example current policies for managing truancy.

Managing Children's Homes

With so few residential establishments, most local authority homes tend to take on a general role, and despite the requirement in the Children Act 1989 that they have a statement of purpose and clear objectives, they are often used as the placement of last resort. Although most establishments now have fewer than a dozen residents, many only three or four, and a staff team that outnumbers them, it is argued that homes can be unmanageable. Reasons include:

- Putting a group of the most 'difficult' young people in one place.
- Problems of staff communication and consistency, given the practical difficulties of shifts and rotas; problems in effectively supervising staff in these conditions, given that managers seldom work alongside their supervisees.
- Problems in recruiting and retaining qualified staff, given the nature of the work (unsociable hours, either crisis work or little to do) and the better terms and conditions and status offered by fieldwork. Successive attempts have been made to increase the proportion of qualified residential workers, but most seek to develop their career elsewhere upon qualification. Perhaps subprofessional qualifications through NVQ are the way forward in increasing the skills of the residential workforce.
- The young people have little incentive to make an investment in the placement given its temporary nature, and professional considerations make it difficult for staff to form proper 'relationships' with residents.
- Issues around discipline and sanctions. In the current culture corporal punishment is forbidden and the human rights of the child must be considered in imposing lesser sanctions. Some workers feel that there are insufficient sanctions to impose effective control, while others argue that despite the difficulties the key to control lies in creating positive relationships with the young people.
- Dilemmas about how to handle 'difficult' behaviour, especially when it is illegal or 'immoral' or where issues of control and restraint present themselves.
- Public relations issues when poor behaviour spills over into the community or affects other agencies – for example, the police complaining about timewasting when residents are reported missing.

Good Practice in Residential Care

Despite the difficulties, some young people do experience their period in residential care positively. However, a well-run home is vulnerable to upset, for example when new residents arrive or a powerful manager leaves. The overriding factor in creating a successful residential experience is to create a culture in which the residents and staff feel valued and respected.

Research suggests that the following factors are associated with running a successful residential home:

- involvement of the children in their daily lives and planning for their future;
- ensuring their right to privacy;
- stability in daily routines;
- consistent practices in control and discipline;
- promoting positive relationships between children;
- acknowledging the sexuality of residents;
- addressing cultural issues;
- working with issues relating to the abuse of tobacco, drugs and alcohol. (Kahan 1994)

A study of 48 children's homes by Sinclair and Gibbs (1998) found the following factors associated with good quality care:

- homes were small;
- the head of the home was empowered (by senior managers) and able to provide strong leadership and create clear roles;
- consensus among staff.

Another study by Berridge and Brodie (1998) added the following factors:

- the ability for a head of home to be able to state their methods of work;
- staff stability.

These factors can be synthesized into the following components of quality:

- understanding the needs of individual children and groups of residents, including listening to them;
- the promotion of children's rights;
- the development of sound management practices, including supervision and support for staff;
- effective leadership;
- consistent daily routines.

The following exercise invites the reader to consider some of the practical problems in putting these principles into practice:

FOCUS ONP RACTICE 6.1

Managing residential care: discussion examples

1. You are on sleep-in duty. You are about to go to bed but decide to first check the bedroom corridor. You smell pot coming from a bedroom. You hear laughter and three or four different voices. You're on duty on your own (the waking night person phoned in sick). What do you do?
2. You know that 15-year-old Dave is grounded. Another resident tells you that he's about to go out and intends to buy drugs. You see Dave heading for the front door. What do you do?
3. 15-year-old Sharon is refusing to get out of bed to attend her court hearing for theft. What do you do?
4 You're duty senior. The assistant director phones at 7 p.m. to say that you must take a very difficult young man as an emergency. You know that your manager turned him down earlier in the day as being unsuitable, especially in terms of your present volatile resident group. He's been a resident before, wrecked the place and bullied other children and threatened staff. What do you do?

In considering these, think about:
■ the legal position;
■ the professional position;
■ an assessment of the risks and benefits of each course of action;
■ what the underlying power issues are;
■ whether there are issues to raise with the manager or staff team.

See the end of the chapter for suggestions.

Control and Restraint in Community Homes

While best practice suggests that control is achieved by making young people feel valued and motivated to conform, and by establishments providing good structures and a sense of order, the bottom line is the use of control and restraint.

Unless an establishment is registered as a secure unit or part of the youth custody estate, there is no legal permission to detain a young person, so they cannot be locked into an establishment. However, the Guidance and Regulations to the Children Act 1989 allows staff in residential settings to take emergency action to restrain a child or young person when they are likely to seriously injure themselves or others, or seriously damage property (Section 8(3)b, Children's Homes Regulations 1991). Concerns about the way words such as 'significantly and 'serious' are interpreted in individual cases and establishments have prompted considerable further guidance from the government. For example, a circular issued in 1998 suggested that residential care staff have the same rights and responsibilities as parents in interpreting these terms, but that individual decisions should be related to factors about the particular child including their 'Gillick competence' (LAC circular CI(97)6).

The Role of Advocacy

Advocacy is an important aspect of work with looked-after children, especially as they have the right to an advocate to assist them with their statutory meetings and in making a complaint (see chapter 2).

Special Residential Facilities

As well as being placed in children's homes, children may be placed in the following parallel systems:

- health services establishments including hospitals, adolescent psychiatric units and therapeutic establishments, for example, dealing with eating disorders or addiction problems;
- education facilities including special boarding schools and boarding houses attached to schools;
- prison service establishments: young offenders' institutions and secure training centres (run by private companies).

In terms of placements it seems likely that the same group of young people, that is those who suffer a high level of social deprivation, are likely to find themselves identified as needing care or control. Whether they are identified as having special educational needs, in need of social services, youth justice or child and adolescent mental health services, seems to be largely a matter of chance. It is likely that the implementation of the Common Assessment Framework will reduce this apparent lottery.

Figure 6.2 maps the routes through these systems.

Secure Accommodation

There are around 22 secure units with some 390 places in the UK. In 2004, 25 per cent of residents stayed for over six months, while 15 per cent stayed 3–6 months. (Department for Education and Skills 2006e)

Secure accommodation is run by or on behalf of local authorities and are effectively locked children's homes. Their residents fall into three distinct categories:

- vulnerable young offenders under detention and training orders sponsored by the Youth Justice Board (around 40 per cent of beds);
- looked-after young people deemed by a court on the application of a children's trust to be a danger to themselves or others (around 60 per cent of

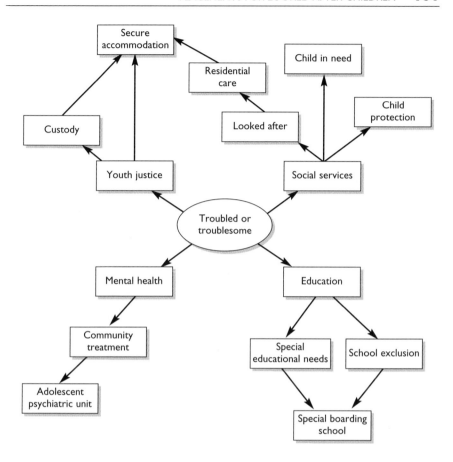

Figure 6.2 Routes into residential care

beds). A placement of up to 72 hours can be authorised by the Director of Children's Services (or their delegate);
■ those detained under Her Majesty's pleasure, mainly murderers.

These are expensive placements (at over £3,000 per week) and in many cases placements are made a long distance from home. The challenge is to devise alternative 'close support packages' that avoid the need for children's trusts to use secure accommodation. This can involve using an empty staff flat and assembling a team of workers, at least two on duty at all times, to work with a young person in a state of acute crisis. While such a package can contain a young person with their consent, there is no legal permission to detain them, so if they are determined not to co-operate, a decision has to be made as to whether the situation justifies a secure placement.

Some young people who have lived chaotic, perhaps dangerous, lives value a period in a secure unit as it provides a safe place in which to regain control.

Some placements are probably inappropriate, for example, when it appears to be used as a punishment for those who are misbehaving in the care system. Placements may also be made to try to rescue a young person from an adverse situation such as prostitution, although there are serious doubts as to the effectiveness of such placements as the young people seem to quickly return to their former lifestyle.

There is debate as to the kind of regime that should operate in these establishments, whether it is to be punitive or liberal. Some see control as the main aim of secure accommodation while others argue that the security offered by the establishment allows workers to confront the young person's issues in a safe way. Others suggest that young people should just be given time and space to work through things in their own way within a liberal and supportive regime.

'Therapeutic' Establishments

There are now relatively few establishments based upon 'therapeutic' principles and those that have survived tend to be within the private and voluntary sectors. This is due to the substantial cost, concerns about their effectiveness and the distance of most placements from the child's home.

Prison Service Establishments

The welfare of children in custody is discussed in chapter 4.

The Case For and Against Residential Care

The arguments in the highly contested debate about the value of residential care are summarised below.

The Case For:

- Residential care should be a 'positive choice' (Wagner 1988). Current problems result from it being used inappropriately as a placement of last resort. It might be particularly valuable in offering respite care (when natural parents might feel threatened if their child goes to another family), to keep siblings together or where the complexity of the case needs intensive resources or therapeutic intervention.
- Young people themselves often see residential placements positively. Kahan's (1994) study supports this view as do some young people's organizations which argue that choice should be offered. Young people often see residential homes as avoiding conflict between natural and substitute families and creating less pressure than foster homes where relationships can be more intense.
- Fostering and adoption breakdowns indicate that some young people are too damaged to be expected to survive in 'normal' families and communities.
- Some young people will end up in 'res. care' anyway. It's perhaps better to place them there in a planned way rather than expecting them to suffer numerous placement breakdowns before a residential placement is made.

The Case Against

- Residents can become contaminated by each other's problems, for example, when a burglar and serious drug user are placed together.
- While 'res. care' is assumed to provide a safe place for young people who might already have suffered abuse, they may suffer abuse by staff or by other residents. Bullying is often reported.
- Factors discussed above may make young people unmanageable.
- Residential care is expensive and arguably the money could be spent more effectively on other placements and services in the community.

In the 1980s Warwickshire closed all its residential homes. Research showed that:

- young people were denied choice;
- placement moves were higher than the national average;
- some residential placements were still made in the private and voluntary sectors but only after a number of breakdowns had been experienced (Cliffe 1991).

Frampton (2003) writes a sensitive account of growing up in Barnardo's care in the 1950s and 1960s. Despite a catalogue of what we would now see as inhumane and abusive treatment in one of their residential homes, he is in favour of residential placements. This is largely as a result of two failed fostering placements at the ages of 4 and 15 from which experience he argues that substitute families cannot meet the needs of all children. Like other personal historic accounts, this has to be viewed with caution. On the one hand, Frampton was unfortunate in his experiences of foster care, and on the other, those were the days when children's homes housed a variety of children, not just the 'hard to place', and although they were institutional, at least there were groups of long-term children, and often long-stay resident houseparents who could provide some semblance of consistency and relationships.

A journalistic account of abuse in children's homes is provided by Wolmar (2000). The book examines the now compelling evidence that widespread abuse took place in residential care in the 1960s to the 1980s, and considers the harm done and some of the wider issues, for example, attempting to dispel the myth that former residents are alleging abuse many years later in the hope of compensation.

Foster Care Placements

The term 'foster care' reflects the changing social construction of the task of caring for looked-after children in one's own home. It moves away from the concept of care being provided within traditional families to embrace a broader range of provision. Foster parenting fails to recognise the complexity of some caring tasks in managing difficult behaviour, which is understated in the word 'parenting'. Some older children with a series of negative experiences of 'families' are seeking a living experience beyond the normal concept of 'parenting'.

Most foster placements are now supported by two social workers: the child's and the foster carer's link worker. Aside from possible differences of perception between the two individuals, it is usual for them to be managed by two separate line managers in two separate units.

The Carer's Perspective

The changing social constructions of parenting, 'families' and the roles of adults and children in our society, can lead to misunderstandings between participants in the fostering process, which often suggests a lack of openness and an inability to achieve consensus about the roles and functions of foster carers. These disagreements are often rehearsed around relatively minor things such as differences between a birth parent and a foster carer over control issues and boundaries, for example, smacking (carers cannot use corporal punishment in any circumstances), bedtimes or the child's freedom to choose their own clothing or hairstyle. Social workers are often unclear as to whether foster carers are service users, volunteers or colleagues, which can lead to unclear expectations, especially in relation to authority and power. Some social workers want to be very controlling ('I must have control of the case' was the catchphrase of one), while others leave the carer to it. Similarly, some foster carers want firm direction, while others are happy to make their own day-to-day decisions.

Despite the lack of clarity about their role and unclear expectations from the various stakeholders in the caring process, foster carers are the people in day-to-day charge who often have to think on their feet in response to difficult situations in and around the living environment. An example might be the embarrassment felt by a foster carer whose charge is swearing or otherwise misbehaving in public or, worse, when restraint has to be used in a public place.

Foster carers can have a negative view of the department. Under-resourcing is often a major issue, with carers sometimes feeling that they have been left with a very difficult young person without the promised level of support. It might involve a fairly fundamental resource like a school place, although regulations now require schools to accept looked-after children promptly in their locality; they can no longer argue that they are full. It is clearly very demanding to have to be with a young person all the time. A social worker who has had a bad day can eventually go home and relax, but a foster carer is denied that luxury. Carers can feel that they are being used, that by taking yesterday's emergency they have been left with the problem while the department moves on to another higher priority today. Frustration can also result from what can feel like dysfunctional Departmental policies. For example, they do not have the money to fund the child on the carer's family holiday, but will pay for the child to be placed elsewhere while the carer is away.

Many of the problems faced by foster carers go beyond individual placements, and often the local foster care association and the department clash over fundamental issues such as support and payment. These often reflect national issues. It can be frustrating for carers that while some departments claim they cannot afford to pay foster carers decent allowances, they can still find large sums of money for an expensive residential placement. The government has recognized that foster carers should be properly trained and rewarded for the complex task (Department for Education and Skills 2006), but with insufficient funding progress towards achieving this is slow.

There can be a major role conflict when the foster carer has to advocate for the young person against the department or wider local authority. This can involve anything from a dispute between the child and their social worker, to contesting an exclusion from school or whistleblowing (see chapter 4) when a child discloses abuse within the care system. The issue here is whether the carer's primary loyalty is to the young person or to the department and whether they should simply keep their head down for fear of being branded a trouble-maker. Foster carers have no conditions of service, and while there are proce-dures for deregistering an unsuitable carer, there is nothing to stop a department simply not using a carer whom they deem to be troublesome.

The rules can get in the way of normalisation. Young people resent such things as reviews and statutory medicals, although a young person deemed 'Gillick competent' can decline their medicals. Until recently when the regula-tions were changed to allow greater discretion to carers, looked-after children couldn't stay overnight with friends unless their parents had been police-checked.

Another uncomfortable issue arises from the concept of 'safe caring'. To protect young people from abuse and carers from allegations, rules have been established which again undermine household normality. However, carers afraid to touch or be alone with a child could feel that they cannot meet the emotional needs of that child, particularly when a young child is distressed and in need of close physical contact such as a cuddle. This is another example of defensive practice. An alternative approach to this dilemma is to undertake a risk assessment of each caring situation so that blanket restrictions can be replaced by individually agreed boundaries.

What Participants Say

Below is a summary of a report from the Children's Rights Director which considered the views of the main stakeholders in the foster care process (Morgan 2005).

What children said

- Many children said they didn't get enough information about their foster families before they moved in.
- The best thing about being fostered was the care and support they received in their foster homes and being part of a family.
- Very little or no choice was given to children as to where they were placed.
- Most children felt they were being treated the same as their foster carer's own children.

- The worst things for children about being in foster care was not seeing their family and feeling the odd one out because they were in care.
- Being in foster care made a huge difference to young people's lives. They told us they were better looked after and achieved more at school.

What foster carers said

- Like the children, foster carers didn't feel they were given enough information about the young people before they moved in.
- Most support for foster carers came from social workers.
- The best thing about being a foster carer was seeing the foster child happy.
- The worst thing was not getting enough support and communication from social services.

What birth parents said

- They would have liked more information about what was happening to their children.
- Birth parents thought the best thing about foster care was knowing their child was safe and well cared for.
- The worst thing was missing their children.

Foster Care: What Works?

Sinclair (2005) summarised the research on what works in foster care. The analysis fits well with the systems approach in that it identifies foster care as a part of the wider care process and suggests that foster carers should have broader roles in supporting both children who return home and those who move on to independence. It stresses that foster care is not just a set of tasks but is about forming relationships and showing commitment, especially for those children who have insecure attachments elsewhere. It suggests that there are a group of older children for whom a return home is unlikely and adoption not a realistic option, and for them the fostering system should provide a 'family for life'. Particularly for younger children, greater decisiveness, especially about the viability of their natural family, could promote the greater use of adoption. It acknowledges that for a group of quite damaged older children 'treatment foster care' is needed. The study also argues that foster carers should be adequately recompensed for and supported in their work.

A research study by Sinclair et al. (2005) considered some 596 children who were in foster care in 1998 and followed them over a three-year period, whether they returned to their natural family, were adopted, moved to independent accommodation or remained in foster care. The study emphasises the importance of proper planning and proper support for placements, which is often about resources. However, whatever statistical research suggests, the reality in individual cases is often different; for example, one cannot plan for adoption until the possibilities for restoration have been exhausted. The study recognises that while many restorations are planned, and the commitment of both children and parents is a crucial variable of success, in a number of cases restoration occurs because of events, and often reflects the strong attachments between natural parent(s) and child. It is perhaps most dramatic when restoration occurs because of difficulties faced by a young person in settling in a placement, or when no suitable placement can be found.

Although adoption is seen as most successful in terms of outcome indicators, the study mainly looks at the placements of under-6s and is thus not able to inform the current Government policy of placing more looked-after, often older, children for adoption. The research also suggests that child-centred fostering by child-orientated foster carers is recognised as a major variable in success, and a major factor in this is listening to children.

Are All Children Fosterable?

There are really two debates, one about the behaviour of particular children and the need to contain this, and the other as to whether it is reasonable to expect ordinary people to cope with what can be quite extreme behaviour in their own homes and private lives. The two debates can arguably be reconciled by broadening the concept of fostering beyond that of the average family; one sometimes needs 'odd carers for odd kids'. Some examples might be placing a gay teenager with gay carers, an alleged perpetrator of sexual abuse with a couple without children, or someone very mistrusting of traditional families with a single carer.

Some of these options are politically contested, especially that of recruiting gay carers. The unjustified stereotypical assumption is that gay carers are motivated by a desire to sexually abuse the young person, whereas in reality most sexual abuse by foster carers has been heterosexual and in two-parent situations. This, however, should be treated with caution since most foster carers are still heterosexual couples.

It may be argued that very difficult behaviour is more easily contained in a small domestic situation than in a group where a young person can play to the audience, and because one or two carers can provide more consistent boundaries than a rota of staff. It is also possible that the young person will perceive the foster carer(s) to be more caring than employed staff who do it as a job and are therefore more likely to make a commitment to the placement, which in turn promotes more acceptable behaviour.

There are other positives that one or two carers can offer, such as providing positive role models to a young person who has learned to mistrust adults, and providing formal or informal support after the placement has ended, especially as the young person moves to independence.

For professional practitioners there can be a number of dilemmas. One arises from the assessment of potential carers: should carers conform to an image of Mr and Mrs Clean or should a broader range of lifestyles and behaviours be acceptable? In terms of the expectations placed on carers, is it also acceptable that they, for example, drink alcohol, have sexual relationships outside marriage, are obese or smoke? Similar issues arise when considering how carers should manage the behaviour of their foster children which is illegal or seen as immoral, for example, when they bring stolen property into the house, are violent or use drugs.

In carrying out assessments of potential carers and foster carer reviews it is important to consider the amount of damage placing very difficult children might do to the carers and their families. An example might be the effect on a marriage or on the natural children in the family. There are also wider issues of risk, such as from violent behaviour, damage to property or arson.

Recruiting carers is often emphasised more than retaining existing carers. The latter is about providing proper support, not just social work, but practical packages of assistance. In some cases it is necessary to get beyond the essentially 'voluntary' nature of foster caring towards providing professional terms and conditions, allowing carers to make their living from caring and to live a personal life beyond.

The wishes and feelings of the young people are important in making placements. However, like the general public, young people have stereotypical views of various caring environments. For example, they may fear being bullied if they are placed with lesbian or gay couples. They need to be given accurate information upon which to make informed decisions that should then be considered in accordance with their age and level of understanding. It is folly to push a young person into a placement to which they are strongly opposed.

It can be argued that if a child is deemed unfosterable and must be placed in residential care, then, given the concerns about running residential units, they should really be placed in secure accommodation. This might apply for example to young people who self-harm, persistently commit offences, or abscond.

The answer as to whether there are unfosterable children lies in whether it is possible to recruit and support people willing and able to undertake the complex and demanding task. Some practitioners remain sceptical about some children with severe behavioural problems (perhaps on the autistic spectrum), those with learning difficulties and challenging behaviour, or those with severe physical disabilities. But there are examples of carers who have successfully fostered such children.

Other Placements

Kinship Care

When a child can no longer live with their natural parents it is now commonplace for first consideration to be given to options for care within their extended family. Often grandparents are the first option, sometimes aunts and uncles, and occasionally older siblings. Sometimes the proposed carer is not actually related to the child but has a meaningful relationship with them, for example, a former partner of the natural mother.

Kinship care is on the threshold between private and public care arrangements (Farmer and Moyers 2005). Some kinship arrangements are negotiated between family members outside the care system, perhaps during a family group conference (see chapter 7), or less formally, which makes the arrangement private fostering (see below). In other cases the prospective carers are assessed as state foster carers and paid accordingly, although in some areas they receive only the basic payment rate, irrespective of the difficulty of the child.

The clear benefit of kinship care is that the child can retain their sense of family and cultural identity and can continue to have a more natural relationship with their birth parents. This can also be a disadvantage, however, where birth parents disrupt the care or confuse the child as to caring roles.

It might be argued that lower standards should be used to assess potential kinship carers in order to take advantage of the benefits of a kinship placement, and that the decision should be based upon what they can offer in comparison with a traditional foster carer.

The research by Farmer and Moyers (2005) considered the characteristics, progress and outcomes of 270 children living with kinship carers compared to a control group of children living with unrelated foster carers. A major finding was that kinship carers often struggled more with the placement, often due to poor support and payment but sometimes due to personal factors, for example the age of grandparent carers. The outcomes for children were generally better than those in unrelated foster placements, but sometimes it was felt that these were achieved at the expense of the carers. Worryingly, in 10 per cent of the kinship placements the standard was judged to be 'very poor'. In terms of placement stability the best results were achieved by grandparent carers, with 86 per cent remaining in placement after a 2-year follow-up period compared to 72 per cent of all family and friends placements and 55 per cent of those with unrelated carers.

In some cases the kinship carer will apply for a residence order or special guardianship (see below).

Private Fostering

The term 'private fostering' is an ambiguous one. It can refer to the fostering of looked-after children arranged by private fostering agencies, or to arrangements made directly between parents and carers outside of the care system. In the former case the statutory duties remain with the placing children's trust, so the term is probably being misused. In this section 'private fostering' is used to refer to direct arrangements between parents and other carers.

The death of Victoria Climbie, a privately fostered child, raised a number of issues. First, Victoria was one of an apparently large number of children being sent to Europe by their parents, often from Africa, in search of better education. Secondly, it gave rise to debate about the poor level of regulation of such arrangements. Under the Children Act 1989 there is a duty for private foster carers to inform the local authority that they are privately fostering, but there are few requirements regarding what is expected of children's services. It is argued that it is the duty of parents making the placement to satisfy themselves as to the suitability of the carers. However,

Victoria (and presumably many other children), was placed at a distance with a distant relative, so it is questionable how able the parents were to adequately vet the proposed carers.

Many hoped that Victoria's death would promote new legislation to bring private fostering in line with state fostering, but sadly under the Children Act 2004 (Sections 44–7) there has been only a minimal tightening of the previous duty to report such arrangements. However, the Act gives the Secretary of State a power to issue further regulations, which sadly has not been used.

The Rush for Permanence

Government policy is to increase the number of looked-after children and young people who are adopted. The target of increasing by 40 per cent between 2000 and 2005 the adoption of looked-after children was met. The major issue is whether it is sensible to pursue a high proportion of adoptions given that up to 50 per cent of placements made from the age of 10 break down (Parker 1999). Another debate is whether carers should be asked to take legal responsibility for a child who might be highly emotionally damaged and may suffer severe emotional and behavioural problems in adolescence or adulthood. On the other hand, modern adoptions often offer continued financial and social work support and continuing contact with the birth family (80 per cent of adoptions are made with some contact). The issue then becomes whether adoption is really different from long-term fostering.

In considering the value of adoption an analogy may be made with getting married as opposed to living together. For some couples the legal cementing of a relationship is highly important, for others less so. In terms of adoption of looked-after children (3,700 in the year to March 2004; 6 per cent of placements), it is debatable whether the current policy of increasing the number of children offered 'permanence' through adoption is more about getting children out of care, rather than meeting their needs. Even with open adoptions (where there is some contact with birth parents), it is questionable whether it is right to legally sever a child's links with their past, even if they are unable to live with their birth parents. This in the context of often lengthy and highly contested court cases aimed at 'freeing' a child for adoption.

Residence Orders and Special Guardianship

Residence orders and special guardianship orders provide a middle ground between being looked after and adopted. They involve the sharing of parental responsibility between the long-term carers obtaining the order and the original holders of it (mother or parents). Although social services might continue to be involved and can pay an allowance, they lose parental responsibility. This can inhibit applications, for example where a relative has cared for a child due to the incapacity of the birth parents and continue to have concerns about the ability or willingness of the birth parent to act in the best interests of the child.

Adoption Practice: Some Issues

Adoption is one of the most contested areas of childcare practice, both in terms of the emotions it elicits (such as giving up one's baby or finding one's birth parents) and the policies employed by adoption agencies, which often hit the media, centring mainly on issues of political correctness.

There are two different marketplaces for adoptive children: healthy white babies, and more difficult-to-place children who are older, in sibling groups or have special needs. The demand for babies (only around 10 per cent of adoptions) far outstrips the supply and tough choices have to be made as to who are accepted as adopters (there are age limits, and smokers and obese people may be ruled out). With difficult-to-place children, where the demand for placements far exceeds supply, debates arise as to how to widen the resource base, for example by advertising individual children, and accepting applications from a wider range of people (such as lesbian and gay couples and from single people).

In the year to March 2004 5 per cent of adopted children were black and 9 per cent of mixed race, which is a bit disproportionately low, and one in five children awaiting adoption is black (Department for Education and Skills 2005). Selwyn et al. (2004) studied black children awaiting adoption who remained in the care system longer. The study identified problems with recruiting black carers and achieving appropriate racial and cultural matches. Poor recruitment derives from demographic factors in black communities, including not having sufficient space for an adopted child, myths and stereotypes within black communities as to suitable adopters, and a reluctance to approach white-dominated social work agencies.

A further area of adoption is adoption by a step-parent, numerically the largest but outside the public care system. This is used to give a new partner parental status over the children from their partner's former relationship.

The average age for being adopted is four years and five months, and 80 per cent of children are placed within twelve months of the decision that they should be adopted (Department of Education and Skills 2005). There is now a national adoption register to match children who wait with approved adopters who don't achieve a local placement. In practice some of the most difficult-to-place children are referred to specialist voluntary agencies, for example Parents for Children, who place children for a fee.

There is a debate about whether foster carers should be allowed to adopt. Some argue that legally and practically fostering and adoption are separate forms of care and shouldn't be mixed, while others welcome a long-term fostering arrangement that has worked progressing to adoption. There are other difficult areas, for example, when a child is placed as a foster child with a view to adoption (perhaps while a freeing order is sought). This can lead to major disappointment if the plan cannot proceed, for example if a court rules that the child should be restored to their natural parent(s). One aspect of this is referred to as 'direct placement', that is, when a baby is placed with prospective adopters direct from the maternity hospital. These cases can lead to 'tug of love' scenarios if the birth mother changes her mind about consenting to adoption. By the time the matter is decided in court the child may have been with the prospective adopters for a considerable period and could have bonded with them.

The Adoption and Children Act 2002 has increased the amount of support available to adopters and given the right to adoptive parents to an assessment of their support needs. It allows unmarried couples to adopt jointly (previously only married couples or single people could adopt), and creates a right to independent appeal for unsuccessful adoptive applicants. It is supported by National Standards for Adoption.

As well as the core tasks of finding and assessing adopters and placing children, an adoption agency will also be involved in counselling people who were adopted and wish to find out about their past, and birth mothers wishing to find their adopted children, and in re-establishing links between adopted children and birth parents.

Adoption: Some Special Areas of Practice

Inter-country adoptions

In 2000, 350 adoption applications were made in respect of children from abroad (Department for Education Skills 2005). While it is tempting for unsuccessful UK adoption applicants to seek a child from abroad, there are moral issues around removing a child from their own culture (where they may face severe poverty and deprivation) and bringing them to the UK where they might be living with a white middle-class family.

The Adoption (Inter-Country Aspects) Act 1999 places inter-country adoption on the same legal footing as UK adoptions. It closes a loophole whereby prospective adopters could pay for a private home study, hence avoiding the need for a full adoption assessment. It also rules out paying for children and makes the UK a signatory of the 1993 Hague Convention on the protection of children, which governs inter-country co-operation. Children adopted from abroad are entitled to the same post-adoption support services as other adoptees.

Unusual applicants

Should adoptions be made to Mr and Mrs Average or should we, especially in the light of the supply–demand situation, accept applicants from more unusual circumstances? This debate tends to focus on lesbian and gay applicants. Some take a moral stance against such applicants, others a more pragmatic but negative one, arguing that a child might get bullied because of the sexuality of their parents. Some argue that such applicants should be seen as second-best and only be offered children who would otherwise not be placed. Others argue that a diverse society should positively welcome a diversity of applicants and that placements with unusual applicants can be a positive choice – 'odd applicants for odd kids'! Best practice suggests that each applicant should be assessed fully on all aspects of the care they are able to offer and that any unusual factors should be viewed only as part of this wider picture.

In some areas local politicians have been involved in these politicised aspects of practice and have sanctioned area-wide policies to inform practice so that each case does not have to be individualised. In the voluntary sector, management boards have been similarly deployed to make clear policies, although some have wrestled with moral debates, for example whether the Catholic Adoption Service should be forced to accept gay adopters.

Improving Placement Practice: the Systems Approach

Applying the systems approach to placements aims to get beyond regular placement crises to a point where a department or team are able to deliver on their objective of meeting the assessed need of each child when they need it.

The first stage in the process is to consider objectives. These might be quite practical, (for example, identifying a placement within four hours of a request), to ideological (such as minimising the use of res care or out-of-area placements).

The next stage is to identify how the current system operates and what problems it generates. Part of this data-gathering phase should involve comparisons between how one's authority or team compares with others. Department for Children, Schools and Families statistics of looked-after children provide a starting point for a comparison of one authority's performance with comparator (broadly similar) others. For example, are we making more use of res care? Are our costs per foster placement higher than others? Local comparisons can then be applied, for example, why does one area team use more residential placements than its neighbours?

The next stage analyses the system in terms of its inputs, internal processes and outputs (see Figure 6.3). The major inputs will be the children who need placement and the resources available to provide for and manage them. Information should be gained about the children's age, gender, ethnic group and religion. It might be found, for example, that a large proportion of the children are older adolescents misplaced in the system and that another scheme could more appropriately focus upon preventing adolescent family breakdown (see chapter 7). Gatekeeping is the process of checking that inputs to the system are appropriate, how and why the children are referred for placement. It might found, for example, that the out-of-hours team are removing children inappropriately because they have insufficient resources to manage crises in other, more proactive ways.

After examining the system inputs, the next issue is the functioning of the system itself. Again objectives need to be set. Some will come from government targets under the Quality Protects initiative, such as to minimise placement moves and to maximise educational achievement among looked-after children. Some will be local; perhaps a rule that prohibits the placement of under-10s in residential care, or gatekeeping systems designed to minimise the number of placements in the private and voluntary sectors. In addition to examining statistics, it is often valuable to create some qualitative data, perhaps examining files to track particular cases though the system, finding out what worked and what didn't, in particular identifying cases that were escalated up the placement tariff for resource reasons, for example someone being placed in a residential unit

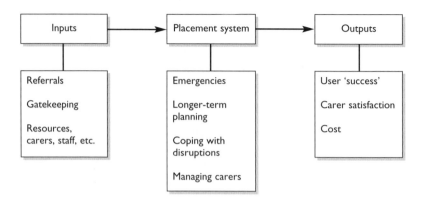

Figure 6.3   Placement system

due to the lack of a bed in a foster home. Better still, undertake some customer research to establish not only what happened but how service users, carers, parents and other stakeholders evaluated the system and how they felt about their participation in it.

A consideration of internal processes, policies and resources might suggest that there are insufficient placements available, with children placed, often inappropriately, in the only bed available, precipitating further moves. Policies might promote numerous moves, perhaps by defining some resources as available for 72 hours only. Recruiting more foster carers will create some slack that will enable the system to function more effectively, and broadening the function of carers can provide greater flexibility and fewer placement moves. It may be necessary to question a poor retention rate among carers.

The final area of analysis is the outputs from the system. This might include where the young people go on exiting the system and such factors as the wastage of carers. For example, where placements are in great demand there is a tendency to try to move over 16s from foster placements towards independence, although this might not be in their best interests.

With the young people the big question is whether the system delivered desired outcomes, for example did destinations match care plans? As Sinclair et al.'s (2005) study suggested, some of the saddest outcomes are when carefully planned work is abandoned in favour of damage limitation, when either the correct resources cannot be made available or the young person is unwilling or unable to use them. An example of the former is when a child is sent to an out-county boarding school despite a plan that they should remain in mainstream education because no school will take them, or where a young person is returned home to an environment recognised as abusive because they cannot 'settle' in the care system.

In evaluating systems effectiveness care should be taken to be realistic about expectations. For example, given that one of the inputs is severely damaged children, some degree of placement breakdown is inevitable, but it doesn't negate the validity of the systems approach in identifying deficiencies.

In childcare people are the most valuable resource. Wastage is not only a financial cost in terms of assessment and initial training, but also a loss of expertise and a scarce resource. Carers exiting, especially after short periods, should be interviewed to establish their reasons for departing and what could have been improved. This information should also be requested from representative agencies, such as the local Foster Care Association.

Collecting information about the nature and effectiveness of the placement system can allow proposals for change to be drafted, consulted upon and finally implemented. However, since systems are not static entities, after a period to allow changes to properly embed, another process of evaluation should commence.

In terms of finance, some 'pump-priming' money is probably needed to implement the proposals from a systems analysis, but in the longer term a more functional system will yield considerable cost savings as well as a higher quality of service, for example, by reducing the need for costly and ineffective out-area placements.

KEY POINTS

- Childcare placements are some of the most contested aspects of childcare practice, particularly the use of residential care and adoption issues.
- Foster care is successful but there is still confusion about the role of foster carers, especially those who care for the most damaged children.
- Kinship care is growing in significance as a placement option but there is debate about its value in comparison with foster care
- Many placements are made in crisis. The systems approach can be used to maximise the proportion of planned and therefore productive placements.
- There is debate about the value of the current policy of increasing the proportion of older, more 'difficult' looked-after children being adopted.

RESOURCES

Residential care

Clough, R., Bullock, R. and Ward, A. (2006), *What Works in Residential Child Care,* reviews the research and practical considerations around what works in residential care on behalf of the National Centre for Excellence in Residential Child Care at the National Children's Bureau.

The Care Leavers Association website offers a useful history of abuse in residential care: www.careleavers.com.

Foster care

Sellick, C. and Howell, D. (2003), *Innovative, Tried and Tested: A Review of Good Practice in Fostering.*

Wilson, K. et al. (2004) *Fostering Success: An Exploration of the Research Literature in Foster Care.*

The Fostering Network is the leading voluntary organisation for those involved in fostering. Many downloadable resources are available to members only: www.fostering.net

Adoption

Most up-to-date material is on websites. The two major interest groups are membership organisations:

- British Association for Adoption and Fostering, which is influential in policy making, etc.: www.baaf.org.uk.
- Adoption UK, mainly a support group for prospective adopters and adoptees. They also advertise difficult-to-place children awaiting adoption in a monthly magazine to members: www.adoptionuk.org.uk.

Rushton, A. (2003), *The Adoption of Looked-After Children.*

Research in Practice (2002), *Adoption and Permanence.*

The Adoption and Permanence Unit is accessible from www.everychildmatters. gov.uk.

Selwyn, J., Frazer, L. and Fitzgerald, A. (2004), *Finding Adoptive Families for Black, Asian and Mixed Parentage Children.*

Many of the more moral aspects of this work are regularly debated in the social work press and in journal articles.

Suggestions for Focus on Practice 6.1   Managing residential care: discussion examples

1 You shouldn't be on duty on your own and should seek back-up. Raise this later with your manager. Although your unit has a firm anti-drugs policy, your first priority is the safety of residents, and secondly your own safety. There is nothing to suggest that these residents are at risk, and you could be if you confront a group of 'stoned' youths. You could call the police but that would unsettle the others and damage staff–resident relationships. You decide to go to bed and deal with the situation in the morning and log your reasoning.

2 You have no legal permission to detain him unless you feel that he is a danger to himself or to others, in which case you could use restraint. This is unlikely to be the case here. You talk to Dave, trying to persuade him to stay in. He brushes past you and leaves. He knows that he will be reported missing under the usual rules at 11 p.m. You raise this case in supervision and at the next staff meeting discuss whether grounding was a sensible strategy with Dave as non-compliance was predictable.

3 This should be dealt with by a female member of staff if it's necessary to enter her bedroom. If normal persuasion fails, in view of the importance of attending court and the consequences of failing to do so, every effort short of physical intervention should be tried. Some form of compromise or deal might work.

4 If a manager is available, that is a decision for them. However, this kind of requirement is sometimes made and is difficult to resist, partly because you know the young person needs somewhere to go and partly for fear of disciplinary action. You might be able to negotiate additional resources in an attempt to safeguard residents and staff, and the suggestion that your establishment is being used inappropriately should be raised as a policy issue later.

CHAPTER 7

Children in Need: Making Prevention Count

Prevention became unfashionable in the Thatcher years as effectiveness is difficult to measure in terms of performance-driven outcomes, and as financial stringency led to a retreat into statutory duties and case work. New Labour revived many aspects of preventative interventions and this chapter identifies how positive interventions which offer real assistance to those in need are preferable to blaming victims. It uses a three-stage model of preventative interventions: structural, focused and remedial. Innovations such as Sure Start, the Children's Fund and Connexions are evaluated as examples of practice which empower individuals and communities. With more children getting sucked into 'welfarist' strategies which then identify them as in need of punitive interventions, the danger of undesired consequences of the targeted approach is discussed.

Prevention in Childcare Work

Prevention in childcare work is a very general concept. There are three preventative strategies:

- Structural interventions aimed at changing factors in society that impact upon childhood misery. Examples are attacking child poverty, poor housing and run-down neighbourhoods, and improving services available to all parents and children, or those in a defined neighbourhood or minority group.
- Targeted work with children in need or other identified at-risk groups in the hope of preventing specific undesirable outcomes, for example a child protection referral, care or custody. Family support is a phrase often used.
- Work with children already in the system to prevent a worsening of the situation, for example moving from a foster home to residential care (see chapter 6).

The role of childcare social workers is firmly established in the second and third areas but more controversial in the first. Radical social workers argue that it is legitimate to address these wider social issues through community work or welfare rights advice, or through more general political intervention aimed at promoting change. Certainly many childcare charities have seen campaigning as a legitimate part of their role in recent years, and other charitable groups exist purely to campaign, for example, the Children's Rights Alliance.

History of Childcare Prevention

The 1950s and 1960s saw numerous projects aimed at building communities, initially aimed at post-war reconstruction and then addressing specific social ills, for example the adverse effects of tower block living. Prior to that there was a long history of community development within the charitable sector, most famously the Settlement Movement.

A significant piece of legislation was the Children and Young Persons Act 1963 which for the first time placed a duty on local authorities to 'promote the welfare of children by diminishing the need to receive them into care'. This was the birth of the 'preventative budget' that allowed packages of 'family support' to be provided in kind, exceptionally in cash. This duty is now Section 17 of the Children Act 1989.

The Seebohm Report (1968) saw the proposed social services departments as having a far more universal role than they were ever funded for. It discussed wide concepts of deprivation and concluded that 'it is crucial therefore that the vicious circle is broken by a forceful and widespread commitment to prevention'. Operationally this would have meant a commitment to community development promoting neighbourhood cohesion and maximum citizen participation. Sadly the legislation that followed, the Local Authority Social Services Act 1970, did not incorporate this vision.

The new social services departments tended to lack vision, instead retreating into bureaucracy and the familiar territory of case work. Research has identified that the departments and social workers were 'in retreat from the earlier commitment to prevention' (Gibbons and Wilkinson 1990). Part of the reason was the increasing number of child protection referrals which consumed time as 'cases' and concentrated upon 'the poor' as abusers despite the view of David Thorpe and others that 'the new ideology appears to have succeeded in changing the role of child welfare agencies from predominantly one of service provision to one of policing' [the poor], (Thorpe 1995). Herein lies the origin of victim-blaming or mother-blaming, rather than offering explanations for personal difficulties that reflected wider disadvantage.

Some aspects of social work in the 1970s and 1980s did reflect the concern for communities, with some departments organised along the lines of generic social work and 'patch' teams. A social worker or small team working a patch could come to appreciate the wider social ills in the area, but were largely being required to work on cases. As legislation became more prolific and scandals, especially relating to child deaths, rocked the departments, there was a retreat from generic practice and the patch system towards specialism.

Departments did develop some preventative resources in the 1980s, notably family centres. This accompanied the retreat from residential care and the realisation that more should be done to maintain children in their birth family. Rather than looking at the wider needs of parents or communities, however, 'family support' was heavily targeted at those deemed to be 'at risk' or 'problem families'.

Ironically, although the Children Act 1989 used the language of prevention in many areas, its prescriptive regulations and guidance sucked resources away from prevention and work with children in need towards meeting statutory requirements, largely child protection and looked-after children. Although few doubted the value of family centres, it was difficult to evaluate and cost their output, and they therefore couldn't compete with the menu of statutory visits and child-minder and foster carer annual reviews.

The Government became increasingly concerned about the demise of prevention and the disproportionate deployment of resources on child protection investigations, many of which came to nothing. The 1995 report *Child Protection: Messages from Research* (Department of Health 1995) promoted a policy known as 'refocusing' which was aimed at persuading social services departments to move some resources from child protection and refocus them on earlier intervention and prevention. An evaluation in 1999 suggested that families that had received family support expressed a high level of satisfaction, but concern was expressed by the Inspectorate that some children suffering abuse or neglect were being left dangerously exposed; in 40 per cent of cases they examined, indicators of abuse were not adequately addressed (Department of Health 1999).

Whether there are too many or too few children in the child protection net is discussed in chapter 3. Groups who currently at best receive non-statutory preventative services or are seen as children in need should be seen as in need of protection, for example trafficked children and others in the child sex industry.

The bottom line for many front-line childcare managers was that: 'no further action' could not be written on a child protection referral to send a social worker out to do some community work! As long as child protection referrals kept coming in, and the resource base was not significantly increased, prevention remained a low priority in many areas.

From 1979 the Labour government tried a new approach by initially not entrusting new preventative initiatives to local authorities, but using the partnership model and quangos (Sure Start, the Children's Fund and Connexions), although some of these services are now part of children's trusts.

New Labour Initiatives

Individualist Interventions

At an individualist level separate initiatives have been implemented to work with children of different ages and their families.

Sure Start

Sure Start has been the flagship policy to provide support to the most deprived young children and their families. It operates in the most deprived areas, although with the growth of children's centres under the Children Act 2004 services will become more universally available. It is based upon largely American research which suggests that providing a stimulating first few years impacts upon a child's whole life and can reduce such things as crime and mental illness in adolescence and adulthood (Karoly et al. 1998).

As well as offering childcare facilities and support to parents, Sure Start provides a range of other services aimed particularly at getting parents into work or education, and there are often good links with other agencies such as Jobcentre Plus. Projects are usually staffed by a wide range of professionals from health, education and social care.

Sure Start espouses the feminist perspective on childcare social work in that nearly all of its participants, staff and service users are women, and mothers are seen as the focus in both parenting and communities. Some projects have attempted to address the gender imbalance by offering schemes aimed at fathers.

Research into the new early years provision has confirmed previous studies that good quality pre-school provision can have long-term beneficial effects upon intellectual and social/behavioural development and that pre-school can play an important part in combating social exclusion by offering disadvantaged children in particular a better start at primary school (Sylva, Melhuish et al. 2004). Interim reports from evaluations of early 'Sure Start' projects suggest benefits both to the development of individual children and to their parents, and wider benefits to the deprived communities served. In particular, marked improvements have been noted in family functioning and interactions between parents and children. The empowering and community development style of the projects and the emphasis upon partnership with other agencies have been factors in the overall success, but attempts at improving the employability of parents and the involvement of fathers have met with limited success (Sure Start 2004).

However, a report by the National Audit Office (2006) was less positive, claiming that fewer than a third of the Sure Start centres had identified and were reaching the most disadvantaged families. It suggested that some 'hard-to-reach' groups were unlikely to visit Centres and services needed to be taken to them.

In discussing the shift from Sure Start to early years provision in children's centres managed by children's trusts, some commentators fear that the service-user and community-orientated approach developed by Sure Start will be lost as the more bureaucratic model associated with state providers takes over (Glass 2004). Given limited finance within children's trusts, it is worrying that the preventative aspects of these services could be engulfed by child protection and statutory care services.

The Children's Fund

This is a pool of government money available to local partnerships designated to meet the needs of children in the middle years of childhood. The local partnerships are representative of the major agencies involved with children and a lead agency, often one of the major voluntary organisations, manages each local scheme. They evaluate local need and grant aid groups offering high-value services. The model is designed to promote local voluntary activity to meet identified needs, with most schemes focusing upon the most deprived areas and/or identified problem groups, for example young offenders.

Concern has been expressed that the funding is insecure, which means that workers are often employed on temporary contracts. The government view is that Children's Fund money should be used to 'pump-prime' and successful schemes should be funded long term from other budgets. Extended schools will provide the sorts of services commonly funded, such as after-school clubs and holiday play schemes.

Connexions

Aimed largely at young people aged 14–19, Connexions was designed to assist in the transition from school to work, incorporating the functions of previous careers services. Through a network of personal advisers young people are offered advice and support. In practice services are targeted at the NEET group ('not in education, employment or training'). Some have criticised this focus saying that 'ordinary' young people are not getting decent careers advice. Most of the functions of Connexions will be absorbed into children's trusts from 2008, while retaining the brand name, but schools will be able to purchase careers advice from Connexions or elsewhere. This will offer an opportunity for a joined-up strategy for work with young people in need, including the youth services and specialist projects that currently function within education or social services.

Parenting initiatives

It is now recognised that parenting has been an underrated role in society. Various initiatives from a national helpline through to parenting classes and mutual support groups are being developed, and there is a 'parenting academy' aimed at training workers to support parents. Most of this activity is within the voluntary sector.

While there is widespread support for the general government strategy for training and support of parents, there is concern that this is focused largely on those felt to be 'poor parents' who are being offered assistance, but with the threat of compulsion if they decline to participate. While it is clear to many professionals who work with young children that it is possible to predict those likely to become problematic teenagers, there is widespread concern that the government, by labelling such families, is likely to achieve the opposite of the desired objective. Those working within youth justice are particularly concerned that the proposal for 'super-nannies' is being fronted by the Department for Justice to divert children from crime. Many people are in favour of advising and assisting parents, but are concerned about both locating this work within youth justice and the element of compulsion. Strategists are concerned that this is another example of net-widening, sucking children into the youth justice system at an even earlier age, which, as they proceed through their childhood, could lead to even harsher interventions inevitably propelling many towards custody.

Family support

'Family support' is a general term covering a wide range of interventions aimed at promoting good quality parenting, often in very disadvantaged families. This approach aims to identify strengths and offer solutions based upon families taking responsibility for their own problems, rather than pathologising situations and providing casework. It tends to be community-based, often operating from buildings called family centres.

A difficulty with this approach is that resources have been stretched and there has therefore tended to be an emphasis upon preventing undesirable outcomes and dealing with crises rather than promoting wider well-being. Thus the emphasis remains on individual 'problems' rather than on a consideration of wider neighbourhood or community based issues.

Structuralist Perspectives

At a structuralist level the biggest initiative has been the drive to end child poverty through policies such as tax credits and the minimum wage. Allied to this are the childcare strategy, giving working parents affordable childcare options, and various welfare-to-work schemes following from the connection between deprivation and worklessness.

When Labour came to power in 1997, over a third of UK children lived in poverty (defined as living in a household with less than 60 per cent of median income). The UK ranked third from the bottom in an international league table of 17 industrialised countries. By 2002/3 child poverty had fallen to 28 per cent of children, with an estimated 550,000 children expected to cross the poverty threshold by 2004/5 (End Child Poverty 2005). Figure 7.1 shows the progress in attacking child poverty.

There has been some progress, but much still to do. One problem is that poverty is a relative concept, and in a period of prosperity median incomes will rise, so anti-poverty strategies have to ensure that the incomes of the poorest, including benefit levels, rise even faster.

A more radical approach to poverty is to tackle fundamental inequalities in income and wealth to create a fairer society (Adams 2002). However, neither of the two major political parties see this as politically feasible.

The End Child Poverty Alliance (ECP) summarises the impact of child poverty as follows:

> Research shows that children growing up poor not only suffer as children, but are also less likely to be successful in education and, as adults in the labour market. Poverty in childhood is scarring, with poor children at increased risk of low income, benefit dependency and homelessness in adults. (End Child Poverty 2005)

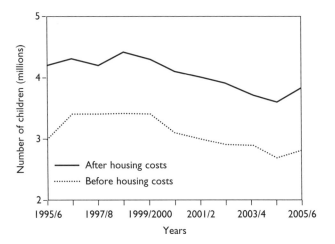

Figure 7.1 Children living in poverty, 1995–2006 (Department for Work and Pensions)

Policies aimed at rejuvenating neighbourhoods recognise that social exclusion results from a combination of adverse factors, including links between poor housing, poverty, deprivation, crime, educational under-achievement and ill health. People living in such communities are discriminated against in looking for work or using services and suffer from poor community facilities, for example affordable shops, leisure facilities and transport links.

The Youth Matters Agenda

Young people are disproportionately blamed for problems of disorder in troubled neighbourhoods (see chapter 2). While large sums of money are expended on controlling or 'treating' troublesome youths (see chapter 8), relatively little has been available for diverting young people from problematic behaviour. Connexions has focused upon the transition from school to work but arguably has had little impact in meeting the wider need of young people to live stimulating private lives. The youth service has done excellent work in both universal social education projects, and in reaching out to many disaffected youths through detached youth work, although funding for youth services has been both patchy and inadequate.

The Green Paper 'Youth Matters' (Department for Education and Skills 2005) proposed a radical reshaping of services to young people flowing from the 5 key outcomes in 'Every Child Matters' (see chapter 1). Following some pilot schemes (for example, the Connexions Card, since abandoned), the government announced a 10-year strategy, Aiming High for Young People (DfCSF 2007), to improve leisure activities and support services for young people to be developed in consultation with young people themselves. While generally welcomed by professionals in this area, they remain sceptical about whether such an ambitious programme will be adequately funded.

Effective Social Work Practice: Interventions that Work

Children's trusts expend preventative money in a targeted way on the assumption that money spent now will avoid the need for greater spending in the future. A systems approach examines referrals received and what happens to them. It also examines the careers of children already in the systems (looked-after or child protection systems for example), the care they receive, how long they remain in the system and particularly the factors that escalate them from low to higher (and more expensive) levels of intervention.

An analysis of the referral system is likely to uncover two major scenarios:

- young children being referred because of child protection concerns, often by health visitors
- teenagers being referred (by teachers, parents or self-referring) as a result of family conflict and often other associated behavioural factors.

A systems approach will consider the rate and appropriateness of referrals. It might be found, for example, that other professionals are unaware of what social services can realistically offer, and hence make fewer or more referrals than appropriate. Often the solution is to convene regular liaison meetings, perhaps based around families of schools and professionals working with young children. These meetings not only oil the wheels of communication and promote better understanding, but can combine the knowledge and expertise of the various agencies in addressing individual needs and wider problems. For example, it might be felt that the use of illegal drugs is growing among teenagers locally and so a strategy can be devised to address that. Such meetings are a means of avoiding bombardment leading to referrals being better handled, and the other agencies experiencing a better service to subjects of appropriate referrals.

With young children it is often appropriate to provide a package of support monitored by the Health Visitor in cases where there are not significant child protection concerns.

Practice Areas: The Systems Perspective

Avoiding Teenager Accommodation

Many authorities now have specialist youth support teams aimed at avoiding the need for teenagers to be accommodated. Strategies vary, but most are able to provide intensive help at a time of crisis and can build packages of care to support families suffering tension at home. The main emphasis is usually upon conciliation rather than 'therapy'. It is easier to avoid the young person from being removed than to restore them home, so many schemes are able to respond at short notice, often outside office hours.

If accommodation is requested the tactic is to make it fairly difficult to achieve. Gatekeeping can be operated by Managers or by setting up a panel where the parents or child must put their case for removal from home. Many appointments at such panels are missed indicating that families have found a way to resolve their problems. There are however potential concerns about this approach to gatekeeping. For example, if children approach children's services are refused a service, they might take matters into their own hands and run away (see chapter 4).

Family Group Conferences

A last strategy is to attempt to keep the responsibility within the family by holding a family group conference. This is a coming together of wider family members to plan for a child. Conferences are used to promote kinship care, to assist where there are child protection concerns or where there is delinquency. However, practitioners should not see family group conferences as an alternative to child protection procedures; families should be given responsibility only when it is consistent with keeping the child safe.

A social worker will usually act as a facilitator for a conference, finding out who the significant people in the child's family (often broadly interpreted) network are and bringing them together. The social worker is usually present at the start of the meeting to set the boundaries and outline the tasks. They then withdraw and allow the family to arrive at their own solutions to the identified problems. The social worker then returns to assist in the development of a care plan based on the family solutions.

This is a particularly empowering form of intervention as service users feel listened to and it challenges the power imbalance between professionals and service users.

Community Development

A more structuralist approach is found in community development. It aims to encourage and enable people to take collective action to address perceived problems, usually on a neighbourhood basis, although the concept can also be applied to communities of common interest across a wider geographical are, for example the gay community or people with particular disabilities. Some projects adopt a community development approach to engage difficult-to-reach groups such as child prostitutes or runaways.

Community workers act as catalysts to promote the formation of groupings and to support community groups in furthering their goals. They might provide advice, access to resources and emotional support. Much community development work has been allied to the radical tradition in social work as it tends to define problems in terms of structural issues rather than isolating individual sufferers.

One reason it is difficult to fund such projects is that results are seldom tangible. Another is that potential governmental funders are likely to be those criticised as part of this approach. Thus most community work that has survived is in the voluntary sector.

Practitioners argue that there is a link between community work and childcare referrals, especially child protection allegations, although this is difficult to prove. However, it might be because communities that are working together are more able to support families in need, or because they are less likely to scapegoat such families. An alternative view is that, by increasing knowledge of available services within a community, the demand for those services might increase, putting further strain upon statutory resources.

In terms of critical analysis, community development is probably the most important tool within social work for empowering individuals and communities. A piece of community work will usually commence with a community audit to find out what provision exists and to identify deficits. It will involve consciousness-raising to assist residents to develop a real and broad analysis of the real nature of community problems, perhaps employing a Marxist perspective to explore the class-based issues associated with deprived communities. A feminist analysis will identify ways in which families, neighbourhoods and communities and the associated oppressions are largely the domain of women.

The government's strategy for tackling social exclusion continues to focus upon individual pathology among the small group of hard-to-reach families who are identified as suffering multiple social exclusions, often across several generations. In the 'Action Plan on Social Exclusion' it is argued that this group often fails to benefit from the more structural interventions, and probably needs a more personalised approach (HM Government 2006). It is recognised that many such families are unwilling or unable to navigate the complex array of services on offer from various agencies, and there are proposals suggesting a new role of a budget-holding lead professional who can harness the resources of the various providers and, *in consultation with the family* offer a joined-up and coherent package of services. However, this should be by consent and not punitive, to avoid the negative cascades of intervention experienced by many young people who have been unwilling or unable to comply with ASBOs or current punitive truancy policies (see chapter 8).

KEY POINTS

- 'Prevention', which largely disappeared in the Thatcher years, has been revitalised by Sure Start, the Children's Fund, parenting initiatives and projects aimed at neighbourhood regeneration.
- Some aspects of prevention, such as community work, have been associated with the radical tradition in social work, especially as they take a structuralist view of problems.
- In terms of individuals at risk, targeted prevention can avoid less desirable and often more expensive outcomes, although it is difficult to evaluate and cost the benefits.

RESOURCES

Community development
Community Development Exchange is a membership-based voluntary organisation that promotes the community development approach to achieving social justice: www.cdx.org.uk.

Parenting
Parentline Plus is a national charity supporting parents. They offer a national helpline, web-based support and local support groups for parents. www. parentlineplus.org.uk

Family support
Gardner, R. (2003), *Family Support*.
Research in Practice (2005), *Supporting Families*.

Family group conferences:
The NSPCC offer a resources list: www.nspcc.org.uk/inform.

CHAPTER 8

Working with Young People in the Authoritarian State

The Labour years have seen an increasingly punitive stance towards young people: harsher sentences, ASBOs, truancy sweeps and fast-track to prosecution, even prison for the parents of truants. In the context of anti-social behaviour, youth justice and education, the chapter considers strategies to deal with young people unwilling or unable to conform to increasingly prescriptive standards of behaviour. It examines the effectiveness of current policies, the divergence between research and rhetoric, and the clash between traditional social work values, especially 'empowerment', and current policy implementation. It suggests alternative strategies to create a better balance between meeting the needs of 'problematic' young people and promoting a 'civilised' society. It reflects upon learning by practitioners in the 1980s using the systems approach to juvenile justice management that saw dramatic cuts in custodial sentences, and why we should now be reinventing the same wheel.

The Authoritarian State

The first section aims to consider the reasons for the rise in authoritarian governance, and the effects this has on service users and professional value systems and practices.

Caring professionals need to stand back from the pressures of everyday practice and consider the operational context and the culture that underpins it – so important in working with young people in the authoritarian state. An 'authoritarian State' is where the state has a view of what is right, is prepared to impose legislation that restricts individual freedoms beyond that necessary to maintain social order, and to use punitive intervention to enforce it, including the use of both the traditional agencies of social control (the police) and the 'caring professions' as enforcers (Sayer 2006). This doesn't just involve social workers; a parallel can be seen in the trend towards defining more young people as having mental health problems and 'treating' them within the medical model (see chapter 9).

In discussing the rise in authoritarian policies towards young people, there are two considerations. First, parallels with the restrictions on civil liberties justified by the 'war on terrorism' suggest a general move towards authoritarian governance, for example, the debate about identity cards provides a good example of the state hijacking legitimate concerns in order to propose more authoritarian intervention.

Secondly, society has demonised successive post-industrial generations of young people, and the perceived fear of (especially violent) crime has been used to justify a punitive stance. Even repressive measures designed to counter sub-criminal, largely nuisance, behaviour are justified by these largely irrational fears. The media, by creating a 'moral panic' around the latest youth cults, paint a picture of people afraid to leave their homes because of marauding youths in the neighbourhood, although this affects only a small minority of people (Home Office 2007; see chapter 2).

A media analysis by the magazine Young People Now highlighted the negative media portrayal of young people: 71 per cent of press stories about young people were negative and 33 per cent concerned crime, with very little reporting of positive activity by young people (Young People Now 2004). Politicians cannot escape blame for the demonisation of youths, with both major political parties competing for the vote-winning tough-on-crime agenda.

Of course 'freedom' has never been an absolute concept: one person's freedom of speech is another person's racial hatred. Social workers have traditionally taken a liberal stance towards freedom, using words like 'empowerment' to justify allowing individual service users the right to make choices that might not sit easily with those in power.

Care versus control has always been a contested issue within social work, but modern social workers are arguably more controlling. For example, we have truancy sweeps – social workers going into shopping centres alongside police officers to 'catch' truants and return them to school (see below). This contradicts the traditional approach of education social workers, based on a welfarist discourse (that truancy is a symptom of wider social problems in the child's life), of assessing the reasons for truancy and offering assistance and exhausting all options before resorting to prosecution. Now we define truants as 'bad' and blame their parents, essentially mothers. Victim-blaming absolves society of responsibility for wider social ills such as poverty which radical social workers would argue causes 'personal' problems; it also masks the need for wider discussion around why schools are failing so many young people.

A number of underlying influences can be identified in the trend towards authoritarianism. First, the retreat from collective morality into a culture of individuality in a postmodern world, whether seen from the Marxist perspective (which saw religion as the opium of the masses), or from Victorian morality (where children were seen and not heard), we as individuals now demand greater freedom of expression, and possess greater knowledge on which to base our views, choices and identity. Thus, from an establishment perspective there is greater potential for 'deviance', giving rise to pressure for controls to maintain the status quo, which arguably benefits those in power.

Secondly, governments have a greater legitimacy to intervene in the private lives of individuals and families due to the demand for better public services, for example, the broad consensus that education, socially constructed as 'schooling', is beneficial to the individual child and wider society, and therefore that truancy is unacceptable. There are, of course, other discourses, including the now seldom discussed concept of de-schooling society (Illich 1971) and the more commonly raised possibilities for educating children out of school, including home education, and those students procedurally excluded from school.

However, more intervention need not mean authoritarianism. Good public services and individual choice about using them could be offered instead.

How Professionals Can Have a Greater Impact

The existence of the 'problem' of unruly teenagers and children cannot be totally denied. No doubt there are some communities where lives are blighted by unruly groups of youngsters, and many young people do face lifelong social exclusion through poor educational achievement fuelled by truancy and poor behaviour in school. However, we need to question, first, whether current penalties are disproportionate to the wrongdoing and harm and, secondly, their effectiveness in meeting set objectives.

The first approach is to redefine the problem, to ask basic questions about prevalence (going beyond the moral panic and political rhetoric) and seek different constructions, for example 'youthful high spirits' rather than 'anti-social behaviour' or 'Attention Deficit Hyperactivity Dosorder (ADHD)'. We could consider the way systems impact upon young people and practices that promote bad behaviour, rather than blaming the individual for that behaviour. For example, the current culture in schools offers little to low-achieving or unmotivated young people, and for some truancy and misbehaviour is a rational response to the repression of their spirit and individuality. The solution is to create a system more tolerant of diversity and deviation.

Where there is a problem, alternative strategies could be considered, perhaps a community development approach, and listening to young people to understand their analysis of the situation. Many will attribute anti-social behaviour to boredom and lack of leisure opportunities, so funding could be used to create real opportunities for these young people. After all, it is estimated that obtaining an ASBO cost an average of £4,800 in 2002 (Home Office, 2002).

Some young people do live chaotic lives, where poor parenting is an issue. Rather than blaming parents, making them the subject of parenting orders and in extreme cases imprisoning them (almost always the mother) for their child's truancy, families could be listened to and offered proper support with the difficult task of parenting. Rather than blaming families, a consideration of the wider social conditions that impact upon them should inform practice, poverty, poor housing and run-down neighbourhoods, for example. Radical social work is unfashionable in the culture of managerialism but individual practitioners and teams can and should be challenging and promoting an alternative discourse to the current authoritarian culture.

As well as fighting through pressure groups, professionals can counter the authoritarian culture in their own workplace. One example, discussed below, relates to how in the 1980s practitioners working with young offenders hijacked what was a punitive juvenile justice system and used the systems approach to keep many young offenders out of care and custody.

Workers who feel that their professional values are being undermined by authoritarian interventions may be relatively powerless as employees of the state, but through continual questioning, pressure group activity and adopting a humane approach to individual service users, all is not lost.

Practice Areas

This chapter will now consider the 'culture of authoritarianism' within the practice areas of anti-social behaviour, youth justice and education.

Practice Area 1: ASBOs and Authoritarianism

The application of authoritarian values by the state can be illustrated by the rise of anti-social behaviour orders or ASBOs, and a raft of linked orders (for example, dispersal orders) designed to restrict the activities of some young people who are regarded as problematic.

Professionals contesting the ASBO culture have come together to form a new pressure group, ASBO Concern, highlighting some of the perverse outcomes of ASBOs. One is that between June 2000 and December 2003 991 ASBOs were issued on 10–17-year-olds, of whom a frightening 18 per cent ended in custody for breaching their orders which were imposed for sub-criminal behaviour (Home Office, cited in Young People Now 2005). This is worthy of challenge under human rights legislation. Secondly, ASBOs have been used in individual cases where behaviour could be a result of learning difficulties, mental health problems or conditions such as Asperger's syndrome (British Institute for Brain Injured Children 2005). Thirdly, there are concerns about the 'lottery' of ASBOs: some areas use them extensively and others hardly at all, because anti-social behaviour is defined differently across areas. A group of grumpy people can press for ASBOs for behaviour that another community might find tolerable and regard as normal childhood enjoyment, even acceptable naughtiness.

Practice Area 2: Youth Justice

For a critical thinker youth justice policy presents many interesting challenges, especially the divergence between rhetoric and research. This is a highly researched area in social science and almost all the research suggests that the most punitive interventions, particularly custody, are the least effective (Muncie 2004), yet politicians and the media would have us believe that being 'tough on crime', popular punitivism, is the only way forward. Despite evidence that the public are not as punitive as they are portrayed (Rethinking Crime and

Puishment 2004), custody has been and remains the gold standard of provision. This contradicts an assumption underlying liberal democracies, and enshrined in the UN Convention on Human Rights, that governance should be about maximising individual freedom within the context of the greater good.

Another interesting factor is that the 1980s systems approach proved beyond reasonable doubt that minimal intervention did work and yet there is now a highly interventionist approach. Pre-court diversion did not promote a juvenile crime wave; in fact youth crime was widely believed to have fallen in areas adopting this approach, and most young people treated minimally did 'grow out of crime' by their mid-twenties (Rutherford 1992). Intervention itself can be damaging and lead to a cascade of further interventions promoting unforeseen and undesirable consequences such as custody. For example, when a young person is first taken to court their peer status can be enhanced; they accept the label of 'offender', and thus are more likely to re-offend.

A third, seemingly contradictory position arises from the justice versus welfare debate. It might be expected that social workers would adopt a welfarist perspective, arguing that interventions with young offenders are in their own best interests. However, what practitioners in the 1980s learned was that the welfarist approach of the 1970s, following the Children and Young Persons Act of 1969 which sought to remove the distinction between offenders and others now described as being 'in need', sucked more young people into the net of juvenile justice (net-widening) and escalated them up the care and justice tariffs towards care orders and custody. This happened because, when those who had been involved in programmes following minor crimes or broader concerns in their younger years eventually appeared before a court, the options had been exhausted; for example, they were seen to have failed to respond to supervision, and were therefore in need of further intervention. Thus, young people, in the name of their own welfare, were being treated more harshly than adults charged with similar offences. They could be placed in care indefinitely or sentenced to borstal training (now detention in a YOI) lasting for up to two years, until the system thought that they had been reformed. However, matters were usually worsened by separating offenders from their families and communities and placing then in oppressive institutions. In the 1980s what practitioners argued was that it was fairer and more effective to treat young offenders from a justice perspective, that their crimes should be evaluated in court in a similar way to those of adults.

There are of course parallels, or a failure to learn from the past, in the present system, with the Youth Justice Board funding a number of schemes aimed at identifying potential offenders early and targeting resources at them. Several years on, the massive increase in custodial sentences can be explained, in part at least, by these early interventions. Even worse is government rhetoric on 'baby ASBOs' and the suggestion that children who are likely to become offenders can be identified and targeted at birth. While there is nothing wrong with assisting parents with the complex task of parenting, to deliver these interventions under the auspices of offender services, is to give rise to a new wave of net widening, and as these young people grow older more of them will be incarcerated.

The Crime and Disorder Act 1998 is the basis for modern youth justice policy including the creation of the Youth Justice Board and local youth offending teams (YOTs). For the first time the aim of youth justice interventions to prevent offending and re-offending has been made explicit. Youth justice policy focuses upon three areas:

- prevention
- restorative justice
- rehabilitation.

The Department for Children, Schools and Families (DfCSF) and the Ministry of Justice share governmental responsibility for the youth justice system, except for courts which are the responsibility of the Department for Constitutional Affairs. Young offenders institutions are managed by the prison service, an executive agency of the Ministry of Justice, secure training centres are run by private companies and secure units by children's trusts. It may be argued that, in order to bring youth justice in line with the rest of children's services, it should be the sole responsibility of the DfCSF where the rest of children's provision is located.

The Youth Justice Board is a quango responsible to government for youth justice strategy, commissioning and purchasing. It has an important role in piloting new schemes in chosen YOTs and is also taking a lead in funding staff training and promoting a career structure for workers in the youth justice system.

Each local area has a youth offending team led by a team manager, with accountability to a lead agency (a participant children's trust) and a partnership board mainly representative of the partner agencies. The partnership has a duty to produce an annual youth justice plan. The workers consist of staff from the children's trust (social work background), probation, education, police (usually on fixed term secondments), health (often a drugs focus), and maybe others, for example, from the voluntary sector. Some staff, especially those on pilot projects, will be directly funded by the Youth Justice Board, often on temporary contracts. Thus a local YOT team manager might feel accountable to their Line Manager, the Partnership Board and the YJB for different aspects of their role.

Youth Justice Law: Another Ambiguity

There is a clash of intention between current youth justice and other children's legislation. First, Section 44 of the Children and Young Persons Act 1933 provides that all courts should consider the welfare of any child, whereas youth justice legislation places the reduction of offending before the bests interests of a particular child. Similarly, the provision in Section 1 of the Children Act 1989 that the child's best interests be paramount has not applied in youth justice cases. However, a High Court ruling in 2002 determined that child protection procedures should apply to young people in custody being the responsibility of local social services (*Howard League for Penal Reform* v *Secretary of State for the Home Department* 2002).

Some argue that youth justice legislation contravenes Articles 37 and 40 (others might also apply) of the United Nations Convention on the Rights of the Child, suggesting that within the justice system there should be a right to treatment that promotes dignity, takes age into account and promotes integration into the community (Stuart and Baines 2004b). The abolition of *doli incapax* in 1998 (an additional test for 10–13-year-olds; that the child knew the action was wrong) could be particularly open to challenge as 10-year-olds can now be held as fully criminally accountable as adults (Muncie 2004).

Facts about Youth Crime

This section examines statistics about youth crime and suggests why current practices can contradict ther aim of reducing offending and re-offending.

Young people commit crime

In a survey, 28 per cent of 10–17-year-olds questioned admitted to committing a crime in the past year (Home Office 2006a). Since some kind of minor law-breaking is common in adolescence, it is arguably wrong to severely punish those who are unfortunate enough to be caught, especially since only one in six had been detected (NACRO 2006).

This is particularly true if those in certain social groups are most likely to be detected, for example, if law enforcement agencies are geared up towards policing the poor. It is possible that a child from a middle-class home background accused of an offence will be dealt with differently; for example, the parents might be better able to suggest that the offence be defined differently. For example, student drunken damage is likely to be defined as 'high spirits' the damage paid for and forgotten, whereas the same damage committed by a working-class young person may be defined as criminal damage and lead to possible prosecuted.

Known offending is falling

The media lead us to believe that we are experiencing a juvenile crime wave, whereas in the last 10 years overall crime levels have fallen, and it is almost certain that youth offending is falling in line with the general trend. There was a 21 per cent fall in convictions/cautions of 10–18-year-olds in the period 1992–2004 (Home Office 2006) and yet more young people are in custody.

The peak age of offending for boys increased from 15 to 17 in the last 20 years (15 for girls) (NACRO 2006). To account for the increased peak age, a social constructionist might argue that this reflects the elongation of the period of adolescence, that some young people are no longer offered the routes to more attachments to mainstream society (often referred to as 'work, women, and wheels' in the 1980s), which enabled them to 'grow out of crime'.

Youth crime is mostly non-violent

Total violent crime in 2004 was less than 17 per cent of all crime, an increase from 12 per cent in 1993, and most of this was at the lower end of the spectrum, with half involving no injury to the victim and 63 per cent resulting in a reprimand or final warning (NACRO 2006).

Although we should be concerned by the rise in violent crime, especially gun and knife crimes and gang warfare, the current moral panic around violent crime is exaggerated. One reason is that much recorded violent crime is less serious robbery, for example young people stealing mobile phones and other portable electronic equipment from other young people. A second factor is the greater likelihood of reporting low-level violence, especially robbery if the property was insured, and hence it becomes a recorded crime; thus the apparent increae in crime could be a symptom of a more civilised, rather than a more violent, society (Pearson 1983).

Drug use is a common factor

While it is difficult to quantify the cost of drug- and alcohol-related crime, research suggests a strong link between the two (Bennett 2000). Drug-related crime refers to offences related to the possession of illegal drugs and the possible effects of consuming those substances, but more significantly to the fact that many substance users have to engage in substantial amounts of property crime to fund their substance use. While recent legislation recognises this by introducing drug testing and rehabilitation orders, and drugs referrals workers are now widely available in custody centres to offer immediate help and advice to arrested users, there are still concerns about the availability of treatment facilities, and the little attention paid to why so many young people turn to damaging escapist behaviour. This links with concerns about increasing numbers of young people with mental health problems (see chapter 9).

Black young people are discriminated against

Black young people are over-represented in the youth justice system, especially in the more serious interventions such as custody (Youth Justice Board 2004). The Macpherson report (1999) into the death of Stephen Lawrence described the Police as 'institutionally racist' and it seems reasonable to assume that other parts of the youth justice system also engage in practices that suck more black young people into the system where they receive harsher outcomes (Youth Justice Board 2004). Critical practitioners need to undertake an audit of their local youth justice system to uncover these practices and take steps to eliminate them.

Custody

The number of young people in custody rose by some 90 per cent between 1992 and 2002, following a decade of decarceration (minimal use of custody). There are now around 3,000 under-18s in custody at any time. Average sentence lengths have almost doubled from 1994 to 2004, for example for burglary from 3.8 to 7.8 months (NACRO 2006).

The Children's Rights Alliance (2002a) argues that the UK imprisons more young people at an earlier age, for longer periods and in inhumane conditions, compared with our European partners. Unsatisfactory conditions, poor education and training facilities, extensive drug abuse, suicides and bullying are all features of custodial regimes (see chapter 4). To protect innocent potential victims, prison should arguably be reserved for very serious and violent offenders, whereas most young prisoners are there for minor, albeit numerous, offences.

In 2001 82 per cent of young male offenders released from custody were reconvicted within two years (Youth Justice Board 2006). Given these reconviction statistics, worse figures for 14–16-year-olds, and the possibility that even more have re-offended but not been caught, it is difficult to justify the continuing mass use of custody as a means of preventing re-offending.

Prior to custody:

- 25 per cent of young males were homeless
- over half of under-18s have been in care
- over half have been excluded from school
- 80 per cent of 15–17-year-olds have no formal qualifications
- one in six admit to being abused
- one in 10 have self-harmed.

Source: Social Exclusion Unit 2002

These statistics suggest that young offenders are children in need of assistance rather than pure punishment. While few people would condone offending, a real attempt at addressing it needs to get away from punitivism to address the wider social issues around the causes of crime. Especially at a time when cost effectiveness is the buzzword and decisions are meant to be made on the basis of evidence, it is difficult to justify the Youth Justice Board spending two-thirds of its annual budget on custody (Youth Justice Board 2006).

A More Positive Approach

The 1980s showed beyond reasonable doubt that pre-court diversion works and yet its use declined from an average of 73 per cent of disposals in 1992 to 56 per cent in 2000 (NACRO 2006). Approximately 80 per cent of those cautioned in the 1980s were not reconvicted within two years, a figure that applied to first and subsequent cautions (author's unpublished research in one authority).

Under the current reprimand and final warning scheme, the use of more than two cautions is largely outlawed despite the use of pre-court diversion being crucial if young offenders are to be kept out of the system, which propels them towards custody.

While community sentences cannot 'cure criminality' (the causes are too complex), they have slightly lower re-conviction rates than for those in custody, and subsequent offences tend to be less serious (NACRO 2006). The content of such programmes can actively address the issues underlying an individual's offending behaviour whereas custody achieves little more than 'warehousing'.

The Youth Justice Process

This section summarises the functioning of the youth justice system. Decision-making stages are shown printed in bold and centred on the page; important factors affecting the decision are outlined; and suggestions (in italics) are made as to how a systems strategist might operate.

Crime prevention/reduction strategy

- target individual potential offenders
- target the wider causes of crime

Work with local crime reduction partnership (convened by the Chief Executive of each district council/unitary authority) to tackle social exclusion. Develop specific schemes to target particular problem groups and problematic areas. If offering work with individuals, be aware of concerns about net-widening. Prevention should not be the remit of YOTs. Argue against the use of ASBOs.

Figure 8.1 The youth justice process: early stages

Crime detected on the street
Decision by police officer

Officer discretion, informal action and resolution on the streets have declined in favour of formally reporting incidents. Arrest targets for police officers work against informal action, especially as minor crime by young people is seen as relatively easy to detect and process. Force and local policy might vary from zero tolerance of some crimes to a more liberal approach. This leads to inconsistency across areas.

Training for local police officers to encourage a return to informal action.

At the police station

A young person taken to a police station will be processed, which includes the taking of photos, fingerprints and DNA samples. There are civil liberties concerns about taking samples from children, especially if they are retained when no charges are brought against them. Most offences are now 'arrestable', although if the evidence is unclear the young person might be 'helping with enquiries'.

FOCUS ON PRACTICE 8.1

At the police station

Options at police station:
- no further action;
- issue a reprimand or final warning including referral to YOT;
- charge, with police bail;
- put before a special court.

Police and Criminal Evidence Act 1984 (PACE) allows:
- parent or other 'appropriate adult' to be present during interviews;
- accused can call a solicitor or make another phonecall;
- can access their own custody record (which constrains how prisoners are treated in police custody) and can read the code of practice on custody.

Provide a responsive 'appropriate adult' service so that good advice and systems management is provided at the police station in the early stages. Be proactive in liaison meetings between the police and children's trusts/YOT management. Make available immediate and credible community package such as bail support and remand fostering. Be available to troubleshoot problematic cases, for example, when the police want to put a young person straight before a court. Know some tame solicitors.

Referral to Crown Prosecution Service (CPS)

The CPS should not prosecute unless there is a greater than even chance of conviction and prosecution is in the public interest.

Be prepared to advocate in individual cases, for example, by suggesting that a prosecution is not in the public interest

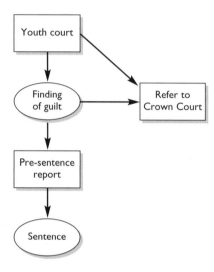

Figure 8.2 The youth justice process: court stage

FOCUS ON PRACTICE 8.2

The Youth Court

In the Youth Court:
- There are three specially trained Magistrates (two in exceptional circumstances);
- Legal representation must be offered;
- Parent or other appropriate adult must be present.

Decisions:
- If the offence is too serious to be heard at this level or defendant wishes trial by jury, refer to Crown Court.
- Finding of guilt.
- Request YOT to provide pre-sentence report (normally within two weeks).
- Sentencing: if the Youth Court feel they have insufficient sentencing powers they can refer to the Crown Court.

ASSET Assessment and Pre-Sentence Report

Will address:

- the reasons for offending
- proposal to reduce offending (sentencing recommendation)

Ensure that the YOT has clear policy guidelines about sentencing, for example, about when an author can recommend custody. These should incorporate 'tariff management' (that a recommendation should be as low as possible on the sentencing tariff). Make sure that all low-tariff disposals are available locally. Have a clear value base supported by evidence (that custody is harmful and doesn't work).

Sentencing philosophies of the local courts

There is concern over the wide disparities in sentencing practices between courts resulting in wide regional differences in the use of custody.

Proactive meetings with court clerks and magistrates using comparative figures about sentencing practices. Use evidence that the least punitive approaches are most effective in reducing crime.

Use of appeals

Some participants in the process, including solicitors, are reluctant to support appeals as they argue that it undermines their reputation with the courts. Individual injustice should clearly override this. It can be argued that all custodial sentences should be appealed as it holds courts to account for their interpretation of the custodial threshold (that the offence is so serious that only a custodial sentence can be justified).

Functions of sentencing/punishment

To question the effectiveness of the principle aim of the youth justice system, preventing offending and re-offending (Crime and Disorder Act 1998), it is important to consider the possible purposes of sentences, especially custody, and whether they focus effectively on this objective.

Functions of sentencing/punishment

Protection of the public/incapacitation (removal from the public)
In custody offenders cannot inflict further crimes on the public, although they might commit offences 'inside'. With relatively short sentences and high reconviction rates it is questionable whether this function can be justified. Only custody achieves incapacitation, although similar claims can be made for curfews, intensive supervision and tagging. There is a debate about whether serious offenders who pose a continuing threat to society, perhaps child sex abusers and psychopaths, should be detained indefinitely (Pritchard and Sayer 2006; see chapter 2).

Retribution (pure punishment)
It is questionable whether pure vengeance has a place in a civilised society, but there is a debate about victims' wishes being considered in sentencing. Arguably this introduces an unacceptable element of inconsistency, and sentencing should be based upon seriousness, tempered only by the personal circumstances of the offender.

Crime reduction
Reducing crime requires evidence about what sentences work and strategies to promote wider crime reduction (preventative) policies.

Deterrence of this offender
With such high reconviction rates it is difficult to argue that custody deters prisoners from re-offending.

Deterrence of others
Arguably the threat of custody deters other potential offenders. However, this assumes that people make rational choices when they commit crime, whereas much youth crime is impulsive and based upon other factors such as drink, drugs and peer influence. Poor clear-up rates (solved crimes) undermine deterrence (around 70 per cent of property crimes are not cleared up by the police), challenging the argument that crime doesn't pay.

Reform and rehabilitation
Reform requires meaningful life chances and attachments to mainstream society. It is difficult to see how positive work in custody affects lives back in the community when offenders return to the problems that contributed to their criminality. Often custody worsens community situations; loss of job, home or relationship.

Reparation (restorative justice)
Restitution: aims to correct wrongs, making good either to the victim or to the wider community through some form of community service.
Mediation: involves the offender and victim in 'offence resolution', meeting together to discuss each other's feelings. The offender usually offers an apology.

Sentencing Proposals

In this section proposals to reform the youth justice system are critically evaluated.

- Proposals to simplify sentences by replacing the existing nine non-custodial sentences with a broader action plan order complemented by child behaviour contracts, parenting contracts and family group conferences. Systems thinking suggests that with fewer sentencing options the custodial stage will be reached more quickly by those persistently before the courts.
- Custodial remands continue to be a concern, especially if the young person is subsequently cleared or given a non-custodial sentence. Their use should be minimised by more intensive community supervision and remand fostering schemes.
- Greater emphasis upon restorative justice to make young offenders appreciate the costs of their actions and the effects upon victims, although it is doubtful whether a court order is required, as in the 1980s schemes aimed at lower-level offenders could be part of pre-court diversion. Current referral orders can be criticised for double jeopardy: low-level offenders have to attend court and appear before the referral order panel. The intervention would be better as pre-court diversion.
- More use of ISSOs as alternatives to custody, although care has to be taken that alternatives to custody are not used when custody was not likely. By failing an ISSO young people face almost inevitable custody for breaches and for future offences.
- More purposeful use of custody, including sentences nearer home, more attention to individual deficits (educational and health) and more 'treatment'-focused approaches, especially related to addiction issues and anger management. While more constructive custodial regimes would be welcomed, the weaknesses of this argument are the negative culture of custody (school for crime) and problems in changing behaviours in a closed institution unrelated to a young person's life in the community. There is also a danger that if custodial provision is of high quality, sentencers may use custody as a means of getting help for needy young people not at that point on the sentencing tariff.

It can therefore be argued that it is almost impossible to effectively reform the current sentencing system without creating undesired consequences such as propelling more offenders towards custody. What is required is a return to more liberal diversionary approaches.

Working in Partnership

Youth offending teams are examples of partnership working both in terms of their organisational arrangements and of the composition of the multi-professional team. The rationale of partnership working is that service users receive a seamless service as various programmes come together to meet an identified

need. Similarly, at a strategic level a multi-agency approach can effectively identify and meet local need.

Working in partnership in youth justice is not new, but YOTs date from
around 1999. Banks (2004) studied a youth offending team to uncover the
complexities of inter-professional work. On the whole, workers and services
users identified good outcomes in term of joined-up programmes, but noted a
number of tensions and ethical challenges associated with inter-professional
working:

- Compatibility of different systems, hierarchies, procedures and criteria.
- Issues of different professional identities, values and cultures. Perhaps the
  most complex area concerns matters of confidentiality. Health professionals
  see confidentiality as a one-to-one relationship between the professional and
  the patient (except with serious child protection issues), whereas social services see confidentiality as belonging to the agency as a whole.
- Some workers felt uncomfortable that their professional identities were being
  undermined as functions became merged with workers performing the roles
  traditionally occupied by others. This caused confusion between the roles of
  (say) a social worker and a YOT worker.

Operationally, in managing YOTs, it must be decided whether all workers
carry out similar (case-holding) tasks, or whether specialisms should be used.
The former is likely to enhance relationship formation with fewer workers
being involved in each case, while the latter utilises the individual expertise of
each team member.

Partnership Work: A Systems Approach to Change

A systems analysis of a youth offending team is constrained by the highly
restrictive and prescriptive legislative framework, but there is scope for
creative action, for example by being proactive in monitoring progress and
selling ideas to other players in the system such as front-line police officers
and magistrates; producing a youth justice plan including local and comparative statistics, and tracking individual groups through the local system, for
example black boys. Individual case studies can be used to illustrate concepts
like net-widening, that the young person sent to custody today would not be
there if they had been diverted from 'the system' three years earlier. Talking
to other partners can emphasise common ground to reduce offending and
help us live in a civilised society. It is only the means to that end that are
contested.

Workers in youth offending teams see the main positive as the time they
spend in face-to-face work with service users but are disillusioned with the
managerialist agenda of meeting targets rather than focusing upon the best
interests of individual young people. The short-term nature of most interventions is an obvious example, closing cases at the end of an order when it is clear
that the young person has ongoing needs.

As YOTs become more integrated into the overall programme for children in need within children's trusts, as workers become better trained and more embedded in their multi-disciplinary roles and functions, the scope for influencing policy and practice away from the current punitive and managerialist agenda should increase.

The Association of Managers of Youth Offender Teams is already acting as a pressure group to argue against current punitive policies, and the Youth Justice Board is arguably also becoming more critical in its approach to Government policy.

Youth Justice: The Way Forward

Former Prime Minister Tony Blair's famous sound bite 'Tough on crime, tough on the causes of crime' (1997) echoes in the ears of critical thinkers. Petty offenders, including those accused of sub-criminal (anti-social) behaviour, may have been hammered, but little has been done to tackle the causes of crime. The government has presided over a system that has locked up more young people at a time when youth crime is falling. The same government claims not to be promoting youth custody and exhorts sentencers to use it as a last resort. If custody were a cheap option the paradox could be explained, but it is the most expensive option. The answer lies in politics, each of the two major political parties wanting to occupy the moral ground of being toughest on law and order. The big issue has to be why we persist with the flagship policy of custody when it's an expensive way of making bad people worse.

The new youth justice is based upon principles and policies that reflect a 'do something now' reaction to moral panic in the media, which arguably leads to poor legislation. The current approach is managerialist, based upon standards, systems and targets which undermine professional discretion and a real ability to help young people in trouble.

Muncie (2006) examines the systematic retreat from the welfare principle towards popular punitivism since the Crime and Disorder Act 1998. He conceptualizes the 'new youth justice' in terms of a number of ideological influences. A major factor has been 'responsibilisation', whereby young offenders, parents and communities are held fully responsible for being anti-social and delinquent in a 'no excuses' culture. This sits alongside other neo-liberal policies in a globalised world, which is increasingly promoting worldwide policies of welfare residualisation, and punitive penal policies. Alongside this is the neo-Conservative agenda of remoralising the poor and conditional inclusion (the tough welfare State), in other words, do what society requires of you or face compulsion.

In short, the Youth Justice Board is leading a highly centralized system that functions to the detriment of its own objective to reduce offending and re-offending, which arguably leads to outcomes for individual young people that will further label and socially exclude them, and further increase the risk of their re-offending. Arguably the current system is not fit for purpose but within current parameters it is not suitable for reform either.

However, there is some indication of a softening in the punitive approach by government, seeing the use of restrictive approaches such as ASBOs as an acknowledgement of failings in wider policies to tackle crime and disorder.

Practice Area 3: Social Work in an Educational Context

The third featured practice area where practitioners work in an authoritarian context is education. While truancy policies provide the most overt example of authoritarianism, this section aims to show how the wider education system is authoritarian in promoting conformity, largely denying individuality and severely punishing those unwilling or unable to conform to this ethos. Education policy is located in its wider social context, examined in terms of the impact of recent reforms upon students and other stakeholders, and the winners and losers uncovered.

Education provides an example where professional values and expectations can clash. A major cause is that while social workers tend to deal with individuals and families, schools deal with classes of students in a climate of managerialism, where even the best-meaning educational professionals must put the education of the majority and the success of the school before individual need.

What is Education?

A starting point is to explore the purpose of formal education in modern society. There is often confusion between 'learning' (a lifelong process that doesn't necessarily require a classroom and indeed is often arranged by the individual using modern technology such as the Internet) and 'schooling' (a part of childhood and adolescence as a life stage).

Education is seen as a tool:

- To promote equality of opportunity and a more equal society. This gives legitimacy to state intervention into the private world of the family.
- To meet the needs of capitalists for a skilled and compliant workforce (the Marxist perspective).
- To socialise individuals into the values of society, promote social order and arguably support current power relations.
- for childminding (looking after children in a society where most parents work).
- For personal growth and development: liberal, child-centred education versus instrumental learning (leading to a vocational model). Liberal approaches to education are now highly unfashionable.

It is debated whether education is a 'moral good', crucially whether it is right that rich people should be allowed to purchase a superior education for their children, or whether resources should be allocated according to need or ability. Should need be defined as the most disadvantaged, developing potential across the board or focusing on the most able (the argument for grammar schools)?

This is important as education is the single most important factor in social mobility, and there is a strong link between educational attainment and lifelong outcomes, with better education leading to higher incomes and less risk of wider social exclusion due to poverty and unemployment (Social Exclusion Unit 2003).

The history of education is largely about class and gender; initially largely only rich boys were educated. The state then increased its role, but there remains an uneasy coexistence between private and state education. Post-war Labour intended to abolish private (public) schools, but for largely political reasons never dared do so. Whether early state intervention was largely philanthropic (provided out of kindness) or was about meeting the needs of capitalists for a skilled and compliant workforce is hotly debated (Lauder et al. 1997).

Post-war, the Labour Party sought to improve educational opportunities for all by abolishing grammar schools (though some still exist) in favour of comprehensive schools. It is doubtful whether comprehensives delivered on their educational and social agendas, largely because the early comprehensive idealists underestimated the complexity of educating poor people. The assumption that if you gave people good opportunities they would take them proved simplistic, and many factors that promoted class bias (see below) were found even within comprehensives.

There is a strong link between educational outcomes and social class. Top achievements are by the privately educated, next come the motivated middle classes in grammar schools and top streams in comprehensives, leaving the poor in the lower streams in comprehensives struggling to achieve. This is not just about exam results; it impacts upon the power, status and contacts young people take into the adult world.

Arguably we now have a four-tier system in education:

- public/private schools for children of the rich who, via the elite universities, get top jobs in law, politics and the major professions (the 'old school tie').
- grammar schools or top streams of comprehensives for the middle classes who then inhabit professional and business jobs;
- secondary moderns or lower streams of comprehensives for the working classes who work in semi-skilled or manual jobs;
- an educational underclass who have little engagement with the formal education system hence creating the likelihood of lifelong social exclusion: truants, those excluded and those with special needs. Traditionally many looked-after children were in this group.

Although the feminist perspective has been remarkably successful in countering the general stereotype that girls don't need a 'proper education' as their role is in the home (girls now outperform boys in most educational outcomes), persistent gender biases in subject choices indicate continuing gender inequality.

There is also a racial dimension as some black groups achieve poor educational outcomes. In 2002 only 30 per cent of black students achieved five or more good GCSEs (51 per cent nationally) and black students are three times more likely than white students to be excluded from school (Department for Education and Skills 2005). The government is addressing this through its Aiming High strategy, the African Caribbean Achievement Project (DfES 2003) which aims to work with leaders of schools to develop whole school approaches to raising the achievement of African Caribbean pupils, often using mentoring schemes. The racialised failure of working-class boys is discussed in chapter 2.

Educational Reforms in the Thatcher years

Thatcher's New Right Conservative government from 1979 set a new agenda for state education based upon market forces with the introduction of competition aimed at increasing standards through less power for teachers and local education authorities and more to parents, head teachers, governors and central government – a shift from professional power to managerialism.

Major changes included:

- Schools were able to opt out of local authority control. Foundation schools and grant maintained schools were funded directly by a central quango, the Funding Council for Schools.
- In the local management of schools, budgets management and more decision-making were given to heads and governors.
- The national curriculum was established, prescribing most of what should be taught in schools, with an emphasis upon academic, classroom-based subjects.
- Standard assessment tests (SATs) were instituted, measuring attainment to national standards from age 7.
- Performance indicators and league tables for schools were set up to complement parental choice by giving comparable information on competing schools.
- The establishment of independent inspection by Ofsted, which could define a school as a 'failing school' and place it under special measures.
- The policy of keeping students with special needs in mainstream schools continued.

An analysis of winners and losers suggests that the inequalities within the postwar system were accentuated. In a world of parental choice, middle-class people played the game more successfully to achieve better school places. This was partly by doing research to exercise informed choice, and partly because they lived, or were prepared to move, near a good school, and would even go to church to get a place in a church school.

Oversubscribed and opted-out schools could exercise selection covertly, with successful schools attracting the best students and recruiting the best staff, increasing the gap between top and bottom. A process was established whereby top schools spiralled upwards to more success while failing schools almost inevitably remained at the bottom.

Particularly worrying for social workers was that school cultures changed as schools competed on performance criteria such as exam results and truancy figures. There was little incentive to persist with an individual student who was unwilling or unable to deliver on these outcomes. Heads worry that if they're seen to take 'disruptives', potential parents might go elsewhere. Pastoral care became reframed in terms of discipline rather than welfare. These changes probably benefited those able and willing to achieve academically, but excluded many others.

Under the national curriculum there has been a retreat from sport, creative subjects and vocational subjects where many less able or motivated students traditionally found a niche, towards academic classroom subjects. Arguably this curriculum diet promoted a crisis in classroom control in the lower streams and teachers had little choice but to clamp down. This 'sit down and shut up' class-room culture offers little opportunity for teachers to see students as individuals and to take time to try to understand individual difficulties. There was also little social education, and teachers became wary of discussing personal issues with students, partly due to increased awareness of child protection issues, which required that they not be alone with a child or discuss things that could be misconstrued, together with concerns about being seen to be over-involved.

Although there is some limited potential to disapply those with special educational needs from the national curriculum in mainstream schools, many such children were forced to apply themselves to the curriculum. It seems absurd, for example, that a child who cannot master basic number work is required to study algebra.

The Labour Years

Surprisingly, given its traditional ideology of promoting social mobility through education, the Labour government has continued along Thatcherite lines, although the rhetoric has changed. Rather than competition, the rhetoric is about promoting excellence through 'beacon schools' (whose excellence is meant to trickle down to other schools) and specialist schools (the new form of opting out). Parental choice is maintained, although even the government recognises that middle-class parents are able to achieve better outcomes.

Targets were at first toughened and the curriculum became more prescriptive, for example through the introduction of literacy and numeracy hours in primary schools. Then there was a relaxation with a reduction in the national curriculum, for example foreign languages are no longer compulsory at Key Stage 4, and the creation of vocational options for 14–16-year-olds. The introduction of citizenship studies into the national curriculum has been significant in allowing students to move from pure knowledge to awareness of wider issues in society.

Most significant has been the commitment to increase funding to achieve the European Union average. Much has been spent on initiatives outside school, for example, provision for under-5s, including Sure Start, the Children's Fund and Connexions. Also, specific initiatives such as Education Action Zones and improving the education of looked-after children. In school there have been improvements (reductions in primary class sizes, building programmes, more ancillary staff), and results, as measured by exams, have improved (despite the annual debate about whether exams are getting easier).

The Education and Inspections Act 2006: Indicating the Future

Government policy towards children has evolved from the Green Paper 'Every Child Matters' which informed the Children Act 2004. The introduction of children's trusts and the development of childcare provision in the form of children's centres for younger children and extended schools for older ones is widening the concept of education in terms of both provision and the roles of educational professionals.

Earlier trends have been developed with more specialist schools, schools becoming self-governing trusts and a lesser role for local education authorities, although with some measures to address inequalities, for example subsidised transport so that poorer students can access schools further from home, and advisers to assist parents in making school choices. Tougher discipline and parenting contracts characterise school life and extra resources aim to make the curriculum more personalised, with more students having personal education plans. Head teachers can now apply directly to court for parenting orders.

Work with Disaffected Students

Engaging those students who are disaffected from school is one of the greatest challenges for the new inter-professional working arrangements. Such students fall into a number of categories: truants, those excluded and, numerically more significant, a large group who remain within mainstream education but largely fail to benefit from it, those who 'muck about' or appear to conform while

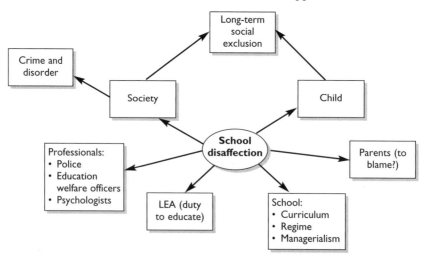

Figure 8.3 Impact of disaffection from school

failing to study. There are commonalities between young people in these groups, for example they come from a poor background. The impact of educational disaffection is felt by the individual student, whose life changes are jeopardised, and by wider society.

Truancy

This section uses truancy to illustrate how current policies are failing, and suggests more effective strategies.

Social workers in education welfare identify as their major issue the clash between traditional social work values (especially empowerment) and punitive policies towards truancy. Alongside policies that clamp down on anti-social behaviour and offending, policies relating to truancy are authoritarian, expensive and ineffective. The test of effectiveness has to be the truancy figures themselves. Sadly, these have remained roughly unchanged over 10 years with nearly 1.4 million children playing truant last year, despite estimated government spending of £885 million on tackling truancy from 1998 to 2004 and 16,000 police hours expended annually on truancy sweeps (Action on Rights for children 2007).

Truancy model

A more effective approach to truancy flows from a systemic analysis of why children truant. This is an interaction between personal factors (in children or their families), wider structural factors relating to peers or neighbourhoods and factors relating to schools or wider educational policies. Some children run from school and others are predominantly sucked away by other opportunities or duties.

Truancy is a social construction. Arguably, if the concern is about the impact upon learning through missing school, greater emphasis should be placed upon authorised absences, for example family holidays in term time.

The National Audit Office (2005), a body charged with seeking cost-effectiveness in government, identified a number of factors influencing school absence:

PRACTICE CONTEXT 8.2

Factors influencing absence from school

School factors
Attractiveness and relevance of curriculum
Quality of teaching
Management of behaviour, including bullying
School–parent relationships
School policies

Pupil
Genuine illness (and medical appointments)

Behavioural problems
Learning difficulties
Personal problems
Influence of friends and peers
Being bullied

Home
Parental attitudes to education
Holidays during term time
Other leave (e.g. for bereavement or religious observance)
Familial problems
Children with caring responsibilities
Difficulties in getting to and from school
Frequent movers

Source: National Audit Office (2005).

It is evident that many of these are personal problems which can be more effectively addressed through a welfare rather than a punitive approach.

Interface with Social Work

Social workers in childcare teams are likely to work in partnership with education in:

- Child protection referrals from schools: each school should have a dedicated child protection lead teacher who will have attended the multi-agency training.
- The education of looked-after children: each school should have a lead teacher for looked-after students who will take responsibility for their personal education plan (see chapter 5).
- Advocating for parents and children in cases of truancy and exclusion.
- Contributing to common assessments where there are special educational needs (SEN) and involvement in negotiating personal educational plans. The issue about SEN is the extent to which children with disabilities should be educated in mainstream schools. In addition, how should disruptive students be dealt with: should they be seen as having special educational needs or should they be excluded?

A clash in values: confidentiality as a case study

The caring professions have a commonality of values, for example respect for the individual. However, the way in which the value system is interpreted and acted upon can cause strains between professionals working together. Confidentiality provides an example of a possible clash in professional values between social work and education. Social workers see the right to confidence on an individual level and within the constraints of policy (that the confidence is with the agency and not an individual worker, and that certain factors, especially child protection concerns, override the normal assumptions of confidentiality), and information is normally shared on a need-to-know basis.

Schools, on the other hand, deal with large numbers of students, many of whom have particular problematic issues, and confidential material may be shared more openly. For example, profiles of students with SENs can be posted on staffroom notice boards, or students who are experiencing problems may be mentioned in staff meetings or in widely circulated staff bulletins.

Positive Approaches to Working with Schools

While different professional cultures and organisational arrangements can make it difficult for professionals to work together to meet the needs of individual children and promote wider social improvement, there are strategies that can be employed to achieve those goals.

First, at a team level social workers should forge links with their schools so that understanding and mutual trust can be established before they need to discuss individuals. For example, a termly liaison meeting involving a secondary school and the wider group of professionals involved with it can discuss matters of concern from all perspectives. A school could feel that social services do not respond adequately to child protection referrals. There may be concerns about delays in getting therapeutic interventions from child and adolescent mental health services (CAMHS), or wider concerns about issues in the community, perhaps a rise in truancy or the consumption of drugs. Greater understanding is achieved by sharing information and agencies can deploy resources to work on a particular problem. Such meetings can also be powerful in pressurizing management to recognise deficiencies and increase resources.

A second approach is to advocate for individual students experiencing problems. It is complex to achieve a balance between the needs of the individual and the wider concerns of the school. Sometimes the offer of additional resources can unstick a situation, for example social services funding an ancillary worker until a special needs statement can be completed. Although at an organisational level such flexibility is difficult to achieve, it can be cost-effective in the long term, for example if school exclusion can be avoided.

A complexity arises where a young person feels aggrieved by a school issue and the social worker has sympathy for that viewpoint. In extreme cases advocacy can lead to a conflictual situation, where for example a social worker is opposing school exclusion by advocating for the child and parents at an appeals panel. Such situations are rare and hopefully, resolution can be achieved through proper negotiations. But because some schools regularly exclude pupils, while others seldom do, finding appropriate balance with certain schools can be challenging.

Structural Changes: The Challenge of Working Together

Time will tell how the merger of educational and social work professionals will impact upon service provision. The experience of earlier attempts at such mergers, for example in mental health, would suggest that social work professionals are likely to be seen as the junior partners, and as such their input could be marginalised.

On the other hand, educational professionals, led by government initiatives, are retreating from seeing children as amorphous groups and returning to viewing each child is an individual. The focus upon special educational needs, personal education plans and the emphasis upon the education of looked-after children support that trend.

KEY POINTS

- Policies regarding 'troubled' or 'troublesome' young people have become more punitive.
- The use of ASBOs is an example of policy that fails to meet its own objectives.
- In youth justice policies, research evidence has been marginalised as political and media rhetoric give rise to ineffective and damaging punitive policies.
- The current education system produces winners and losers largely based upon gender, class and ethnicity. Although the rhetoric is about inclusion the current system excludes and marginalises those most in need.
- The coming together of educationalists and social workers in children's trusts presents challenges to integrating two very different cultures and the worrying possibility that social work may become marginalised.

RESOURCES

ASBOs

The ASBO Concern website has links to a wide variety of critical papers: www.asboconcern.org.uk

Millie, A. et al. (2005), *Anti-Social Behaviour Strategies: Finding a Balance*. Joseph Rowntree Foundation. Downloadable from: www.jrf.org.uk

Youth justice

Home Office Youth Offenders Unit (2003), *Youth Justice: The Next Steps.* Companion report to 'Every Child Matters', downloadable from www.homeoffice.gsi.gov.uk.

Youth Justice Board has briefing papers on sentences, guidance to YOTs: www.youth-justice-board.gov.uk (mostly downloadable series of practice guides).

NACRO (probably the main pressure group in this area) has briefing papers critical of current policies and practices: www.nacro.org.uk.

National Association for Youth Justice, the professional body for practitioners in this area: www.nayj.org.uk.

Barnardo's: www.barnardos.org.uk. As well as its own interests, Barnardo's also fronts the Youth Justice Coalition, which includes the Children's Rights Alliance, Children's Society, Howard League for Penal Reform, NACRO, NAYJ, NCB, NCH and NSPCC. See also the websites of these individual organisations.

Rethinking Crime and Punishment is good on the more philosophical aspects of the debate: rethinking.org.uk.

Youth Justice Coalition (2003), *Children in Trouble: Time for Change.*

Journal of Youth Justice.

Education

The Department for Children, Schools and Families website has a search engine for most issues in education and children's social work.

Website for teachers: www.teachernet.gov.uk

Times Educational Supplement, weekly newspaper for educationalists.

Social Exclusion Unit (2003), *A Better Education for Children in Care.*

Truancy

National Audit Office (2005), *Improving School Attendance in England.*

Action on Rights for Children, a pressure group critical of punitive policies: www.arch-ed.org.

CHAPTER 9

Child and Adolescent Mental Health: A Social Construction?

As statistics indicate that an increasing number of children and young people suffer from mental health difficulties, the chapter explores whether these increases are real or merely reflect modern social constructions around childhood, adolescence and 'normality'. It considers the price paid by individuals and society for a culture based on conformity and achievement, and taking ADHD as an example, whether medication is overused. In the context of children's rights it explores civil liberties issues such as compulsory treatment. Cannabis-induced psychosis is used as an example of an area where 'research' needs to be viewed with caution and alternative discourses examined.

Background

Discussions about child and adolescent mental health are overshadowed by studies that indicate that around one in 10 children suffer from a diagnosable mental health problem at some point in their childhood (Goodman 2000). This is often placed in the context of factors in modern childhood that promote such depressing statistics. The contradiction is that in an affluent period with greater opportunities for young people, they seem less happy than those living in the aftermath of the Second World War (Layard 2005).

The Children's Society are conducting a major national enquiry (due to report in 2008) examining the conditions that promote a good childhood and how childhood has changed from that experienced by previous generations. The initial report based upon a survey of young people identifies a range of factors that can adversely impact upon a modern child, including technological developments, demographic changes and a greater degree of diversity (Children's Society 2006).

Facts and Figures

Statistics are considered before examining the possible reasons for such widespread childhood misery. Findings from the first nationally representative survey of the mental health of children and adolescents (Goodman 2000) are summarised below.

Prevalence of disorders
- Mental disorders were more common in boys than in girls. Among 5–10-year-olds, 10 per cent of boys and 6 per cent of girls, and for 11–15-year-olds, 13 per cent of boys and 10 per cent of girls, had a mental disorder.
- Mental disorders were more likely among children:
  (a) in lone parent families (16 per cent).
  (b) in reconstituted families (15 per cent).
  (c) where parents had no educational qualifications.
  (d) where neither parent worked compared with both parents working (20 paer cent and 8 per cent).
  (e) in families of social class V (unskilled occupations) compared with social class I (professional occupations) (14 per cent and 5 per cent).
  (f) where parents were social sector tenants compared with owner occupiers (17 per cent and 6 per cent).

Link with education
- Mental disorders ranged from 6 per cent of children without special educational needs (SEN) to 43 per cent among children with a statement of SEN.
- 25 per cent of children with emotional disorders had been absent from school for 11 days or more in the past term.

Social functioning of the family
- 47 per cent of children with a mental disorder had a parent who had mental health problem (23 per cent nationally).
- 35 per cent of children with a mental disorder lived in families with a high level of family discord (17 per cent nationally).
- Children with mental disorders were far more likely to be frequently punished: 18 per cent compared with 8 per cent were frequently sent to their rooms; 17 per cent compared with 5 per cent were frequently kept in, and 42 per cent compared with 26 per cent were frequently shouted at.
- Two specific factors associated with the highest rates of mental disorders were: children (aged 13–15) who had split with a boyfriend or girlfriend (24 per cent), and children whose parent had been in trouble with the police (22 per cent).

Social functioning of the child
- Among all 11–15-year-olds, 6 per cent had a severe lack of friendship, 9 per cent of those with mental disorders and 5 per cent of those with no disorder.

- One quarter of young people had sought help with unhappy or worried feelings. Children with a disorder were almost twice as likely to have sought help and advice.

Source: adapted from: Goodman et al. 2000.

These figures paint a picture of children with disrupted lives in families with a multitude of personal and structural problems. Perhaps most worrying is that a similar statistical profile could equally well apply to young people identified as young offenders, or who become looked-after. The same young people seem to go through different systems depending upon who identifies an initial problem (Coppick 1997; see chapter 6).

Child and Adolescent Mental Health: A Social Construction?

A social constructionist considering the extent to which apparently declining child and adolescent mental health reflects more actual mental illness, or whether social factors that define abnormality have impacted on the statistics, would search for consistency across time periods and cultures.

The number of children diagnosed with mental health issues has increased dramatically. Maughan et al. (2004) analysed data from national surveys of 15- and 16-year-olds from 1974, 1986 and 1999, covering a wide range of adolescent difficulties from depression, anxiety and behavioural problems to wider issues such as bullying and fighting. They found that the rate of emotional problems such as anxiety and depression had increased by 70 per cent since the mid 1980s, having previously been stable, and that conduct problems showed a continuous rise over the 25-year period, but this was largely non-aggressive behaviour such as lying, stealing and disobedience. Although this study did not cover more serious difficulties such as suicide and self-harm, other studies also suggest dramatic increases in these categories (Department of Health 2005).

Some of the labels applied to young people defined as having mental health problems are listed below:

- Behavioural or conduct disorders:
    ADHD, hyperkinetic disorder
    Tourette's syndrome
    Inappropriate sexual behaviour
- Attachment disorders:
    Attachment deficit disorder
- Emotional disorders:
    Depression
    Self-harming
    Eating disorders (anorexia and bulimia nervosa; some obesity)
    Anxiety disorder

- Psychosis:
  Schizophrenia
- Psychopathy (sometimes concerns about 'dangerous' personality disorders)
- Autism spectrum disorders (autism itself is usually seen as a learning disability)
  Asperger's syndrome

One explanation for the apparent increase in mental health problems at the lower end of the spectrum could be changes in the way we define deviant behaviour. The post-war period has seen a range of new diagnoses, for example ADHD, Asperger's syndrome, Tourette's syndrome and many others. Clearly these behaviours existed 50 years ago, but were not medically labelled; instead sufferers were likely to be seen as 'odd' or 'naughty'.

Another explanation is that because professional and public awareness of these conditions has improved and services to sufferers have increased, more young people are being presented for diagnosis and labelled. Certainly, until child and adolescent mental health services (CAMHS) consolidated previous child and adolescent mental health services, concerns were constantly being raised about inadequate and patchy services (Street 2000). Work was carried out, largely with sufferers of the more serious disorders, but in many areas waiting lists were so long that potential referrers (GPs, schools and social workers) tended to direct a troubled young person elsewhere, perhaps a counselling project in the voluntary sector. Although resourcing levels remain an issue, there is a greater likelihood of a service being offered to lower-level sufferers through CAMHS. This in turn is likely to generate more referrals, more children labelled and further unsatisfactory waiting times. CAMHS is perhaps a product of its own success.

A third possibility is that in an authoritarian state, with its emphasis upon compliance and conformity, we have become less tolerant of any form of deviant behaviour and more willing to apply labels to explain such behaviour. Additionally, the pressure to achieve within the narrowly defined bands (academic successes) can promote anxiety-linked disorders (see chapter 8). On the other hand, the possibility remains that the incidence of mental health problems has increased, and suggested underlying factors will be discussed in the next section.

A social constructionist would also want to ask if adolescent mental health difficulties have similarly increased in other countries and across cultural groups. The Maughan et al. (2004) study cited research conducted in the US and the Netherlands. The US research suggested increased problems between 1976 and 1989 which were then reversed by 1999 (Achenbach et al. 2003). The Netherlands study found no noticeable increase in problems for children aged 4–16 between 1983 and 1993 (Verhulst 1997). While it is difficult to make detailed and reliable comparisons from such studies due to differences in years, age groups and criteria used, a wider study of Europe and the US by the World Health Organization did conclude that there are worryingly high levels of disturbing behaviour among young people in the UK (Currie 2004).

Whether mental health difficulties are more prevalent in some adolescent ethnic groups is under researched. However, Tolmac and Hooles (2004) suggested that black (African Caribbean) young people are far more likely to be defined as experiencing serious mental health difficulties than other ethnic groups. This relatively small study of 13–17-year-old in-patients in adolescent psychiatric units found that black patients comprised 35 per cent, those of Asian origin 13 per cent and white adolescents 45 per cent (minority ethnic groups comprise about 10 per cent of the overall population), showing that black young people were considerably over-represented in this Tier 4 service. Six out of eight black young people were being treated for schizophrenia at the most serious end of the mental illness spectrum. The study attributes this over-representation of black youngsters to poorer levels of social support and higher levels of exposure to stressful situations, although other explanations are possible. These include black young people being less likely to seek early help due to a mistrust of the mental health system being perceived as white-dominated, or to institutional racism in the mental health system with largely white mental health professionals not fully understanding that some behaviours could be attributed to cultural differences rather than disturbance. It could also be that black young people are treated differently once they are in the mental health system and to be placed in residential units.

There are other inequalities in those diagnosed with mental health problems. Perhaps most disturbing is that 37 per cent of looked-after children in England have clinical conduct disorder (around 5 per cent nationally), 12 per cent have an emotional disorder such as depression and 7 per cent are deemed hyperactive. Of even greater concern is that very young children are being diagnosed with mental illnesses. 42 per cent of looked-after 5–10-year-olds have a mental illness (8 per cent nationally) (Office of National Statitics 2004). It is likely that child mental health issues will have contributed to family breakdown, leading to a care episode, but also possible that aspects of family functioning gave rise to the mental health difficulties of the child (a chicken or egg situation).

Promoting Good Mental Health in Childhood

From a social constructionist perspective, there are many aspects of modern childhood that promote behaviour that is then labelled as mental health difficulties. The first area to explore is the practicalities of many children's lives. The first concern is diet, and the links between a poor diet, as typified by junk food and e-numbers, with behavioural problems. There are also indirect links, for example being overweight can promote bullying, which leads to unhappiness. Another practical area is lack of exercise (which releases serotonin in the brain, a hormone associated with well-being). For some children a sedentary life in front of a computer has replaced the more active life of previous generations (playing outside, for example), which is related to weight gain and less sociability. It is also ironic that parents are scared to allow outside play for fear of 'stranger danger', and yet this might in itself be harming their children.

The second area is about relationships, the main way in which we all feel valued and wanted. There are aspects of modern society working against the formation and maintenance of long-term trusting relationships. Parents should be the front line for providing emotional support to children, but for a variety of reasons – busy lifestyles or being consumed by their own difficulties – this cannot always be relied upon. Demographic factors, particularly the decline in the concept of marriage for life, have meant that a number of children are brought up in households that lack stability (see chapter 1).

A second line of defence in providing children with trusted adults should be teachers, but in the modern culture of schools (see chapter 8) it is difficult for teachers to establish personal relationships with individual children. So children who lack a sense of caring and closeness seek to fill the void elsewhere, perhaps making themselves vulnerable, for example in internet chatrooms where paedophiles can 'groom' them for abuse. Others might seek relationships with peers, some of which might lead to problematic outcomes, for example, drink or drug use, gang membership, self-harm or teenage pregnancy.

Some commentators consider the demands on young people to be excessive, particularly the pressure to achieve educational success and to make the necessary decisions in their own lives perhaps without the advice and support of trusted adults and without a framework of shared morality within modern society.

For some, formal services provide a solution to an emotional void, the almost frightening number of children who attempt to phone Childline being an obvious example. Their research (2005) suggests that in 2004 they counselled 4,000 self-harmers, up 30 per cent on the previous year. Others turn to local advice and counselling services and some can be introduced to volunteers or mentors who can establish themselves in the role of trusted adult. Others suffer in silence, sometimes turning to private coping mechanisms, self-harm, suicide attempts or eating disorders, for example. Some will be identified as problematic and referred to the appropriate services, although as we have seen, many of these are so overstretched that they struggle to meet the demands upon them.

Also important is the role of the media in promoting an image of what a successful child is, or should be, creating strain for those who feel unable or unwilling to conform, or lack the resources to do so. Food disorders, anorexia and bulimia are sometimes attributed to sufferers trying to live up to the media image promoted by celebrities that slim is beautiful.

The concept of self-esteem can provide a valuable insight into how children feel about themselves and thus how they handle the stresses of life. One way of measuring a person's self esteem is to compare the image they have of themselves with what they would see as their ideal self. Those with major differences will be suffering low self-esteem. It's not so much about the objective reality, as about how they feel about themselves. For example, some suffers of anorexia were already thin before they become obsessed with dieting, but that was not how they felt.

A related concept is that of resilience, an inner skill that enables a person to cope well with anything that life throws at them. We can identify factors that tend to make children resilient and others that put them at risk of not being so.

Factors that Improve Resilience

Payne and Butler (2003) suggest that secure early attachments, the confidence of being loved and valued by family and friends, a clear sense of personal, cultural and spiritual self-identity and being able to make and act on one's own decisions constitute the major factors that promote resilience. Even when facing adverse circumstances, for example parental separation, children who are strong in these factors can survive relatively unscathed. Adults helping a child through such a situation can take positive action to help maintain their resilience, for example by ensuring that they are involved in decisions as far as possible, and by making sure that there is a trusted adult in whom they can confide.

Factors that detract from Resilience

There is a correlation between poor mental health and other health issues, including poor physical health and learning difficulties, as well as special educational needs. Parental factors are also important, including parents who themselves suffer from mental health problems and where the family is disrupted or unstable. Abuse and harsh parental discipline can also be associated with mental health difficulties (Payne and Butler 2003). It is also suggested that there is a link between socio-economic disadvantage, poverty and deprivation, and poor childhood mental health (Kay 1999). Kay also suggests that risk factors are cumulative: the more risk factors the greater the probability of mental health difficulties; one risk factor promotes a probability of 1–2 per cent, rising to 20 per cent with four or more risk factors.

Services for Those with Mental Health Difficulties

Services for children and adolescents with mental health difficulties are provided by local multi-disciplinary Child and Adolescent Mental Health Services (CAMHS) teams, although at Tier 1, the usual entry point, low-level services are the responsibility of other professionals.

PRACTICE CONTEXT 9.1

The four-tier framework of CAMHS

Tier I
CAMHS at this level are provided by practitioners who are not mental health specialists, including GPs, health visitors, school nurses, teachers, social workers, youth justice workers, voluntary agencies. Practitioners will be able to offer general advice and treatment for less severe problems, contribute towards mental health promotion, identify problems early and refer to more specialist services.

Tier 2

Practitioners at this level tend to be CAMHS specialists working in community and primary care settings in a uni-disciplinary way (although many will also work as part of Tier 3 services). This can include primary mental health workers, psychologists and counsellors working in GP practices, paediatric clinics, schools and youth services. Practitioners offer consultation to families and other practitioners, outreach to identify severe or complex needs which require more specialist interventions, assessment (which may lead to treatment at a different tier) and training to practitioners at Tier 1.

Tier 3

This is usually a multi-disciplinary team or service working in a community mental health clinic or child psychiatry outpatient service, providing a specialised service to children and young people with more severe, complex and persistent disorders. Team members are likely to include child and adolescent psychiatrists, social workers, clinical psychologists, community psychiatric nurses, child psychotherapists, occupational therapists, art, music and drama therapists.

Tier 4

These are services for children and young people with the most serious problems, such as day units, highly specialised outpatient teams and in-patient units. These can include secure forensic adolescent units, eating disorders units, specialist neuro-psychiatric teams and other specialist teams (for children who have been sexually abused, for example), usually serving more than one district or region.

Source: adapted from: Department of Education and Skills (2003): www.everychildmatters.gov.uk/health/camhs

A Critique of Services

The biggest weakness in CAMHS is that they are neither a completely specialist service nor fully integrated into other children's services.

At Tier 1 the assumption is that other professionals involved with children on a day-to-day basis will identify and support low-level mental health difficulties. There are many reasons why this might not be effective. First, non-specialist staff are not traind and do not have the knowledge and confidence to enter this complex and risky area. Secondly, many professionals are too busy with their key tasks to find time to listen, for example, most GP appointments are for less than 10 minutes. Thirdly, roles might conflict, for example a teacher perceived as authoritarian is unlikely to gain the trust of a student needing to discuss personal problems. Lastly, a professional might not wish to be perceived as being 'too close' to a young person in need of that kind of supportive relationship.

At the other levels where CAMHS specialists are involved there have been concerns that targets have not been met and waiting times remain unacceptable. A government review of success in meeting Standard 9 (the mental health standard) of the National Service Framework for Children, Young People and Maternity Services pointed to continued resource deficiencies, with only 25 per cent of children accessing specialist services from which they could have benefited and patchy services continuing to operate across the country (Appleby et al. 2006).

Another concern is about the nature of treatment. Mental health issues are seen largely on the medical model of diagnosis and treatment, often with medication. Arguably, treatment should address the underlying social conditions that promote mental health problems. An influential report to the Government Strategy Unit relating to the whole field of mental illness suggested that even from a financial standpoint (it estimated that mental illness costs the UK 2 per cent of the gross domestic product), it would be worth addressing social factors. It suggested that early intervention and a greater emphasis upon 'talking therapies' would be cost effective as a means of keeping sufferers off long term incapacity benefit (Layard 2004). Predictably, through the labelling process (see chapter 2) many adolescents now diagnosed as having mental health difficulties will continue these problems into adult life, with consequences for their productive capacity, wider levels of social functioning, and parenting ability.

Practice Areas

Consent to Treatment: the Moral Debate

Work with adolescents with more serious mental health problems can present some complex moral and legal dilemmas: first as to whether treatment can be forced, and secondly, as to who has the power to consent to treatment, especially in contested situations.

It is unclear whether childcare or mental health legislation should be used, particularly where residential treatment is provided. While legislation allows young people to be sectioned under the Mental Health Act, some practitioners argue that wherever possible childcare legislation should be used. Young Minds suggests that in order to consider the wider family, and the educational and social needs of a child, legislation ought to provide the safeguards offered by childcare legislation, for example systematic care planning and review, and the availability of an independent professional outside of the mental health system (Young Minds 2004).

There is a further lack of clarity about whether it is the parent or the young person who should consent to treatment, or indeed withhold such consent. If there is a conflict between the wishes of the parent and the child, best practice is that the child's view be assessed according to their 'Gillick competence', although this can be complicated if it is argued that by virtue of their mental health difficulties they lack competence in law.

This is further complicated by the duty of doctors to preserve life, which in life-or-death situations can involve treatment without consent, for example force-feeding a young person whose life is under threat due to anorexia. In practice many such situations are being resolved in the courts. Such dilemmas can reflect wider debates, for example whether a person should have the right to choose to end their own life.

Young Minds (2004) also expresses concern about the inappropriate detention of children and young people in adult psychiatric wards (said to be 260 cases in 2003), often in an emergency or because of the lack of availability of a dedicated children's bed within reasonable travelling distance.

ADHD: the Medication Debate

This section discusses the contested diagnosis of attention deficit hyperactivity disorder (ADHD) and the debate about treatments for it, especially the controversy about the use of medication, mainly Ritalin, described variously as a 'chemical cosh' and a 'wonder drug'.

In Britain the incidence of diagnosed ADHD has risen sharply to around one in 20 schoolchildren, and many feel that this is an underestimate. The causes of ADHD are heavily contested with some believing that it is genetic because of evidence that many sufferers have parents who also had behavioural problems as children (but might not have been diagnosed) and that often siblings also suffer from the disorder. However, it is difficult to show that these observations suggest a genetic causation; it could be that children in such households learn to behave similarly to their parent or older sibling. Those who support the genetic hypothesis believe that medication is justified to rectify an imbalance in those parts of the brain that control attention, impulses and concentration.

Others argue that ADHD is a convenient diagnosis to justify enforcing conformity in children. Clearly there are some powerful vested interests in the diagnosis, from the drug companies who profit from the estimated 200,000 prescriptions for Ritalin per year, schools whose students are calmer and parents who can avoid an implicit assumption that naughty behaviour results from poor parenting. Parents with children suffering from ADHD can also claim disability living allowance.

Other theories suggest that ADHD is triggered by modern diet, particularly food additives, or that it is related to the pressures of modern life, whether arising from the social constructions of adolescence as a life stage (see chapter 2) or expectations of conformity and achievement. Figure 9.1 summarises these possibilities.

As the amount of drugs prescribed for ADHD rises, the moral issue is whether it is right to medicate children in such numbers, especially if, as I have argued, ADHD is largely a social construction rather than a biological disorder. While most practitioners can testify to individual cases where medication has calmed children to a point where their self-esteem increases dramatically and they start to achieve at school, in other instances young people appear to have used the ADHD label as an excuse their errant behav-

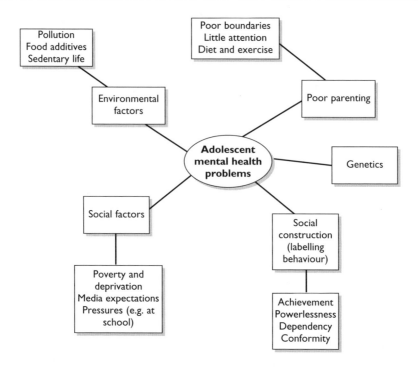

Figure 9.1 Causal factors in adolescent mental health problems

iour and apparent failure: *'I'm going to give you hell today, Sir, because I've forgotten to take my Ritalin.'*

There are side effects associated with Ritalin, including tremors, sleeplessness and possibly growth restriction. It is also likely to increase blood pressure which is linked to heart attack and stroke. Social side effects include the likelihood that Ritalin, as a stimulant, is being sold on the black market and abused.

Ritalin has been in use in the US since the early 1960s, initially as a slimming pill, but there have been no definitive longitudinal studies as to its long-term effects. However, evidence is emerging, largely from the US, that there are both physical and psychological consequences of the long-term use of Ritalin and other similar drugs. As it is a stimulant similar to amphetamine it is hardly surprising that long-term users can become physically or psychologically addicted to the substance.

Hyperactivity: an Alternative Approach

Regardless of the cause of ADHD it cannot be denied that there are children whose lives are blighted by their inability to concentrate and thereby fully participate in a 'normal' childhood. If they cannot achieve in school their long-term prospects are also likely to be damaged. Many would also point to the significant impact the condition has on parents and siblings, and to teachers and other students whose classes might be disrupted.

There are two alternative approaches. First, many parents report massive positive outcomes following lifestyle changes, particularly avoiding sugary foods and food additives. Secondly, cognitive behavioural approaches can be employed to manage the behaviour without resorting to drugs. Effective behavioural programmes depend upon the delivery of positive reinforcers (praise), which can be a real challenge when the instinctive reaction to 'naughty' behaviour is reprimand.

FOCUS ON PRACTICE 9.1

What works with ADHD youngsters

- Clearly established rules and boundaries, enforced by discussion and nego-tiation rather than sanctions. Children with ADHD are like other children: they need to be listened to. They have feelings about their situation, which in their calmer moments they will probably want to share.
- Not picking on all minor transgressions, but instead giving praise in any circumstance possible.
- One-to-one, rather than group, activity works well.
- Establish a personal style based upon consistent reactions with a clear and authoritative tone of voice, and be able to exhibit a sense of humour in times of stress ('I always hated that [broken] ornament anyway!').

People with personal experience might say that this approach sounds good but underestimates the highly demanding nature of such children. The answer lies in the carer's support systems, particularly support from other carers and respite care, a chance to get right away to recharge the batteries.

Cannabis-Induced Psychosis: Evaluating Evidence

This section questions the validity of evidence which links mental health issues with their cannabis use without seeking to minimise the suffering of those involved. Even when evidence comes from a credible source, in this case often practising psychiatrists and psychologists, there is still scope for sceptical inter-pretation. Clinicians who see numerous young people, mainly men in their late teens and early 20s, who present with psychotic symptoms, often paranoia, report that they have often used a considerable amount of cannabis over a long period of time. Patients themselves often associate their mental health difficul-ties with cannabis use, and it is therefore easy to assume a causal link between excessive cannabis use and psychosis.

A BBC *Panorama* programme attempted to unpick this assumption from a review of the evidence, they suggest four alternatives that account for this sad clinical observation:

Cannabis use and psychosis

1 *The causal hypothesis* suggests that heavy cannabis use can cause mental disorders such as psychosis.

2 *The dormant hypothesis* argues that cannabis use may precipitate a mental disorder that was previously dormant in individuals who were prone to mental health disorders anyway.

3 *The common cause hypothesis* states that mental illness and cannabis use may simply occur together as a result of common variables, such as unemployment, family difficulties and other drug use. So, arguably, people take to heavy cannabis use as a means of coping with wider social or personal problems.

4 *The self-medication hypothesis* argues that people use cannabis after experiencing signs of a mental health disorder in order to alleviate symptoms. After all, cannabis was once used in psychiatry.

Source: BBC 2005.

This cautionary tale suggests that while in social science it is tempting to search for causal links, real life is seldom that simple. There are intervening variables that stand in the way, in this case considering the reasons why young people turn to excessive cannabis use in the first place, the link with wider deprivation and unhappiness, or a predisposition to psychosis in the first place which might have been triggered or exacerbated but not caused by cannabis.

KEY POINTS

- It is doubtful whether, as statistics suggest, there are many more young people with mental health problems, and possible that we are instead less willing to tolerate difference and need to label more young people.
- It is likely that those labelled with mental health problems come from similar groups to those labelled differently, for example as 'delinquent'. Interventions are largely about policing the poor.
- The concept of resilience is valuable in discussing how to promote good mental health as well as accounting for problem behaviour.
- There are practical and moral issues relating to the mass use of medication, especially to treat ADHD.
- The issue of cannabis-induced psychosis as a diagnosis highlights the need to be sceptical when simple causal links are suggested. There are often other explanations.

RESOURCES

Childhood mental health in general
Maughan, B., Collishaw, S. and Goodman, R. (2004), 'Trends in Adolescence'.
  Downloadable from: www.nuffieldfoundation.org
Goodman R. et al. (2000), *Mental Health and Adolescents in Britain.*

On ADHD
SCIE (2004a), *Assessing and Diagnosing Attention Deficit Hyperactivity Disorder* (ADHD).
SCIE (2004a), *Treating Attention Deficit Hyperactivity Disorder* (ADHD).
Downloadable from: www.scie.org.uk
Website for sufferers, carers and interested professionals: www.addiss.co.uk.

Cannabis-induced psychosis
Full report of the BBC programme summarising the research: www.news.bbc.
  co.uk/go/pr/fr/-/1/hi/programmes/panorama/4109360.stm.

CHAPTER 10

Conclusion: Childcare Futures

Bringing together the theoretical perspectives from earlier chapters, the conclusion reflects upon the legacy of the twentieth century for children's practitioners. It identifies new challenges arising in the twenty-first century, including the child health agenda. It considers the changing lives of children and parents and their relationships in an increasingly materialistic, globalised and technological world.

It discusses whether work with children and families can best be promoted through the citizenship agenda, whether community development approaches can be revived or whether the consumerist model is likely to predominate. It identifies contradictory trends such as more authoritarianism versus greater individuality within a postmodern world.

The impact upon childcare workers is considered in the light of care management, multi-professional teams and service delivery through the mixed economy. The unique contribution of social work, especially the anti-oppressive value system, is considered in the context of likely workforce reforms.

The intent is not to gaze into a crystal ball to predict childcare futures, but to identify the framework upon which future decisions are likely to be taken.

Children's Social Work: a Critique

Evaluation of post Seebohm Children's Services

A number of critical perspectives have been offered to evaluate the success of recent childcare social work.

- From the left: the Marxist perspective. It is not coincidental that most childcare social work is aimed at policing the poor, keeping control and promoting social order in the interests of capitalists. Social work papers over the cracks of the capitalist system which is based upon fundamental inequalities. Despite its value base around anti-oppressive practice, social work has done little to help poor children.
- From the left: a more moderate socialist perspective. The retreat from more

radical social work discourses, which invited workers to identify structural causes for many social work issues, has detracted from social work as a catalyst for social change. Instead of the more political interventions like community work, we now individualise problems through case work, blaming the victims. Social work has largely failed to tackle social inequality.

■ From the right: the nanny state. There is too much costly intervention into the private lives of individuals and families which encourages welfare dependency.

■ The feminist perspective. Women (mothers) are largely the subject of childcare social work interventions. Although much of the legislation refer to 'parents' it is largely mothers who are blamed for their children's problems and can be the subject of punitive interventions (for example prison for their child's truancy). Even when men are perpetrators, for example of sexual abuse, mothers get blamed for failing to protect. Women are also exploited as informal carers, having to interrupt their careers for childcare responsibilities with long-term consequences for earnings and pensions. Women are also exploited in the social care workforce where poor pay and conditions predominate at the lower levels largely occupied by women.

■ From the margins: pressure groups. A variety of pressure groups point to inadequacies in the system: for example, the Children's Society focusing on lack of services for young runaways (see chapter 4) and child sex workers; the Children's Rights Alliance focusing on the overuse of child custody and the poor treatment of unaccompanied asylum-seeking children (see chapter 4); men's groups focusing upon the apparent bias towards mothers in the Courts in custody and contact issues, and many others. Thus, children's social work has continued to fail many children on the margins of society, arguably the very groups it was set up to assist.

■ From minority groups. Poor services are provided to minority ethnic groups. They are over-represented in the more punitive services, for example youth justice (see chapter 8), and seem to be invisible to many more preventative services.

■ Failure to meet the needs of our most vulnerable children, even those within childcare systems, scandals and enquires. Despite 35 years of social services departments, systems still fail to effectively protect some of the most vulnerable children (see chapters 2 and 4).

Additionally, a critical thinker would identify and critique some of the major trends in childcare policies over the last 35 years:

■ There has undoubtedly been much more centralisation through legislation, regulations and guidance. Set standards are imposed through targets and the national service framework. This allows less professional discretion as workers implement set policies and procedures. National standards are positive in that they minimize local variations in service provision (the postcode lottery) but can stifle initiatives designed to respond to personal circumstances or local factors.

- The culture of managerialism has seen managers/accountants set the agenda based upon the financially driven concept of 'efficiency'. 'Best value' is a more recent concept requiring local authorities to consider not only cost in evaluating their services but also a wider concept of value. This approach should lead to services being evaluated on the systems model, particularly aiming to ensure that value is achieved in the longer term, avoiding 'short-termism' (make a cut today regardless of the longer-term effects).
- Children's work has been largely conducted in a hostile external environment, including the negative effect of the media. Whereas nurses are seen as angels, social workers are demonised.
- The blame culture had led to social workers being blamed for child deaths when it is others who kill the child, arguably promoting defensive practice rather than creativity and risk-taking.
- A narrower focus within case-work on individual 'problem' children and families and, within the current culture of responsibilisation, shifting the blame for social problems from structural factors and the state to individual children, families and communities.
- A focus on child protection to the exclusion of other groups in need. Resources have been expended on child protection investigations, leaving many children in need without services until their problem has deteriorated sufficiently to meet high priority group criteria (child protection, accommodation, youth offending or mental health issues).
- A focus on short-term crises, leading to a lack of vision or strategy as suggested by the systems approach.

New Labour's Impact

Several trends have emerged from the New Labour government:

- A more interventionist and controlling state: youth justice, ASBOs, parenting orders, truancy sweeps.
- Even greater centralisation through national service frameworks and targets.
- More policing of services through inspection.
- Limited progress towards listening to children (for example, Minister for Children, children's commissioners, advocacy projects, independent reviewing officers).
- Structural changes, especially promoting working in partnership.
- More marketisation and service provision involving the private and voluntary sectors.
- The responsibilisation agenda which makes individuals, families and communities more responsible for the behaviour – a 'no excuses' approach.

Social Work: A Positive Contribution

In the light of these reservations it is tempting to conclude that childcare social work has offered little since the early 1970s. That is not the case. Many very needy children and families have undoubtedly been helped by the dedication of numerous social care staff. Like children with teachers, young people who have relied on social workers usually have fond tales to tell of the worker who went the extra mile to help them. Of course these personal testimonies are counterbalanced by tales of poor or indifferent practice and resource shortages.

One of the major lasting impacts of social work on the caring professions has been a commitment to values, particularly anti-oppressive and non-judgemental practice, and respect for the individual. Some of these values are now arguably under threat within the new agendas. Social workers have impacted upon other professionals through networking and inter-professional work. Child protection and youth justice provide obvious examples, as does advocating for the social rather than the medical model of illness or disability.

A Modern Critique

A number of social work academics have revitalised the debate about what is wrong with social work as a profession, and where it should go from here. In their 'Manifesto for a New Engaged Practice', they write:

> Many of us entered social work – and many still do – out of a commitment to social justice or, at the very least, to bring about positive change in people's lives. Yet increasingly the scope for doing so is curtailed. Instead, our work is shaped by managerialism, by the fragmentation of services, by financial restrictions and lack of resources, by increased bureaucracy and work-loads, by the domination of care-management approaches with their associated performance indicators and by the increased use of the private sector. While these trends have long been present in state social work, they now dominate the day-to-day work of front line social workers and shape the welfare services, which are offered to clients. The effect has been to increase the distance between managers and front line workers on the one hand, and between workers and service users on the other. The main concern of too many social work managers today is the control of budgets rather than the welfare of service users, while worker–client relationships are increasingly characterised by control and supervision rather than care.' (Jones et al. 2006)

This is the context in which the future of childcare work lies.

Imagining Childcare Futures

This section discusses what childcare social workers will do in the future, where they will do it and, probably most importantly, what values will govern their work, the culture of the profession and its organisational arrangements.

Legal Frameworks and Structures

Organisational arrangements for the early part of the twenty-first century are governed by the Children Act 2004 and its regulations and guidance. Most significantly, the formation of children's trusts has seen the split of social work services for adults from those for children, and more integration between children's professionals in education, health and social care. These arrangements are seen at the strategic level (children's trusts headquarters) and among practitioners based in children's centres and extended schools.

What is significant about these changes has been the shift from service provision by the state towards greater provision by the private and voluntary sectors, and the development of quangos. Consideration of these reforms and the Education and Inspections Act (2006), which gives more autonomy to successful schools by granting them trust status, shows that both the children's trusts that commission children's services and many major providers will be in quangoland (although local authorities are very major stakeholders in children's trusts). Whether these new governance arrangements are an improvement depends on an evaluation of the loss of local democratic accountability against the possible benefits of smaller, arguably more flexible, self-governing bodies.

With private organisations the major issue is whether care and profit mix. There have been exposés of private providers charging high fees for poor services, and sometimes being slack in their application of such processes as Criminal Records Bureau (CRB) checks. It is debatable whether these failings are an inherent problem of capitalism (where the profit motive predominates), or whether they reflect a market situation where children's trusts are often desperate for a service due to under-investment in their own provision, or whether there is a failure in statutory regulation and inspection. For the voluntary sector the challenge remains whether to embrace the contract culture and prosper, or to remain true to their original mission and potentially struggle.

The National Children's Database (Contact Point) has provoked debate on the civil liberties issues as to what data is held and who has access to it. While it will clearly enhance the ability to track children at risk when they move around the country, and potentially internationally, and help co-ordinate services and avoid duplication, professionals must resist the temptation to record too much and collude with the Big Brother state. Parallel debates centre on surveillance technology, obtaining and storing DNA from children in police stations, and drug testing and searching children in schools.

Organisational and Professional Cultures and Values

Since the 1980s there has been a shift from professional autonomy towards the culture of managerialism, with professional practice becoming more accountable through output measures (such as targets and league tables) and day-to-day practice more standardised through national standards, guidance and regulations, and a reliance on forms (the 'tick box' approach).

There has been a more open approach to rationing resources as the rhetoric has shifted from 'quality' to 'efficiency'. Whether the modern concept of quality as evaluated within the regulation culture equates to a more subjective concept of quality – how service users value their services – is an ongoing debate. Arguably such debates have masked the real problem – under-resourcing.

Although there is a long history of partnership working in child protection, it is interesting that the new structural arrangements for children's services based on children's trusts have not set up specialist child protection agencies following the arguably more sophisticated partnership model used, for example, in youth offending teams (YOT) and child and adolescent mental health services (CAMHS). Given the finding in successive enquires following child deaths, that a contributory factor was the failure of different professional to communicate adequately (Laming 2003) it is surprising that different agencies involved in protecting children will not be sitting together in a specialist setting. Work on partnership arrangements suggests that in order to merge various professional cultures and break down rivalry and mistrust, people need to be organisationally located together (Seden and Reynolds 2003).

A major challenge for the new services is how to meaningfully consult children and young people and their families about the services they want and need, and evaluate their participation in the services they consume, and how to redefine the role of children and young people in modern society (Mason and Fattore 2005).

In terms of social work values, the last 20 years have seen two contradictory trends: a move towards a more authoritarian stance and towards consumerism and empowerment. The former has seen education welfare officers move from 'welfarism' to 'truancy sweeps', 'fast track to prosecution', and Courts imposing prison sentences on parents (mothers) for their children not attending school. Similar trends have been seen in practices with young offenders, where social workers have seen their role change from being champions of liberal approaches, to being officers of the court within current YOTs. Similar, though more subtle trends can be found at work within CAMHS, where social constructions of 'naughtiness' are increasingly adopting the medical model of diagnosis and medication.

There remains an uneasy tension between care and control. For example, in child protection we say we want to work in partnership and to offer help to improve parenting, but eventually the decision might be taken to remove the child and/or take care proceedings.

The role of the new Children's Commissioner in England has been widely debated (England being the last of the UK countries to establish this post). Many argue that their inability to investigate individual allegations of injustice (unless asked to do so by the government) suggests that the role is a largely toothless one. It is disappointing that the opportunity was not taken to remove the funding of such things as advocacy services from local authorities, for, as long as social services directly or indirectly funds and awards contracts in these areas of work, the ability of the appointed agencies to contest decisions will be weakened.

One of the interesting debates about multi-professional, inter-agency work is whether the individual professions will retain their individual identity, especially their culture and values, or become merged so that people become 'youth offending workers' or 'child protection workers'. A concern is that the distinct value system of social work could be lost if social workers become minor partners in multi-agency work, either numerically or as relatively low-status professionals.

Professionals used to have considerable control over how they managed their workload. They did a considerable amount of direct work with children and families, and the social work task was framed in a much more political context, for example taking a structural view of people's problems, with interventions including community work and welfare rights advice and advocacy.

Although care management and the purchaser/provider split is not enshrined in childcare legislation, in practice it dominates what statutory social workers actually do. The top priority must be to ensure that regulations are upheld to meet targets, and that resources are allocated (rationed) 'efficiently'. Hence paperwork and purchasing packages from the private or voluntary sectors, or less qualified in-house providers, has largely replaced direct work.

On the other hand, social work has become more professionalised, with the General Social Care Council (GSCC) and its registration and regulatory functions, and the upgrading of social work training to degree status. Indeed, the basic qualification is now seen as a start to further professional development through the PQ award.

Reinventing the 'Problem Family'

An area of increasing tension has been around the legitimacy of state intervention in the private affairs of children and families, and whether such interventions should be 'helpful' or punitive, linked to the crucial political decision as to whether services should be universal or targeted, and whether their use should be voluntary or compulsory. An example is seen in parenting. Some might argue that all parents should have better access to training and support for the various stages of parenting, a highly complex and underrated task. Some feel that parenting is almost innate and only those who fail should be targeted, through ASBOs, parenting orders and child protection procedures. Whether our failure to provide universal parenting services beyond compulsory education and health visiting is a matter of funding or ideology is an interesting debate. Targeting creates stigma, which can promote mistrust between service users and childcare professionals and deter potential service users from seeking help. The challenge for extended schools and children's centres is to create a culture that attracts the whole range of children, rather than just 'the needy'. What is of concern is that the most disaffected parents, who might for example have felt comfortable with the voluntary-led Sure Start, will be alienated from statutory and school-based programmes.

There has been a marked shift in the relationship between the state and parents and children. The blame culture expects parents and children to take full responsibility for their own misdeeds and the role of the state is largely policing. The welfarist rhetoric that problems within families were exacerbated, if not caused, by deprivation and wider social factors is now unfashionable. The modern rhetoric has in some ways reinvented the 'problem family', but rather than seeing these hard-to-reach families as being in need of help, it portrays them as a threat to wider society, and uses punitive approaches to enforce order and conformity.

A recurrent theme in this book has been the shift away from the structuralist perspective (looking for the causes of individual and social problems in terms of wider social factors), towards greater responsibilisation upon individuals and families (victim blaming). This has involved the demonisation and labelling of increasing numbers of young people, as 'truants', young offenders or 'antisocial'. We are told that it may be possible to predict which infant children will progress to become criminals, and that the intervention of people like 'supernannies' is to be offered, and if declined, imposed.

The Demographic Legacy

The demographic legacy from the twentieth century is largely the greater diversity of domestic living arrangements in our society, notably the number of children raised in single-parent, usually female-led households, and those who experience a number of reconstituted households as their parents shift partners.

Another factor is the ageing population, with a predicted crisis in public sector funding as the ratio of taxpayers to dependants worsens and the demand for services increases. This will clearly impact upon resource availability across the board, arguably not just in providing services to elders (see chapter 1).

Evidence-based Practice

The search for evidence of what works has improved the accountability of professionals, although arguably the standardisation of need has undermined the creativity and individuality associated with professionalism. Some evidence-based approaches can be criticised for missing the big picture in a search for interventions that apparently work. For example, in youth justice individual programmes are researched and monitored but there is little questioning of the effectiveness of the whole system.

Can Childcare Social Work Survive?

One way to approach this question is to imagine the customer and worker in childcare services in 20 years' time. Almost certainly there will be a greater delineation between the purchasers and providers, with central commissioning, and provision largely within the private and voluntary sectors. It is likely that services will increasingly be delivered by multi-disciplinary teams, and eventually these teams will no longer be considered multi-disciplinary; they will have adopted their own job titles and career structures. Hopefully within this the skills and values of social workers can survive, although with social workers as a minority group within many multi-professional groups it is questionable.

The writers of the 'Manifesto' (Jones et al 2006) see the way forward in terms of two approaches:

- Greater engagement between social workers and wider social groupings including service user groups and wider interests contesting such things as global capitalism, the 'new collective movements'.
- Restating the concept of an 'ethical career', contesting managerialisation and marketisation and instead sticking to the traditional social work mission of anti-oppressive practice.

Coming Together: The Children's Workforce Strategy

The Childcare Workforce Strategy Group is considering the future needs of the childcare workforce. It is likely that, as well as traditional professional roles merging, training and qualifications will also come together, promoting greater flexibility and movement between the various aspects of work with children. For example, it could be that qualification courses for teachers, social workers and other children's professionals will contain a common core of knowledge and skills followed by some specialism.

Conceptualising the Service User

There remains a lack of clarity about how we construct childhood, whether children are seen almost as naughty animals that must be tamed, or in terms of an investment for the economic future of the country, or as innocents in need of protection. The increasing influence of the children's rights movement suggests that the child, rather than the adults in their lives, should be the focus of any intervention in modern society.

Social constructions of users of public services have progressed from their being seen as passive recipients of what public services offered (as 'patients', 'clients' or 'pupils'), to more complex and often contradictory constructions. Hughes et al. (1998) developed a model to envisage the future of welfare users in general which can be applied to children's services. They saw future consumers as being:

1 *Customers.* Following from the marketisation of services within the mixed economy of care, service users are now seen as customers or quasi-customers (their purchasing power is exercised by a third party, a care manager or a GP, for example). Customers can expect quality services and where poor services are provided have the right to complain or take their business elsewhere. In a competitive market poor quality providers should lose business and be forced to leave the market and good quality ones will prosper and expand.

The trend towards consumerism has developed from the concept of working in partnership with parents and young people enshrined in the Children Act 1989. Since then we have seen the growth of advocacy services, and children and young people and parents being more involved in care planning. In some cases responsibility has been handed back to children and families, for example through family group conferences and direct payments for children with disabilities.

2   *Citizens.*   New Labour have revitalized the concept of citizenship, whether considering citizenship tests for immigrants seeking British citizenship, the study of citizenship in the national curriculum at Key Stage 4 or a wider concept of citizenship based on a revised contract between the state and the welfare subject based around rights and responsibilities, for example, seeking work as a condition of claiming benefits, making the best of educational opportunities, and the 'respect' agenda.

3   *Community members.*   'Community' can be seen as either a place or a group with common interests, for example the gay community. 'Community' used to be seen as a site for the delivery of state services (see chapter 7 on the demise of 'community work'), and informal childcare services (people supporting each other). In the last half-century demographic and policy factors have promoted a decline in the importance of communities for individuals and in the delivery of welfare. However, Hughes et al. (1998) discuss two models that could revitalize the concept of 'community'. The first, communitarianism, is a largely moral discourse emanating from the political right, suggesting that communities should take a more involved role in the problems facing them, by for example 'owning' anti-social and other problematic behaviour rather than leaving them to the state. A similar discourse from the left argues that communities could be used as a medium for contesting present state authoritarianism and repressive interventions. Either position would require community members to come together in new alliances to promote grass roots service developments. The greater powers given to school governors and the use of lay people on referral panels in youth justice are examples of policies moving in this direction.

Challenges for the Twenty-first Century

Arguably the way to real service improvements lies not in tinkering with existing systems but in adopting some 'blue skies' thinking to create a society that values children and parenting (not in the current blaming and punitive manner through parenting orders) and is prepared to divert the necessary resources to make every child really matter.

A concern is whether the merging of education and social services children's functions into children's trusts under a supreme director will adequately address the issues raised in the Laming Report (2003) and earlier ones about the impact of dysfunctional organisational cultures upon accountability, and hence outcomes in child protection (see chapter 4).

The overall aim of children's work should be ensuring that every child has a happy childhood that prepares them for the challenges of adult life. Although the meaning of 'happy' might be contested (Layard 2005), as will the means of achieving it, what is clear is that major inequalities of opportunity and outcome continue to exist, and these undermine the aspiration of government policy that 'Every Child Matters'. This book has examined a number of cases where groups of children and young people continue to be socially excluded, not through their own failings but because of structural factors in wider society.

The Child Well-Being Agenda

A modern challenge to all workers with children is to recognize that the twentieth century has left a serious legacy in terms of the health and broader well-being of our children.

UNICEF (2007) has argued that children in the UK have the worst sense of well-being among 20 comparable richer countries. The report considered material well-being, health and safety, education, peer and family relationships, behaviour and risks and the child's subjective view of their own well-being.

PRACTICE CONTEXT 10.1

Well-being among UK children
- UK child poverty has doubled since 1979.
- 16 per cent of children living in homes earning less than half national average wage.
- 43 per cent of children rating their peers as 'kind and helpful'.
- 66 per cent of families eating a meal together 'several times' a week.
- 31 per cent of children admit being drunk on two or more occasions.

Source: UNICEF 2007.

The Children's Commissioner for England commented: 'We are turning out a generation of young people who are unhappy, unhealthy, engaging in risky behaviour, who have poor relationships with their family and their peers, who have low expectations and don't feel safe' (BBC News, 14 Feb. 2007).

Chapter 9 focused upon child and adolescent mental health, but equally worrying is the physical health of our children. Obesity and poor diet, coupled with insufficient exercise, are probably the main factors limiting life expectancy through contributing to illnesses such as heart problems and Type 2 diabetes (Foresight Thinktank 2007). For some, overeating is an obsessive compulsive disorder, but the majority of children simply overeat sugary and fatty foods as a normal part of their childhood experience. Worse, the likelihood of change is constrained by modern young parents also tending to consume a diet of junk and convenience food, with little concept of nutrition, the value of home cooking or the social value of eating together. The Foresight (2007) report estimates that, with an emphasis upon individual and societal change, it will take around 30 years to reverse current trends.

Childcare professionals have shied away from engaging in this area, feeling that they could be criticised for interfering in matters private to families, but the problem is now so severe that ways must be found to keep health and wider well-being higher on the professional agenda. It has even been suggested that parents allowing their children to become obese could be subjected to child protection investigations.

Another new area of concern is the impact of the Internet on children's lives. Clearly the biggest challenge is to protect children from sexual grooming through chatrooms and from inappropriate exposure to a wide variety of unsuitable material. A dedicated police squad, Operation Orr, is the major UK contribution to the tackling of this worldwide problem. As usual the most vulnerable children are likely to be least protected, especially as it is almost impossible to effectively police the Internet at national or international levels. The best hope is for controls to be exercised at the point of use by parents and other carers.

Childcare in a Postmodern and Globalised World

The concept of postmodernism arises from the realisation that modernism (associated with 'Fordism', that is, one size fits all), is an outmoded concept, that the modern public, constructed as consumers, want to make a wide range of personal choices that reflect their individuality. While this adequately reflects the development of the industrialised world, arguably children's social services are moving in the opposite direction, with a greater emphasis upon standardisation in our 'tick box' world. Individuality is constrained by requirements to conform and punitive policies towards those who fail to do so.

Globalisation impacts upon childcare services in a number of ways. Muncie (2006) suggests that the needs of international trade and global capital means that individual governments are constrained in the economic and social policies they can follow, and that there has tended to be international harmonisation of policies around social inequality, deregulation, privatization, penal expansion and welfare residualism. This restricts the amount of welfare on offer and promotes a conceptualization of the service user in terms of being either vulnerable or a threat, rather than accepting a more structural view of 'need'.

Global consumerism opens the door to the exploitation of children from across the world who become trafficked internationally, usually being lured to Western countries to enter the sex trade. A similar problem is found in 'sex tourism' where affluent westerners exploit children as sex workers in their home countries.

Childcare and Modern Britishness

This section considers working with children in a multi-cultural society where even something as apparently simple as the concept of 'Britishness' is highly contested. Terms such as 'race', 'colour', and 'ethnicity' are difficult to define, and even more difficult to apply operationally, However, we know that discrimination persists based upon these factors, despite many ethnic minority people being born in the UK, as were their parents and often grandparents. A more helpful approach is to examine where we as individuals seek to gain our sense of personal and cultural identity.

Having a concept of Britishness is important for determining:

- how the nation is run and our relationships with the rest of the world (are we still a 'world power' and how is this connected with our colonial history?)
- our personal sense of identity
- a concept of national 'culture'.

Even being 'British' might be insufficient to locate our identity in the globalised world, our geographic identification presents a number of personal possibilities. Clearly the challenge for practitioners is to get beyond race and religion and consider the multiplicity of factors that impact upon individual identity, for example an Asian teenager who wishes to develop a Western identity which contradicts their family cultural values. The following Practice Context suggests a hierarchy of geographical statuses and some of the reasons why we might relate to them:

PRACTICE CONTEXT 10.2

Sources of Identity

Global	Free trade
	Economic issues (labour outsourcing)
	Migration (economic or refugee)
	Travel and tourism
	The Internet
European Union	United States of Europe
	Policy harmonisation
	Subsidiarity (where policy should be made)
Great Britain/ United Kingdom	Sovereignty (£ v Euro)
	Relations with the US
	Commonwealth legacy
	Role in the world e.g. defence
UK nations	Devolution
	National identities
Regions	Regional assemblies
Local authorities	Decentralisation v standardisation
	Role of local democracy v other modes of decentralization
Communities	Geographical or common interest
Households/families	Nuclear, extended, reconstituted
	Geographically mobile
Other affiliations	Neighbours
	Social groupings (church, union, etc.)
	Friendships

I am English, although my passport says that I am a citizen of the European Union. I travel abroad, so like to adopt a partial global identity. As a consumer I benefit from low-priced imports from developing countries (although I have concerns about the exploitation of workers and wider issues around global capitalism), yet I live in a locality, and in many ways that is the most important place for my sense of belonging and personal security. If my simple personal position seems complex, then the challenge for modern professionals is to appreciate and value the far more complex experiences of many of our service users.

There are two competing visions of our developing multi-cultural society. First, assimilation: the vision that we should fully integrate minority religious and ethnic groups. Political rhetoric suggests that people who wish to live in the UK should be prepared to assimilate into our society, for example being prepared to learn English and undertake a citizenship test to apply for British nationality. The other major discourse is multi-culturalism. This celebrates the diversity of minority groups in society and recognises the rights of each minority group to pursue their own cultural values, from which we all gain enrichment.

A number of significant reports have informed our concerns about failings in multi-cultural Britain and our critical analysis needs to be informed by the wider oppressions faced by minority groups, and the possibility that our services could be contributing to that picture.

PRACTICE CONTEXT 10.3

Racial tensions

Scarman Report 1981 (into the Brixton Riots):

Housing stress (37 per cent on housing waiting list were black)
Disproportionate number of black people unemployed/in poverty
Poor educational achievement
Heavy-handed policing
Lack of social and leisure amenities.

Macpherson Report 1999 (into the murder of Stephen Lawrence):

Metropolitan Police are 'institutionally racist'.

Ouseley Report 2001 (into the Bradford riots):

Fragmented communities
Deteriorating race relations
Recommended neighbourhood renewal strategy.

Cantel Report 2005 (into riots in northern cities in 2001):

Asian and white youths living 'parallel lives'
Recommended strategy for tackling segregation and promoting 'community cohesion'
Danger of 'sleepwalking into segregation'
Ethnic alienation and extremism fostered by people living in ghettos
Muslims are three times more likely to be unemployed than white people.

As with child protection scandals (see chapter 4), this list reflects a sad failure in society to learn the lessons of the past, over 25 years of wasted opportunities to develop a truly inclusive society. Sadly debate around race and inclusion is now often negative, with commentators fearing the further fragmentation of society, for example, the suggested threat posed by asylum seekers and migrant workers, and the supposed link between terrorism and the alienation and radicalization of some young Muslims.

For practitioners there are a number of issues, for example the debate about inclusive schooling with policies to make schools more culturally diverse, versus the demand for more faith schools. For those involved in allocating work, while there is a general aspiration that any particular team should reflect the social mix of the community it serves, the reality is often far from that. The question becomes how to maximize the benefit of minority people in the team: do they act as race consultant, do they undertake work with minority service users, or do we pretend that race is not an issue (colour blindness)?

These two examples illustrate a major theme in this book, and therefore offer a fitting final statement: that critical analysis might not offer definitive solutions to intractable problems, but it can provide frameworks for at least knowing what the problems are.

KEY POINTS

- A critique of children's social work over the last half-century suggests that, despite much valuable work, little has been achieved in creating a more inclusive society and impacting upon fundamental inequalities.
- There are contradictory trends as to whether future users of children's services will be constructed as customers, citizens or community members.
- Social work value systems have been compromised by managerialism and the profession will struggle to maintain its value base given the split between adult and children's social work and under the new inter-professional organisational arrangements.
- Social work has to find a new role within a globalised and postmodern world, just as individuals have to acquire meaningful identities in modern multi-cultural society.

RESOURCES

Jones, C., Ferguson, I. et al. (2006), 'Manifesto for a New Engaged Practice' can be downloaded from: www.liv.ac.uk/sspsw/Social_Work_Manifesto.html

UNICEF (2007), *Child Poverty in Perspective: An Overview of Child Wellbeing in Rich Countries.*

Childhood obesity

A House of Commons Report: 'Childhood Obesity' (2003) introduces this. Downloadable from www.parliament.uk/post/pn205.pdf

Internet protection

A good starting point in this evolving area is the NSPCC resources list (2005), 'Child Abuse on the Internet: a Selection of Materials for Professionals'. Downloadable from: www.nspcc.org.uk.

For parents seeking more information on how to protect their children effectively there is a Home Office recommended helpline (08456 008844) and website: www.iwf.org.uk/safe/tool/htm.

References

Achenbach, T. M. et al. (2003) 'Are American Children's Problems Still Getting Worse?' *Journal of Abnormal Child Psychology*, 31, 1–11.

Action on Rights for Children (2007) 'How Effective are Truancy Sweeps?' Available at www. arch-ed.org/truancy/tsr05.htm.

Adams, R. (2002) *Social Policy for Social Work* (Basingstoke: Palgrave Macmillan).

Adams, R., Dominelli, L. and Payne, M. (2002) *Critical Practice in Social Work* (Basingstoke: Palgrave Macmillan).

Adams R., Dominelli, L. and Payne, M. (2005) *Social Work Futures* (Basingstoke: Palgrave Macmillan).

Adoption and Children Act 2002 (London: HMSO). Available at http://opsi.gov.uk/acts.htm.

Adoption (Intercountry Aspects) Act 1999 (London: HMSO). Available at http://opsi.gov.uk/acts.htm.

Alinsky, S. (1971) *Rules for Radicals* (New York: Vintage).

Allen, M. (2003) *Into the Mainstream: Care Leavers Entering Work, Education and Training* (York: Joseph Rowntree Foundation). Available at www.jrf.org.uk.

Appleby, L. et al. (2006) *Report on the Implementation of Standard 9 of the National Service Framework for Children, Young People and Maternity Services* (London: DfES/DoH). Available at www.doh.gov.uk.

Archer, S. (1979) 'Gender Role Learning', in J. Coleman (ed.), *The School Years* (London: Routledge), 56–80.

Asylum and Immigration Act 2004 (London: HMSO). Available at http://opsi.gov.uk/acts.htm.

Baily, R. and Break, M. (1975) *Radical Social Work* (London: Edward Arnold).

Baldwin, N. and Walker, L. (2005) 'Assessment', in R. Adams, L. Dominelli and M. Payne, *Social Work Futures* (Basingstoke: Palgrave Macmillan).

Banks, S. (2004) *Ethics, Accountability and the Social Professionals* (Basingstoke: Palgrave Macmillan).

Barn, R. et al. (2005) *Life after Care: The Experiences of Young People from Different Ethnic Groups* (York: Joseph Rowntree Foundation). Available at www.jrf.org.uk.

Barnardo's (2006) *Failed by the System: The Views of Young Care Leavers on their Educational Experiences* (London: Barnardo's). Available at www.barnardos.org.uk/failed_by_the_system_report.pdf.

BBC (2005) 'Cannabis: What Teenagers Need to Know', *Panorama* (19 June), BBC.

Beckett, C. (2003) *Child Protection* (London: Sage).

Beishon, S., Modood, T. and Virdee, S. (1994) *Ethnic Minority Families* (London: Policy Studies Institute).

Benjamin, A. (2004) 'Childish Argument', *Guardian*, 'Society' supplement (14 July). Available at www.guardian.co.uk/society/2004/jul/14/childrensservices.schools.

Bennett, T. (2000) *Drugs and Crime: Home Office Research Study 205* (London: HMSO). Available at www.homeoffice.gov.uk/rds/pdfs/hors205.pdf.

Berridge, D. and Brodie, I. (1998) *Children's Homes Revisited* (London: Jessica Kingsley).

Bichard Enquiry Report into the Soham Murders 2004 (London: HMSO). Available at www.homeoffice.gov.uk/pdf/bichard_report.pdf.

Bilson, A. and Ross, S. (1999) *Social Work Management and Practice: Systems Principles* (London: Jessica Kingsley).

Boarding Out Regulations (1955) (London: HMSO).

Bostock, L., Bairstow, S., Fish, S. and McLeod, F. (2005) *Managing Risk and Minimising Mistakes in Services to Children and Families* (London: SCIE). Available at www.scie.org.uk/publications/reports/report06.pdf.

Bowlby, J. (1971) *Attachment and Loss* (Harmondsworth: Penguin).

Brake, M. (1985) *Comparative Youth Subcultures* (London: Routledge & Kegan Paul).

Brake, M. (2005) *Comparative Youth Culture* (London: Routledge and Kegan Paul).

Brammer, A. (2003) *Social Work Law* (Harlow: Longman).

Brayne, S. and Preston-Shoot, M. (2004) *Teaching, Learning and Assessment of Law in Social Work Education* (London: SCIE). Available at www.scie.org.uk/publications/knowledgereviews/kr08.pdf.

Bridget, J. (n.d.) 'Lesbians, Gays and Suicide: Research Findings'. Available at www.lesbianinformationservice.org (accessed 27 December 2007).

British Institute for Brain Injured Children (2005) *Ain't Misbehavin': Young People with Learning and Communication Difficulties and Anti-Social Behaviour* (London: BIBIC). Available at www.bibic.org.uk/newsite/general/pdfs/ASBOandYOTsummary.pdf.

Broad, B. (2003) *After the Act: Implementing the Children (Leaving Care) Act 2000* (Leicester: De Montfort University). Available at www.dmu.ac.uk/faculties/hls/research/cfru/publications.jsp.

Brown, K. and Rutter, L. (2006) *Critical Thinking and Analysis* (Exeter: Learning Matters).

Bullock, R., Little, M. and Millham, S. (1993) *Residential Care for Children: A Review of the Literature* (London: HMSO).

Butler-Sloss, E. (1998) *Report of the Enquiry into Child Abuse in Cleveland* (London: HMSO).

Care Standards Tribunal (2004) 268PC.

Carlile Inquiry (2006) *The Carlile Inquiry* (London: Howard League for Penal Reform).

Casson, R. and Kingdom, C. (2007) *Tackling Low Educational Achievement* (York: Joseph Rowntree Foundation). Available at www.jrf.org.uk.

Census 2001, cited in *Social Trends 2004* (London: HMSO). Available at www.statistics.gov.uk/downloads/theme_social/Social_Trends37/Social_Trends_37.pdf.

Charities Act 2006 (London: HMSO). Available at http://opsi.gov.uk/acts.htm.

Children Act 1989 (London: HMSO) (and associated volumes of Regulations and Guidance). Available at http://opsi.gov.uk/acts.htm.

Children Act 2004 (London: HMSO). Available at http://opsi.gov.uk/acts.htm.

Children and Young Persons Act 1933 (London: HMSO). Available at http://opsi.gov.uk/acts.htm.

Children and Young Persons Act 1969 (London: HMSO). Available at http://opsi.gov.uk/acts.htm.

Children (Contact) and Adoption Act 2005 (London: HMSO). Available at http://opsi.gov.uk/acts.htm.

Children (Leaving Care) Act 2000 (London: HMSO). Available at http://opsi.gov.uk/acts.htm.

Children's Rights Alliance (2002a) *Rethinking Child Imprisonment* (London: CRA). Available at www.cra.org.uk.

Children's Rights Alliance (2002b) *State of Children's Rights in England* (London: CRA). Available at www.cra.org.uk.

Children's Rights Alliance (2003) *Review of UK Government Action on 2002, Concluding Observations of the UK Committee on the Rights of the Child* (London: CRA). Available at www.cra.org.uk.

Children's Rights Officers and Advocates (2000) *Total Respect* (London: CROA).

Children's Society (2004) *Thrown Away: Young People Forced to Leave Home* (London: Children's Society). Available at www.childrenssociety.org.uk/resources/documents/Research/Thrown_Away_The_experience_of_children_forced_to_leave_home_3205_full.pdf.

Children's Society (2005) *Safe and Sound?* (London: Children's Society).

Children's Society (2006) *Good Childhood: A Question of our Times* (London: Children's Society). Available at www.childrenssociety.org.uk/resources/documents/good%20childhood/Executive%20summary%20of%20launch%20report_2723_full.pdf.

Clare, A. (2000) *On Men: Masculinity in Crisis* (London: Chatto and Windus).

Clarke, J., Cochrane, A. and McLaughlin, E. (1994) *Managing Social Policy* (London: Sage).

Clayden, J. and Stein, M. (2005) *Mentoring Young People Leaving Care: Someone for Me* (York: Joseph Rowntree Foundation). Available at www.jrf.org.uk.

Cliffe D. (1991) *Closing Children's Homes: An End to Residential Care?* (London: NCB).

Clough, R., Bullock, R. and Ward, A. (2006) *What Works in Residential Child Care* (London: NCB). Summary available at www.ncb.org.uk/ncercc/ncercc%20practice%20documents/whatworksinrccsummary_ncbhighlight.pdf.

Cohen, S. (1973) *Folk Devils and Moral Panics* (St Albans: Paladin).

Coleman, J. (1999) 'The Trouble with Teenagers', *Community Care* supplement (7 Oct.).

Coleman, J. and Hendry, L. (1999) *The Nature of Adolescence* (London: Routledge).

Community Care (1996) 'Blasts from the Past', *Community Care* (1 Aug.).

Connolly, M., Crichton-Hill, Y. and Ward, T. (2006) *Culture and Child Protection: Reflexive Responses* (London: Jessica Kingsley).

Conrad, C. (2007) *Fathers Matter*, 2nd edn (London: Creative Communication).

Coppick, V. (1997) 'Mad, Bad or Misunderstood', in P. Scraton et al. (eds), *Childhood in Crisis* (London: UCL Press), ch. 7.

Corrigan, P. and Leonard, P. (1977) *Social Work Practice under Capitalism: A Marxist Approach* (Basingstoke: Macmillan).

Cottrell, S. (2003) *The Study Skills Handbook* (Basingstoke: Palgrave Macmillan).

Coxall, W., Robins, L. and Leach, R. (2003) *Contemporary British Politics* (Basingstoke: Palgrave Macmillan).

Crawley, H. and Lester, T. (2005) *No Place for a Child* (London: Save the Child).

CSCI (2002) *Arrangements to Safeguard Children* (London: CSCI).

CSCI (2005) *Arrangements to Safeguard Children* (London: CSCI).

Currie, C. et al. (2004) *Health Policy for Children and Adolescents 4* (Copenhagen: WHO). Available at www.euro.who.int/Document/EHI/ENHIS_Factsheet_2_3.pdf.

Curtis Committee (1946) *Report of the Care of Children Committee* (London: HMSO).

Daniel, B., Featherstone, B., Hooper, C. and Scourfield, J. (2005) 'Why Gender Matters for Every Child Matters', *British Journal of Social Work*, 35(8), 1343–55.

Department for Children, Schools and Families (2007a) *Aiming High for Young People* (London: DfCSF). Available at www.hm-treasury.gov.uk/media/2/6/cyp_tenyearstrategy_260707.pdf.

Department for Children, Schools and Families (2007b) *Care Matters: Time for Change* (White Paper) (London: DfCSF). Available at www.dfes.gov.uk/consultations/conResults.cfm?consultationId=1406.

Department for Education and Skills (2003) *Every Child Matters* (London: HMSO). Available at www.dfes.gov.uk/everychildmatters.

Department for Education and Skills (2005) *Youth Matters* (Green Paper) (London: HMSO). Available at www.dfes.gov.uk/everychildmatters.

Department for Education and Skills (2006a) *Working Together to Safeguard Children*, 2nd edn (London: HMSO). Available at www.dfes.gov.uk/everychildmatters.

Department for Education and Skills (2006b) *Care Matters: Looked After Children* (Green Paper) (London: HMSO). Available at www.dfes.gov.uk/everychildmatters.

Department for Education and Skills (2006c) *Referrals, Assessments, and Children and Young People on Child Protection Registers, England, Year Ending 31–3–06*. Available at www.dfes.gov.uk/rsgateway.

Department for Education and Skills (2006d) *Children Looked After in England 2005–6*. Available at www.dfes.gov.uk/rsgateway.

Department for Education and Skills (2006e) *Children Accommodated in Secure Children's Homes*, March 2006, available at www.dfes,gov,uk/rsgateway.

Department of Health (1995) *Child Protection: Messages from Research* (London: HMSO).

Department of Health (1998) *Modernising Social Services* (London: HMSO).

Department of Health (2000) *Framework for the Assessment of Children in Need and their Families* (London: HMSO). Available at www.doh.gov.uk.

Department of Health (2002) *Children Missing from Care or Home* (London: HMSO). Available at www.doh.gov.uk.

Department of Health (2004) *Best Practice Guidance for Doctors and Other Health Professionals on the Provision of Advice and Treatment to Young People Under 16 on Contraception, Sexual and Reproductive Health* (London: HMSO). Available at www.doh.gov.uk.

Department of Health (2006) *The Needs and Effective Treatment of Young People who Sexually Abuse: Current Evidence* (London: HMSO). Available at www.doh.gov.uk.

Department of Work and Pensions (2007) *Households Below Average Income, 1994/5 to 2005/6* (London: HMSO); available at www.dwp.gov.uk.

Dickens, C. (1839) *Oliver Twist* (Ware: Wordsworth Classics).

Dixon, J. and Stein, M. (2005) *Leaving Care: Throughcare and After Care in Scotland* (London: Jessica Kingsley).

Dominelli, L. (2002a) *Anti-Oppressive Social Work Theory and Practice* (Basingstoke: Palgrave Macmillan).

Dominelli, L. (2002b) *Feminist Social Work Theory and Practice* (Basingstoke: Palgrave Macmillan).

Douglas A. (2006) 'Divorce and Separation: What about the Children?' *Community Care* (7 Sept.). Available at www.communitycare.co.uk/Articles/2006/09/07/55603/divorce-and-separationwhat-about-the-children.html.

Easton, C. and Carpentieri, J. (2004) 'Can I Talk to You Again?' Available at www.childline.org.uk.

Education and Inspections Act 2006 (London: HMSO). Available at http://opsi.gov.uk/acts.htm.

Edwards, T. (2004) 'Sexuality', in J. Roche and S. Tucker, *Youth in Society* (London: Sage).

Edwards, T. (2006) *Cultures of Masculinity* (London: Routledge).

End Child Poverty (2005) *Ten Policies to Take One Million Children out of Poverty by 2010*. Available at www.ecp.com.

Equal Opportunities Commission (2005) *Men into Childcare* (London: EOC). Available at www.equalityhumanrights.com/Documents/EOC/PDF/Research/Occupational%20segregation%20GFI%20Great%20Britain%20progress%20report.pdf.

Erooga, M. (2002) *Adult Sex Offenders* (London: NSPCC). Available at www.nspcc.org.uk/Inform/informhub_wda49931.html.

European Social Network (2005) 'Promoting Inclusion for Unaccompanied Young Asylum Seekers and Immigrants'. Available at www.socialeurope.com.

Evans, G. (2006) *Educational Failure and White Working Class Children in Britain* (Basingstoke: Palgrave Macmillan).

Family Law Act 1996 (London: HMSO). Available at http://opsi.gov.uk/acts.htm.

Farmer, E. and Moyers, S. (2005) *Children Placed with Family and Friends: Placement Patterns and Outcomes* (London: HMSO). Available at www.fipr.org/policy.htmlwww.bristol.ac.uk/sps/research/fpcw/default.shtml.

Fawcett, B. et al. (2004) *Contemporary Child Care Policy and Practice* (Basingstoke: Palgrave Macmillan).

Finkelhor, D. (1986) *A Sourcebook on Child Sexual Abuse* (London: Sage).

Foundation for Information Policy Research (2006) *Children's Databases: Safety and Privacy* (Sandy: FIPR). Available at www.fipr.org/policy.html.

Fook, J. (1992) *Radical Casework: A Theory of Practice* (London: Allen and Unwin).

Fook, J. (2002) *Social Work: Critical Theory and Practice* (London: Sage).

Foresight Thinktank (Government Office for Science) (2007) *Tackling Obesity: Future Choices* (London: HMSO). Available at www.foresight.gov.uk/Obesity/obesity_final/17.pdf.

Fox Harding, L. (1997) *Perspectives in Child Care Policy*, 2nd edn (Harlow: Longman).

Frampton, P. (2004) *The Golly in the Cupboard* (Manchester: Tamic).

Franklin, B. and Larsen, G. (1995) 'The Murder of Innocence', *Community Care* (2 Feb.).

Freedom to Care (n.d.) 'The Charter of Public Accountability' (online). Available from www.freedomtocare.org/page313.htm, accessed 9.03.08.

Frosh, S. et al. (2005) *Emergent Identities: Masculinity and 11–14 Year Old Boys* (London: ESRC). Available at www.esrcsocietytoday.ac.uk.

Galilee, J. (n.d.) *Literature Review on Media Representation of Social Work and Social Workers* (Edinburgh: Scottish Executive). Available at www.socialworkscotland.org.uk/resources/pub/SocialWorkersandtheMedia.pdf.

Gardner, R. (2003) *Family Support* (London: NSPCC). Available at www.nspcc.org.uk/Inform/informhub_wda49931html.

Garrett, P. (2003) 'Swimming with Dolphins: The Assessment Framework, New Labour and New Tools for Social Work with Children and Families'. *British Journal of Social Work*, 33(4), 441–63.

General Social Care Council (2002) *Code of Practice for Social Care Workers* (London: GSCC). Available at www.gscc.org.uk.

Gibbons, J. and Wilkinson, P. (1990) *Family Support and Prevention: Studies in Local Areas* (London: HMSO).

Glass, N. (2004) 'Childish Argument', *Guardian*, 14 July 2004.

Goldthorpe, J., Lockwood, D., Bechhofer, F. and Platt, J. (1969) *The Affluent Worker in the Class Structure* (Cambridge: Cambridge University Press).

Gondolf, W. (1994) *Men Who Batter: An Integrated Approach for Stopping Wife Abuse* (New York: Learning Publications).

Goodman, R. et al. (2000) *Mental Health and Adolescents in Britain* (London: ONS). Available at www.ons.gov.uk.

Gosling, P. and D'Arcy, M. (1998) *Abuse of Trust: Frank Beck and the Leicestershire Children's Home Scandal* (London: Bowerdean).

Green, R. (2002) *Mentally Ill Parents and Children's Welfare* (London: NSPCC). Available at www.nspcc.org.uk/Inform/informhub_wda49931.html.

Grier, A. and Thomas, T. (2005) 'Troubled and in Trouble: Young People, Truancy and Offending', in R. Adams, L. Dominelli and M. Payne, *Social Work Futures* (Basingstoke: Palgrave Macmillan), 128–40.

GTC (2006) 'Inter-Professional Values Underpinning Work with Children and Young People', *Teaching: The GTC Magazine* (autumn 2006). Available at www.gtce. org.uk/shared/contentlibs/145247/145250/176617/GTC_Magazine_Autumn_2 006.pdf.

Hackett, S., Masson, H. and Phillips, S. (2005) *Mapping and Exploring Services for Young People who Have Sexually Abused Others* (London: YJB). Available at www.youth-justice-board.gov.uk.

Halsey, A. H., Lauder, H., Brown, P. and Stuart Wells, A. (1997) *Education: Culture, Economy, and Society* (Oxford: Oxford University Press).

Haynes, K. (2002) 'Youth Justice and Young Offenders', in R. Adams, L. Dominelli and M. Payne, *Critical Practice in Social Work* (Basingstoke: Palgrave Macmillan), 137–48.

Hester, M. and Westmarland, N. (2005) *Tackling Domestic Violence: Effective Interventions and Approaches* (London: Home Office). Available at www.homeoffice.gov.uk/rds.

Hicks, S. (2005) 'Sexuality: Social Work Theory and Practice', in R. Adams, L. Dominelli and M. Payne (2005), *Social Work Futures* (Basingstoke: Palgrave Macmillan), 141–51.

HM Government (2006) *Reaching Out: An Action Plan on Social Exclusion* (London: HMSO). Available at www.cabinetoffice.gov.uk/social_exclusion_task_ force/publications/reaching_out.aspx.

Home Office (2005) *Tackling Domestic Violence: Proving Advocacy and Support to Survivors of Domestic Violence* (London: HMSO). Available at www.homeoffice. gov.uk/rds.

Home Office (2006a) *Young People and Crime: Findings from 2005 Offending Crime and Justice Survey* (London: HMSO). Available at www.homeoffice.gov.uk/rds.

Home Office (2006b) *Criminal Statistics 2005* (London: HMSO). Available at www. ons.gov.uk.

Home Office (2007) *Crime in England and Wales 2006/7* (The British Crime Survey) (London: HMSO). Available at www.ons.gov.uk.

Home Office Youth Offenders Unit (2003) *Youth Justice: The Next Steps* (London: HMSO). Available at www.everychildmatters.gov.uk/_files/EF7067D73CCE91 F94E771F4312C55F3F.pdf.

Homelessness Act 2002 (London: HMSO). Available at http://opsi.gov.uk/acts.htm.

House of Commons (2003) *Childhood Obesity* (London: HMSO). Available at www.Parliament.uk/post/pn205/pdf.

Howarth, J. (1999) 'Inter-Agency Practice in Suspected Cases of Munchausen Syndrome by Proxy', *Child and Family Social Work*, 4, 109–18.

Howe, D. (2005) *Child Abuse and Neglect: Attachment, Development and Intervention* (Basingstoke: Palgrave Macmillan).

Hughes, G. (ed.) (1998) *Imagining Welfare Futures* (London: Routledge).

Human Rights Act 1998 (London: HMSO). Available at http://opsi.gov.uk/acts.htm.

Hunt, G. (ed.) (1998) *Whistleblowing in the Social Services* (London: Hodder Arnold).

Hunt, R. and Jensen, J. (2007) *The School Report: Experiences of Young Gay People in British Schools* (London: Stonewall). Available at www.stonewall.org.uk/documents/school_report.pdf.

Hunter, B. and Payne, B. (n.d.) *Research Programme Series: Being Healthy* (Leicester: National Youth Agency). Available at www.nya.org.uk/shared_asp_files/uploadedfiles/1f2403e8–6564–4dad-8f48-f812fd5b48fb_beinghealthy.pdf.

Hunter, B. and Payne, B. (n.d.) *Research Programme Series: Enjoying and Achieving* (Leicester: National Youth Agency). Available at www.nya.org.uk/shared_asp_files/uploadedfiles/721f25f8–3b8c-4b88–9e57–437fa41028ef_enjoyingandachieving.pdf.

Illich, I. (1971) *Deschooling Society* (Harmondsworth: Penguin).

IPPR (2006) *Freedom's Orphans: Raising Youth in a Changing World* (London: IPPR). Available at www.ippr.org/members/download.asp?f=%2Fecomm%2Ffiles%2Ffreedoms%5Forphans%5Fexec%5Fsumm%2Epdf.

Jack, G. (1997) 'An Ecological Approach to Social Work with Children and Families', *Child and Family Social Work*, 2, 109–20.

Jack, G. and Owen, G. (2003) *The Missing Side of the Triangle* (London: Barnardo's).

James, A. and James, A. (2004) *Constructing Childhood* (Basingstoke: Palgrave Macmillan).

Joint Chief Inspectors' Report (Second) (2005) *Safeguarding Children* (London: HMSO). Available at www.safeguardingchildren.org.uk.

Jones, C., Ferguson, I. et al. (2006) 'Manifesto for a New Engaged Practice'. Available at www.liv.ac.uk/sspsw/Social_Work_Manifesto.html.

Joseph Rowntree Foundation (1996) *Domestic Violence and Child Contact Arrangements* (York: Joseph Rowntree Foundation). Available at www.jrf.org.uk.

Joseph Rowntree Foundation (1998) *Domestic Violence in Work with Abused Children* (York: Joseph Rowntree Foundation). Available at www.jrf.org.uk.

Joseph Rowntree Foundation (2000) *Working with Families where There is Domestic Violence* (York: Joseph Rowntree Foundation). Available at www.jrf.org.uk.

Joseph Rowntree Foundation (2004a) *The Effect of Parental Substance Abuse on Young People* (York: Joseph Rowntree Foundation). Available at www.jrf.org.uk.

Joseph Rowntree Foundation (2004b) *Substance Misuse or Parental Health Problems* (York: Joseph Rowntree Foundation). Available at www.jrf.org.uk.

Joseph Rowntree Foundation (2004c) *Understanding What Children Say about Living with Domestic Violence* (York: Joseph Rowntree Foundation). Available at www.jrf.org.uk.

Joseph Rowntree Foundation (2005) *Drugs in the Family: The Impact on Parents and Siblings* (York: Joseph Rowntree Foundation). Available at www.jrf.org.uk.

Kahan, B. (1994) *Growing Up in Groups* (London: NISW/HMSO).

Karoly, L. A. et al. (1998) *Investing in our Children: What We Know and Don't Know about the Costs and Benefits of Early Childhood Interventions* (Santa Monica, CA: RAND).

Kay, H. (1999) 'The Mental Health Problems of Children and Young People', *Childright*, 155.

Kierney, P., Levin, E. and Rosen, G. (2000) *Alcohol, Drug and Mental Health Problems: Working with Families* (London: SCIE). Available at www.scie.org.uk.

Kierney, P., Levin, E., Rosen, G. and Sainsbury, M. (2003) *Families that Have Alcohol and Mental Health Problems: A Template for Partnership Working* (London: SCIE). Available at www.scie.org.uk.

Kirby, P. et al. (n.d.) *Building a Culture of Participation* (London: DfES). Available at www.dfes.gov.uk/listeningtolearn/downloads/BuildingaCultureofParticipation%5Bhandbook%5D.pdf.

Kohli, R. and Mather, R. (2003) 'Promoting Psycho-Social Wellbeing in Unaccompanied Asylum Seeking Young People in the UK', *Child and Family Social Work*, 8, 201–12.

Laming, Lord H. (2003) *The Victoria Climbie Report* (London: HMSO). Available at www.victoria-climbie-enquiry.org.uk.

Langlan, M. and Lee, P. (1989) *Radical Social Work Today* (London: Routledge).

Lauder, H. et al. (1996) *Education, Globalisation and Social Change* (Oxford: Oxford University Press).

Lavalette, M. and Ferguson, I. (2007) *International Social Work and the Radical Tradition* (London: Venture Press).

Layard, R. (2004) *Mental Health: Britain's Biggest Social Problem?* (London: HMSO). Available at http://64.233.183.104/search?q=cache:rqOeSs_mIyoJ:www.cabinetoffice.gov.uk/upload/assets/www.cabinetoffice.gov.uk/strategy/mh_layard.pdf+Layard,+R&hl=en&ct=clnk&cd=73&gl=uk&client=firefox-a.

Layard, R. (2005) *Happiness* (London: Allen Lane).

Leicestershire County Council (1993) *The Leicestershire Enquiry 1992* (The Kirkwood Report) (Leicester: Leicestershire County Council).

Lovell, E. (2002) *Children and Young People who Display Sexually Harmful Behaviour.* (London: NSPCC). Available at www.nspcc.org.uk/Inform.

MacDonald, R. (1997). *Youth, the 'Underclass' and Social Exclusion* (London: Routledge). Available at www.regard.ac.uk.

MacDonald, R. and Marsh, J. (2005) *Disconnected Youth: Growing up in Britain's Poor Neighbourhoods* (Basingstoke: Palgrave Macmillan).

McLean, J. (2003) 'Men as Minority: Men Employed in Statutory Social Care Work', *Journal of Social Work*, 3(1), 45–68.

Macleod, M. and Saraga, E. (1994) 'Child Sexual Abuse: Challenging the Orthodoxy', in M. Loney (ed.), *The State or the Market*, 2nd edn (London: Sage), 94–135.

Macpherson, W. (1999) *The Stephen Lawrence Enquiry* (London: HMSO). Available at www.archive.officialdocuments.co.uk.

Mason, J. and Fattore, T. (eds) (2005) *Children Taken Seriously* (London: Jessica Kingsley).

Maughan, B., Collishaw, S. and Goodman, R. (2004) 'Time Trends in Adolescence', *Journal of Child Psychology and Psychiatry*, 45(8), 1350–62. Available at www.nuffieldfoundation.org.

Miller, C. (2004) *Producing Welfare* (Basingstoke: Palgrave Macmillan).

Miller, D. (2002) *Disabled Children and Abuse* (London: NSPCC). Available at www.nspcc.org.uk/Inform.

Millie, A. et al. (2005) *Anti-Social Behaviour Strategies: Finding a Balance* (York: Joseph Rowntree Foundation). Available at www.jrf.org.uk.

Mitchell, F. (2003) 'The Social Services Response to Unaccompanied Children in England', *Child and Family Social Work*, 8, 179–89.

Moore, S. (2004) 'Beyond the Double Shift', *New Statesman* (19 July). Available at www.newstatesman.com/200407190024.

Morgan R. (2005) *Being Fostered: A National Survey of the Views of Foster Children, Foster Carers and Birth Parents about Foster Care* (London: CSCI). Available at www.rights4me.org.

Mullender, A. et al. (2002) *Children's Perspectives on Domestic Violence* (London: Sage).

Mullender, A. et al. (2003) *Stop Hitting Mum!* (East Molesey: Young Voices).

Muncie, J. (2004) *Youth and Crime*, 2nd edn (London: Sage).

Muncie, J. (2006) 'Governing Young People: Coherence and Contradiction in Contemporary Youth Justice', *Critical Social Policy*, 26(4), 770–93.

Munro, E. (2002) *Effective Child Protection* (London: Sage).

Munro, E. and Calder, M. (2005) 'Where Has Child Protection Gone?' *Political Quarterly*, 76(3), 438–45.

NACRO (2006) *Some Facts about Children and Young People who Offend, 2004* (London: NACRO). Available at www.nacro.org.uk.

National Audit Office (2005) *Improving School Attendance in England* (London: HMSO). Available at www.nao.gov.uk.

National Audit Office (2006) *Sure Start Children's Centres* (London: HMSO). Available at www.nao.gov.uk.

NSPCC (2000) *Child Maltreatment in the UK* (London: NSPCC). Available at www.nspcc.org.uk/Inform.

NSPCC (2002) *Mentally Ill Parents and Children's Welfare* (London: NSPCC). Available at www.nspcc.org.uk.

NSPCC (2003a) *Domestic Violence and Children: A Resource List* (London: NSPCC). Available at www.nspcc.org.uk/Inform.

NSPCC (2003b) *Briefing Paper: Child Killings in England and Wales* (London: NSPCC). Available at www.nspcc.org.uk/Inform.

NSPCC (2003c) *Abuse of Children in Residential Care* (London: NSPCC). Available at www.nspcc.org.uk/Inform.

NSPCC (2003d) *It Doesn't Happen to Disabled Children* (London: NSPCC). Available at www.nspcc.org.uk/Inform.

NSPCC (2006a) *Talk 'til It Stops* (London: NSPCC). Available at www.nspcc.org.uk/Inform.

NSPCC (2006b) *Key Child Protection Statistics* (London: NSPCC). Available at www.nspcc.uk/inform.

Office of National Statistics (2005a) *Crime in England and Wales*, supplementary vol. 1: *Homicide and Gun Crime* (London: HMSO). Available at www.ons.gov.uk.

Office of National Statistics (2005b) *Children in Need in England* (London: HMSO). Available at www.ons.gov.uk.

Office of National Statistics (2005c) *Social Trends* (London: HMSO). Available at www.ons.gov.uk.

Ofsted (2003) *Boys' Achievement in Secondary Schools* (London: HMSO). Available at www.ofsted.gov.uk/assets/3316.pdf.

Osgerby, B. (1998) *Youth in Britain since 1945* (Oxford: Blackwell).

Packman, J. (1986) *Who Needs Care? Social Work Decisions about Children* (Oxford: Blackwell).

Parker, R. (ed.) (1999) *Adoption Now: Messages from Research* (Chichester: Wiley).

Parmer, A. et al. (2005) *Tackling Domestic Violence: Providing Support to Survivors from Black and Other Ethnic Minority Communities* (London: Home Office). Available at www.homeoffice.gov.uk/rds.

Parton, N. (2006) *Safeguarding Childhood* (Basingstoke: Palgrave Macmillan).

Parton, N. and O'Byrne, P. (2000) *Constructive Social Work: Towards a New Practice* (Basingstoke: Palgrave Macmillan).

Payne, H. and Butler, I. (2003) *Promoting the Mental Health of Children in Need.* 'Children First' research briefing (London: Research in Practice). Available at www. rip.org.uk.

Payne, M. (2005) *Modern Social Work Theory*, 3rd edn (Basingstoke: Palgrave Macmillan).

Pearson, G. (1983) *Hooligans: A History of Respectable Fears* (Basingstoke: Macmillan).

Postman, C. (1983) *The Disappearance of Childhood* (London: W. H. Allen).

Pritchard, C. (2004) *The Child Abusers: Research and Controversy* (Buckingham: Open University Press).

Pritchard, C. and Sayer, T. (2006) 'Exploring Potential "Extra-Familial" Child Homicide Assailants in the UK and Estimating their Homicide Rate', *British Journal of Social Work* (Nov.). Available at www.10.1093/bjsw/bcl333.

Public Interest Disclosure Act 1998 (London: HMSO). Available at http://opsi.gov.uk/ acts.htm.

R (Behre) v *Hillingdon* [2003] EWHC 2075.

R (Howard League for Penal Reform) v *Secretary of State for the Home Department* [2002] EWHC 2497.

Reder, P. and Duncan, S. (1997) 'Adult Psychiatry: A Missing Link in the Child Protection Network', *Child Abuse Review*, 6(1), 35–40.

Reder, P. and Duncan, S. (2004) 'Making the Most of the Victoria Climbie Report', *Child Abuse Review*, 13(2), 95–114.

Refugee Council (2005) *Ringing the Changes: The Impact of Guidance on the Use of Section 17 and Section 20 of the Children Act 1989 to Support Unaccompanied Asylum Seeking Children* (London: Refugee Council). Available at www.refugeecouncil.org. uk/OneStopCMS/Core/CrawlerResourceServer.aspx?resource=063A9362–8227–4 445-AA30-CCE982B3D36A&mode=link&guid=6157b27655574ed4b8fb03 f1a2de4fb7.

Refugee Council and Refugee Action (2006) *Inhumane and Ineffective: Section 9 in Practice* (London: Refugee Council and Refugee Action). Available at www.icar. org.uk/download.php?id=322.

Research in Practice (2002) *Adoption and Permanence*. Available at www.rip.org.uk.

Research in Practice (2003) *Leaving Care*. Available at www.rip.org.uk.

Research in Practice (2005a) *On New Ground: Supporting Unaccompanied Asylum Seeking and Refugee Children and Young People*. Available at www.rip.org.uk.

Research in Practice (2005b) *Supporting Families*. Available at www.rip.org.uk.

Rethinking Crime and Punishment (2004) *Rethinking Crime and Punishment: The Report* (London: Rethinking Crime and Punishment). Available at www.rethink-ing.org.uk/informed/pdf/RCP%20The%20Report.pdf.

Roberts, Y. (2005) 'When Love is Not Enough', *Guardian* (17 Aug.). Available at www.guardian.co.uk/parents/story/0,,1550558,00.html.

Robinson, W. and Dunne, M. (1999) *Alcohol Child Care and Parenting: A Handbook for Practitioners* (London: NSPCC). Available at www.nspcc.org.uk/Inform.

Roche, J. and Tucker, S. (2004) *Youth in Society*, 2nd edn (London: Sage).

Rushton, A. (2003) *The Adoption of Looked After Children*. Knowledge Review (London: Social Care Institute for Excellence). Available at www.scie.org.uk.

Rutherford, A. (1992) *Growing Out of Crime* (Harmondsworth: Penguin).

Ryan, W. (1976) *Blaming the Victim* (New York: Vintage).

Safeguarding Vulnerable Groups Act 2006 (London: HMSO). Available at http://opsi.gov.uk/acts.htm.

Saunders, H. (2004) *Twenty-Nine Child Homicides: Lessons Still to be Learnt on Domestic*

Violence and Child Protection (Bristol: Women's Aid). Available at www.family-justice-council.org.uk/docs/twenty_nine_child_homicides.pdf.

Sayer, T. (2006) 'Working with Young People in the Authoritarian State'. Paper presented at the International Association for Human Caring Conference, Perth, Australia (May 2006).

SCIE (2004a) *Assessing and Diagnosing Attention Deficit Hyperactivity Disorder (ADHD)*. SCIE Research Briefing (London: Social Care Institute for Excellence). Available at www.scie.org.uk.

SCIE (2004b) *Treating Attention Deficit Hyperactivity Disorder (ADHD)*. SCIE Research Briefing (London: Social Care Institute for Excellence). Available at www.scie.org.uk.

Scott, S. (2001) *The Politics and Experience of Ritual Abuse: Beyond Disbelief* (Buckingham: Open University Press).

Seden, J. and Reynolds, J. (2003) *Managing Care in Practice* (Buckingham: Open University/Routledge).

Seebohm Report (1968) *Report of the Committee on Local Authority and Allied Personal Services* (London: HMSO).

Sellick, C. and Howell, D. (2003) *Innovative, Tried and Tested: A Review of Good Practice in Fostering*. Knowledge Review (London: Social Care Institute for Excellence). Available at www.scie.org.uk.

Selwyn, J., Frazer, L. and Fitzgerald, A. (2004) *Finding Adoptive Families for Black, Asian and Mixed Parentage Children* (London: NCH). Available at www.nch.org.uk.

Sexual Offences Act 2003 (London: HMSO). Available at http://opsi.gov.uk/acts.htm.

Sinclair, I. (2005) *Fostering Now: Messages from Research* (London: Jessica Kingsley).

Sinclair, I. and Gibbs, I. (1998) *Children's Homes: A Study in Diversity* (Chichester: Wiley).

Sinclair. I, Baker, C., Wilson, K. and Gibbs, I. (2005) *Foster Children: Where They Go and How They Get On* (London: Jessica Kingsley).

Smeaton, E. (2005) *Living on the Edge: The Experiences of Detached Young Runaways* (London: Children's Society). Available at www.childrenssociety.org.uk.

Social Exclusion Unit (2002a) *Young Runaways* (London: Office of the Deputy Prime Minister). Available at www.socialexclusionunit.gov.uk.

Social Exclusion Unit (2002b) *Reducing Re-Offending by Ex-Prisoners* (London: Office of the Deputy Prime Minister). Available at www.socialexclusionunit.gov.uk.

Social Exclusion Unit (2003) *A Better Education for Children in Care* (London: Office of the Deputy Prime Minister). Available at www.socialexclusionunit.gov.uk.

Social Exclusion Unit (2004) *The Impact of Government Policy on Social Exclusion among Young People* (London: Office of the Deputy Prime Minister). Available at www.socialexclusionunit.gov.uk.

Spotlight (2004) 'Anti-Bullying' edn, *Spotlight* (Nov.) (London: NCB).

Staffordshire County Council (1991) *The Pindown Experience and the Protection of Children* (Stafford: Staffordshire County Council).

Stein, M. (2006) 'Wrong Turn', *Guardian* (6 Dec.). Available at www.guardian.co.uk/society/2006/dec/06/childrensservices.guardiansocietysupplement1.

Stewart-Brown, S. (2004) 'Legislation on Smacking' (editorial), *British Medical Journal*, 329(7476), 1195–6.

Straus, M. and Kantor, G. (1994) 'Corporal Punishment of Adolescents by Parents: A Risk Factor in the Epidemiology of Depression, Suicide, Alcohol Abuse, Child Abuse and Wife Beating', *Adolescence*, 29(115), 543–63.

Street, C. (2000) *Whose Crisis? Meeting the Needs of Children and Young People with*

Serious Mental Health Problems (London: Young Minds). Available at www.young-minds.org.uk.

Stuart, M. and Baines, C. (2004a) *Progress on Safeguards for Children Living Away from Home* (York: Joseph Rowntree Foundation). Available at www.jrf.org.uk.

Stuart, M. and Baines, C. (2004b) *Safeguards for Vulnerable Children: Three Case Studies on Abusers, Disabled Children and Children in Prison* (York: Joseph Rowntree Foundation). Available at www.jrf.org.uk.

Sure Start (2004) 'Summary of Findings from the National Evaluation'. Available at Surestart.gov.uk/research/evaluations.

Sylva, K., Melhuish, E. et al. (2004) *The Effective Provision of Pre-School Education Project: Findings from Pre-Sschool to the End of Key Stage 1* (London: Institute of Education, University of London). Available at www.onderwijsachterstanden.nl/php/download.php/rbx15–03.pdf.

Thomas, N. (2005) *Social Work with Young People in Care* (Basingstoke: Palgrave Macmillan).

Thorpe, D. (1995) 'Some Implications of Recent Child Protection Research', *Representing Children*, 8(3), 45–56.

Tolmac, J. and Hodes, M. (2004) 'Ethnic Variation among Adolescent Psychiatric In-Patients with Psychotic Disorders', *British Journal of Psychiatry*, 184 (May), 428–31.

Training and Development Agency for Schools (TDA) (2007) *Gender Equality Scheme* (London: TDA). Available at www.tda.gov.uk/upload/resources/pdf/g/gender_equality_scheme_7_10.pdf.

Trisileotis, J., Sellick, C. and Short, R. (1995) *Foster Care Theory and Practice* (London: BAAF). Available online to members.

UNICEF (2007) *Child Poverty in Perspective: An Overview of Child Wellbeing in Rich Countries* (Florence). Available at www.unicef.org/media/files/ChildPoverty Report.pdf.

United Nations Convention on the Rights of the Child 1989 (New York: United Nations). Available at www.ohchr.org/english/law/pdf/crc.pdf.

Utting, Sir W. (1997) *People Like Us: The Report of the Review of Safeguards for Children Living Away from Home* (London: HMSO).

Valios, N. (2006) 'Ealing Looked After Children: Education Exam Success', *Community Care* (21 Sept.). Available at www.communitycare.co.uk/Articles/2006/09/21/55793/ealing-looked-after-children-education-exam-success.html?key=SUBSTANCE%20MISUSE.

Verhulst, F. C. et al. (1997) 'Ten Year Time Trends of Psychopathology in Dutch Children', *Acta Psychiatrica Scandinavica*, 96, 7–13.

Voice (2004) *Start with the Child, Stay with the Child* (London: VCC/NCB). Available at www.voiceyp.org/docimages/28.pdf.

Wagner, G. (1998) *Residential Care: A Positive Choice* (London: NISW).

Walby, S. and Allen, J. (2004) *Domestic Violence, Sexual Assault and Stalking: Findings from the British Crime Survey* (London: Home Office). Available at www.home office.gov.uk/rds/pdfs04/hors276.pdf.

Wardhough, J. and Wilding, P. (1993) 'Towards an Explanation of the Corruption of Care', *Critical Social Policy*, 13(37), 4–31.

Warner, N. (1992) *Choosing with Care* (London: HMSO).

Waterhouse, Sir R. (2000) *Lost in Care* (London: HMSO). Available at www.lga.gov.uk/lga/executives/socialaffairs/00_2_28/item4.pdf.

Watts, J. (ed.) (1977) *The Countesthorpe Experience* (London: Unwin Education).

Williams, W. (1986) *The Spirit and the Flesh* (Boston: Beacon Press).

Willis, P. (1978) *Learning to Labour* (London: Saxon House).

Wilson, D. and Rees, G. (eds) (2006) *Just Justice: A Study into Black Young People's Experiences of the Youth Justice System* (London: Children's Society). Available at www.childrenssociety.org.uk.

Wilson, K. et al. (2004) *Fostering Success: An Exploration of the Research Literature in Foster Care.* Knowledge Review. Available at www.scie.org.uk.

Wolmar, C. (2000) *Forgotten Children: The Secret Abuse Scandal in Children's Homes* (London: Vision).

Young Minds (2004) *Compulsory Treatment and Children* (London: Young Minds). Available at youngminds.org.uk.

Young People Now (2004) 'Who are You Calling a YOB?' *Young People Now* (13 Oct.).

Youth Justice Board (2004) *Differences or Discrimination* (London: YJB). Available at www.youth-justice-board.gov.uk.

Youth Justice Board (2006) *Annual Statistics 2004–5* (London: YJB). Available at www.youth-justice-board.gov.uk.

Youth Justice Coalition (2003) *Children in Trouble: Time for Change* (London: Children's Rights Alliance).

Author Index

Subject Index